25

Stupid Mistakes
You Don't Want to Make
in the Stock Market

25

Stupid Mistakes

You Don't Want to Make in the

Stock Market

David E. Rye

Contemporary Books

Chicago New York San Francisco Lisbon London Madrid Mexico City
Milan New Delhi San Juan Seoul Singapore Sydney Toronto

We wish to thank the publishers of *Smart Money* magazine (smartmoney.com) and *Money* magazine (money.com) for granting us permission to use many of their respective Web site screens to illustrate important points throughout this book. All of the Web sites that we referenced in the book were thoroughly checked out. However, as we all know, Web site addresses can change at any time and we apologize if any address changes were made after this book went to press.

Library of Congress Cataloging-in-Publication Data

Rye, David E.
    25 stupid mistakes you don't want to make in the stock market / by David E. Rye.
        p.   cm.
    Includes bibliographical references and index.
    ISBN 0-7373-0617-3 (alk. paper)
    1. Stocks—United States.   2. Investments—United States.   I. Title:
Twenty-five stupid mistakes you don't want to make in the stock market.
II. Title.

HG4910.R93   2001
332.63'22—dc21   2001042233

Contemporary Books

A Division of The McGraw·Hill Companies

1 2 3 4 5 6 7 8 9 10   AGM/AGM   10 9 8 7 6 5 4 3 2 1

ISBN 0-7373-0617-3
P 4-29-02   1073707
This book was set in Stone Sans and Stone Serif by Robert S. Tinnon Design
Printed and bound by Quebecor Martinsburg

Cover design by Laurie Young
Interior design by Robert S. Tinnon

McGraw-Hill books are available at special quantity discounts to use as premiums and sales promotions, or for use in corporate training programs. For more information, please write to the Director of Special Sales, Professional Publishing, McGraw-Hill, Two Penn Plaza, New York, NY 10121-2298. Or contact your local bookstore.

This book is printed on acid-free paper.

Contents

Preface

THE DECADE OF THE NINETIES WAS NOT A DECADE FOR FAINT-OF-HEART stock market investors. It was laced with dramatic changes during which astute investors were forced to surf swelling waves of volatility to achieve financial success. Although many of them made lots of mistakes and consequently didn't make it back to shore, more millionaires were created in the past decade than ever before. A steadily growing economy helped even average investors obtain stellar financial gains from their stock market investments as long as they paid attention to where they were going. It all began with a stock market that started to soar in the early 1990s, then plummeted in 1998, then soared again before the bears took over the market in 2000, forcing investors to tear up and reconstruct their financial strategies.

Throw in rising wages and interest rates, the biggest merger boom ever, the upheaval in the Clinton White House, and the late nineties were a chaotic picture for all of us. Even with all of the chaos, a lot of people did better than they ever dreamed they might in the stock market.

Add to the game the international economic crisis that spread like a contagion throughout much of the world, bringing near panic to Wall Street in 2001. For companies in Asia and much of the developing world, the mixture of plummeting currencies and depressed economies put pressure on the earnings of U.S. firms, whose export markets were virtually slammed shut.

No matter their age, race, or background, thousands were able to find the path to invest successfully in the market of the nineties—and they're believers in the future despite the turmoil of the early twenty-first century. Most of these people are just average Joes like you and me. Most weren't born with a silver spoon in their mouth, and yet they've become wealthy or well on their way to it. How did they do it? They set goals and created a plan—and then just plunged in and learned from their mistakes.

Learning how to invest systematically in the stock market and avoid the twenty-five classic investment mistakes most people make isn't complicated. If you're willing to spend a few hours reading this book, you too can invest with confidence.

Introduction

*U*NLESS YOU WERE LIVING ON MARS FOR THE PAST DECADE, YOU COULD hardly have missed the country's torrid love affair with the Dow Jones Industrial Average (the Dow) and the NASDAQ. As the indexes raged to record heights, the great bull run of the nineties was front-page news. It's easy enough to see why. If in 1990 you had invested $10,000 in the thirty industrial stocks that make up the Dow index, your money would have quadrupled to more than $40,000 by 1999. If you had invested $10,000 and added an additional $100 each month, your total would have soared to almost $100,000.

The question is, why weren't more people buying stocks in 1991, the year the bull market began? Back then, Wall Street was about as popular as the radiation activity on Three Mile Island. Two market crashes, a debilitating banking crisis, and an economy flirting with recession had soured people on investing. As Gulf War euphoria faded, the idea that the stock market would grow explosively was viewed as absurd. That says a lot about conventional wisdom, doesn't it?

The truth is, you shouldn't pay too much attention to what the pundits are thinking when it comes to investing in the stock market. More often than not, they are wrong. We saw vivid examples of that throughout 2000 and into 2001 when the market got badly mauled by the bears and the NASDAQ sank to half its high point in March 1999. How many times have you heard the "experts" claim that the market has "hit bottom" only to find out that the bottom was deeper than predicted?

Unfortunately, many people believe that some kind of magic order controls the stock market and that only the "chosen few" know how it works. It's those chosen ones who make all the money in dynamic markets. The rest of us spend our time traveling down the "yellow brick road" trying to get to Oz to discover the secrets of their success. Well, my friends, that is just not true.

There's a financial opportunity on your doorstep that's not pie in the sky—if you want to make it happen and are willing to learn how to avoid the common mistakes most investors make when they invest in the stock market. Americans are retiring with more money today than at any time in our nation's history. And they're doing it by investing wisely in stocks, mutual funds, and even in bonds. A couple of years ago, investors were satisfied with just a 10 percent return on their money. If you were thirty years old and your investments returned that 10 percent, all you had to do to become a millionaire at age sixty-five was to save $3,500 a year. In today's market, you can cut that time at least in half. Smart investors are demanding a 20 percent or more return from the stock market—and they're getting it.

WHAT THIS BOOK WILL DO FOR YOU

During the height of the great bull market of the Roaring Twenties, Will Rogers was asked what he thought of the market's returns. "To tell you the truth," he said, "I'm more concerned about the return of my money than the return on my money." As you will learn in this book, I'm not promising you high returns without any risk whatsoever. But I will show you how to avoid or control—how to minimize—many of the common investment risks so that you can enjoy high rates of return on your money. I'll make the same promise to you that I make to my seminar participants. If you will spend a couple of evenings reading this book, I will show you how to avoid twenty-five common mistakes that people make when investing in the stock market. If you follow my advice, you'll be able to make sound investments that will pay off. And once you set up your investment program, you won't need to spend a lot of time managing it.

Much of what I discuss in this book is based on common sense. Facts and ideas are important, but applying common sense to every investment decision you make is perhaps more so. Here's how my common sense philosophy works. Suppose you've been invited to participate in a twenty-mile race down a wide, straight road with no traffic. You're racing against Lance Armstrong, three-time winner of the Tour de France, the Super Bowl of bicycle races, and one of the best cyclists on earth. He'll be riding the most sophisticated racing bike ever built.

You're going to race him in your vintage 1961 Volkswagen Beetle. Even though the body has some rust spots on it, the engine still runs and the gear box works. Who do you think will win the race? No matter how good Lance is, there is no way he is going to beat a car. Although he'll probably get off to a faster start than your VW, you will eventually overtake him and win the race.

This analogy forms the basis of the investment approach I take throughout this book. Over the long haul, stocks have historically outperformed bonds, savings accounts, certificates of deposit and just about any other investment option available to most investors. The only thing you have to do to make it happen is to invest in the right stocks and not make any stupid mistakes.

You'll find, as you read these chapters, that I caution against getting talked into buying some hot initial public offering (IPO) or the stock of some startup that a friend tells you about over dinner. Why? It's simple. Don't make stupid mistakes! You don't have to buy highly speculative stocks to enjoy high rates of return. Instead, control your risk. Invest in stocks and funds that are in the top 10 percent of their class, have proven track records, and consistently earn high rates of return. That's how to make real money in the market while at the same time minimizing your risk. I will show you how easy it is to find winning stocks and funds throughout the book.

THE FOLLY OF PROCRASTINATING

It takes more than a good head for numbers to be successful in the stock market. You need patience and persistence and, at times, courage and conviction. The dizzying twists and turns of the market have sunk more than a few rookie and expert investors alike who simply didn't have the mettle to stick with their strategy. But those who continue to invest and diversify invariably find themselves richly rewarded for their diligence.

Investing in the stock market is not rocket science. What trips up most people is that initial hurdle, the act of actually putting some money in the market in the first place. Millions of would-be investors never succeed because they never take the initial step: They never take the money out of their bank accounts and put it into the market. Their excuses are many—"The market is down right now," "The market is too high now," or simply, "I don't know anything about the stock market"—but the result is the same. You can't make money in stocks if you don't buy some.

If you let yourself get caught in this trap, you'll never know the benefits of participating in the stock market. But if you have the courage to take the plunge, you can look forward to the rewards of a lifetime of wise investing. You'll succeed, not necessarily because you are lucky or even very smart, but in large part because over the long term, the stock market has produced an average rate of return of 12 percent.

WHY IT'S HARD TO LOSE

In spite of what your friends may have told you, investing in stocks bears little resemblance to gambling at a casino. At a casino, the odds always favor the house. But in the stock market, the odds favor the investor. Over time, the vast majority of quality stocks increase in value. In fact, the overall stock market tends to move up most years. In the sixteen-year period from 1983 through 1998, the Dow Jones Industrial Average set new highs in fourteen of those years. (The Dow, as it's called, measures price movements in thirty widely held stocks that trade on the New York Stock Exchange. It's a good barometer of what's happening in a certain segment of the market.)

That's not to say there won't be some ups and downs, as we all saw very clearly in 2000 and 2001. There will be slow periods, there will be volatile periods, and there will even be dramatic declines in stock prices from time to time. Experienced investors like to refer to those periods as "buying opportunities." But those who invest for the long term clearly have the odds in their favor. Since 1900, there have been five years when the market dropped more than 20 percent. But there have also been twenty-seven years when the market rose by 20 percent or more.

When you invest in a stock, you become part owner in a corporation that is in business to make a profit. The corporation typically has hundreds or thousands of employees all working for you, striving each day to increase the company's sales and profits. As a company's profits climb, the value of the company increases, which in turn boosts the value of the company's stock. One key to beating the market is finding the companies that are growing the fastest. This book will teach you how to recognize them—and about other factors that will contribute to your success as well. At the end of *25 Stupid Mistakes You Don't Want to Make in the Stock Market*, you'll find an appendix filled with information to help you successfully invest in the stock market—a sample investment plan, books and publications to check out, associations to consider joining, and great Web sites to visit. And if you run into terms you don't understand as you're reading, check the glossary at the end of the book.

Investing in the stock market is a high-energy game. This book will teach you how to play the game, have fun while you're doing it, and make some money at the same time.

MISTAKE 1

I Already Know Everything There Is to Know

*Investors who tell me they already know
everything there is to know are fools. I don't
pretend to know everything and I'm not a fool.*

PETER LYNCH

WELCOME TO THE STOCK MARKET GAME. ANYONE CAN PLAY SIMPLY by picking up the telephone or turning on the computer. In a few words or keystrokes, you can own a piece of a company or several companies in a mutual fund. You don't have to attend a board meeting, develop a product, or devise a business plan. It has become that easy. Many of us think we already know everything there is to know about how to play the game, but nobody does! Before picking up your telephone or sitting down at your computer to buy some stocks, spend a few minutes taking the following quiz designed to help you identify your investment strengths and weaknesses.

THE INVESTMENT-SAVVY QUIZ

1. Which of the following would you consult to track the performance of small-company stocks?
   a) Wilshire 5000 index
   b) Russell 2000 index
   c) CNN *Moneyline*

2. A downward-sloping advance/decline line means:
   a) the market has bad breadth, and more stocks are declining than advancing
   b) the market has good breadth because more stocks are advancing than declining
   c) the market has halitosis and needs a swig of Listerine
3. Diversifying your portfolio among a variety of assets that don't all move in lockstep:
   a) allows you to achieve a better balance between risk and reward
   b) decreases the odds that all your investments will decline at once
   c) both of the above
4. A bear market is typically defined as:
   a) a decline of 10 percent or more in the market value of a major stock index, such as the Standard & Poor's 500-stock index (S&P 500)
   b) a decline of 20 percent or more in the market value of a major stock index, such as the S&P 500
   c) what happens just after you move your money into stocks
5. An inverted yield curve is often a sign that:
   a) the economy is headed for a recession
   b) the economy is poised for robust growth
   c) darn kids have been fooling around with the traffic signs
6. A tax-efficient fund is one that:
   a) delivers its gains in dividends and capital gains distributions
   b) delivers its gains in share-price appreciation
   c) delivers its gains without blabbing to the IRS
7. A study of more than sixty-six thousand households with discount brokerage accounts found that investors who traded most frequently earned:
   a) the highest returns
   b) average returns
   c) the lowest returns
   d) the undying affection of their brokerage firms
8. The statistical gauge that measures the degree to which two assets move in sync is:
   a) coefficient of correlation
   b) duration
   c) moving average
9. When the price/earnings ratio for the stock market is way above its historical average, it's a sign that:

a) investors are optimistic about stocks' prospects

b) the market is headed for a crash

c) Alan Greenspan is about to make another "irrational exuberance" speech

10. If a stock is trading at $10.50 a share, but you want to try to buy it for $10.25 or less, you would give your broker a:

    a) stop order

    b) limit order

    c) market order

    d) restraining order

11. Value investors often look for stocks that:

    a) trade at high price–earnings ratios

    b) trade at low price–book value ratios

    c) are recommended by a friend

12. If the *Investors' Intelligence* Sentiment Index shows that 55 percent or more of investment advisers are bullish, it's a sign that:

    a) stock prices are likely to surge to new highs

    b) stock prices are likely to stagnate or even fall

    c) the other 45 percent of advisers are just being jerks

13. What is typically the main cause of a bear market?

    a) bloated stock prices

    b) rising interest rates

    c) a right-wing conspiracy

14. To get a sense of whether an advance or a decline in a stock index is the beginning of a significant move, a breed of market watchers known as technical analysts will often.

    a) plot the index against its moving average

    b) pore over the annual reports of companies in the index

    c) consult a Ouija board

15. Standard deviation is:

    a) the amount by which stock returns usually deviate from bond returns

    b) a measure of volatility that tells how much an investment's returns bounce around its average return

    c) an oxymoron—can something be both standard and a deviation?

16. You can effectively build your own tax shelter by:

    a) buying and holding growth stocks that pay dividends

    b) buying and holding growth stocks that pay no dividends

    c) buying a tax-shelter kit at Home Depot

17. Which of the following is often used to gauge the value of companies with large noncash expenses such as depreciation?
    a) price to earnings ratio
    b) price to cash flow ratio
    c) price to book value ratio

18. If a bond has a call feature, then:
    a) the issuer has the right to repay the bond's principal before its stated maturity date
    b) the issuer has the right to extend the bond's maturity date
    c) you have the right to call the issuer and complain if the bond goes into default

19. The S&P 500-stock index contains:
    a) the 500 U.S. stocks with the highest market values
    b) the 500 top-performing stocks in the United States

20. Interest and dividends earned by municipal bonds are exempt from federal income tax.
    a) true
    b) false

21. All else being equal, the lower a bond fund's average credit quality, the higher its yield.
    a) true
    b) false

22. Index funds:
    a) seek to track the investment returns of a specified stock or bond benchmark
    b) try to beat the investment returns of a specified stock or bond benchmark
    c) buy only stocks in the S&P 500-stock index
    d) seek to invest in the best-performing sectors of the stock market

23. If interest rates declined, the price of a bond or bond fund would generally:
    a) increase
    b) decrease
    c) stay about the same
    d) it is impossible to predict

24. Dollar-cost averaging is:
    a) a strategy that entails buying low and selling high
    b) a way to sell fund shares to minimize capital gains

    c) an approach in which you invest the same amount of money in a
       fund at regular intervals
    d) none of the above

25. If your investment portfolio contains only U.S. stocks, you will reduce
    your overall risk by adding international stocks.
    a) true
    b) false

26. Which market benchmark or stock exchange is the best gauge of the
    performance of the entire U.S. stock market?
    a) S&P 500-stock index
    b) Wilshire 5000
    c) Dow Jones Industrial Average
    d) NASDAQ Composite Index

27. If you invest in a 401(k) plan at work, you are not eligible to contribute
    to an IRA.
    a) true
    b) false

28. How long must you hold a stock or stock fund to receive the lowest cap-
    ital-gains tax rate?
    a) more than one month
    b) more than six months
    c) more than one year
    d) more than five years

29. The long-term historical return on U.S. stocks has averaged:
    a) 5 percent a year
    b) 11 percent a year
    c) 19 percent a year
    d) 28 percent a year

30. Which of the following is *not* an attribute of mutual funds?
    a) diversification
    b) professional management
    c) guaranteed return
    d) none of the above

31. If your investment returned 10 percent last year and inflation was
    3 percent, your "real" return was:
    a) 3.3 percent
    b) 7 percent
    c) 13 percent
    d) 30 percent

32. A mutual fund that invests in government securities is guaranteed not to lose money.
    a) true
    b) false

33. The average stock mutual fund charges an annual expense ratio ranging from:
    a) 0.5 percent to 0.99 percent
    b) 1 percent to 1.49 percent
    c) 1.5 percent to 1.99 percent
    d) more than 2 percent

34. Contributions to a Roth IRA are tax deductible.
    a) true
    b) false

Answers to Investment-Savvy Quiz

1. (b) The consulting firm Frank Russell Company tracks the small-cap market.

2. (a) The advance/decline line is a running tally of the difference between the number of stocks with price gains and the number with losses. When falling stocks outnumber risers, the line points downward, which is considered a negative sign for the market.

3. (c) Diversification decreases the odds that all your holdings will get clobbered at once, while helping you get the maximum reward for the level of risk you're willing to take on.

4. (b) A decline of 20 percent or more is a bear market. A drop of more than 10 percent but less than 20 percent is considered a correction.

5. (a) An inverted yield curve is what you have when short-term Treasury securities yield more than long-term ones. This usually occurs when the Federal Reserve pushes up short-term rates to slow the economy and stem inflation. That strategy can lead to recession.

6. (b) Unlike dividends and capital gains distributions, which are taxed yearly, share-price appreciation isn't taxed until you sell a fund. As a result, funds whose gains come from share-price increases generate fewer tax bills, making them more tax-efficient.

7. (c) Researchers found that the most active traders earned 7 percentage points a year less than the least active traders.

8. (a) The higher the correlation between two assets, the more they zig and zag in unison. For example, large-cap stocks have a higher correlation with small-cap stocks than they do with bonds.

9. (a) Above-average price–earnings (PE) ratios indicate that investors are willing to pay more than usual for future corporate earnings, which means they're optimistic about stocks' prospects.

10. (b) A limit order may get you a stock below the prevailing price. But if no one meets your limit price, you won't get the stock at all.

11. (b) The price to book value ratio is calculated by dividing a company's share price by its book value (assets minus liabilities) per share. The lower this ratio, the more assets you're getting for your buck.

12. (b) When 55 percent or more of advisers are bullish, market watchers take it as a sign that stock prices will likely fall. The theory is that a high percentage of bulls means most people have already put their money in stocks, leaving less cash on the sidelines that can drive up prices.

13. (b) Rising interest rates cause bear markets by raising borrowing costs for businesses (which hurts profits) and by making interest-paying investments, such as bonds, more attractive relative to stocks.

14. (a) A moving average dampens the effect of daily stock-price fluctuations and helps analysts get a fix on where the market is heading.

15. (b) Standard deviation measures the volatility of returns. If a fund has a 12 percent average annual return and a standard deviation of 20 percent, annual returns will be 20 percentage points above or below the average.

16. (b) Growth stocks that pay no dividends offer a superior tax shelter because taxes can be as high as 39.6 percent on dividends, but no higher than 20 percent on long-term capital gains.

17. (b) Since noncash expenses depress reported earnings, analysts often look to cash flow (earnings before deducting noncash charges) to gauge the earning power of a company with large noncash expenses.

18. (a) A call feature gives the issuer the right to repay, or call, the bond on certain dates prior to maturity.

19. (b) The S&P 500 index committee chooses stocks that in its judgment represent leading companies in leading industries, which are not necessarily the biggest or top-performing companies.

20 (a) Although dividends and interest are exempt from federal income tax, they usually pay lower interest than corporate bonds.

21. (a) The yield that you will earn on a bond will typically increase if you're willing to accept a lower credit rating on a given bond that you are considering.

22. (a) As the name implies, index funds generally consist of a portfolio of stocks designed to track the total performance of an index of stocks in a specific sector, such as technology or retail.

23. (a) If you buy a bond today at the current market interest rate, and the market rate increases tomorrow, chances are that the price you paid for your bond will increase.

24. (c) When you dollar-cost average, you invest a given amount of money at regular intervals. In this way, you buy more shares when the share price is low and fewer when it is high.

25. (a) Not all economies go up and down together. If your portfolio includes stocks from outside the United States, you avoid the risk of loss if the only economy that you are in goes down.

26 (b) The Wilshire 5000 literally represents the performance of 5,000 stocks as opposed to just 500 that are in the S&P 500 index.

27. (b) Revisions in the tax laws in 1997 allow you to participate in both plans.

28. (c) It is more than one year, but watch for changes in the tax code that could shorten that period.

29. (b) Since 1929, the historical average has been 11 percent.

30. (c) No mutual fund can guarantee a return on your investment.

31. (a) This is easy because 3 divided by 10 is 0.33 or 3.3 percent.

32. (b) Although most U.S. government securities are among the safest investments you can make, there are never any guarantees.

33. (c) Be wary of investing in any mutual fund that charges an annual expense ratio that's greater than 2 percent.

34. (b) Although you pay taxes on the money you invest in ROTH IRAs, you pay no taxes when you withdraw your money from a ROTH IRA.

How Did You Score on the Investment-Savvy Quiz?

Give yourself three points for each correct answer, total your score, and see how you measure up on the scale below.

96 to 102   Wow, you really know this stuff. Maybe you should be writing this book instead of reading it.

84 to 93   Terrific score. You've managed to learn quite a bit about investing. If it weren't for those questions on standard deviation and correlation, I bet you would have aced this quiz.

69 to 81   You've built a solid foundation of investing knowledge. But until you fill in a few gaps, I'd suggest exercising caution when making investment decisions.

51 to 66   You're obviously no Warren Buffett, but you still managed to answer at least half of the questions correctly. Work on the topics that tripped you up, and you'll be in good shape.

Below 50   I'm not going to sugarcoat it—you flunked. But don't despair. You'll move up in the rankings by the time you finish reading this book.

WHERE TO FIND INFORMATION

According to the Security and Exchange Commission's (SEC's) Office of Investor Education and Assistance, online trading may make it easier for investors to execute trades, but it doesn't mean that investors do the necessary homework. And without research, investors are flying blind. Even Tiger Woods couldn't win at golf with a paper bag over his head.

The Internet makes improving your investment knowledge as easy as trading. For a crash course, take the interactive Money 101 seminar at www.money.com. You can also learn a lot by visiting Morningstar's University (www.morningstar.com), the Motley Fool's School (www.fool.com), and the 401Kafe (www.401kafe .com). Also check out resources like the Road Map to Investing (www.sec.gov).

THE LEAST YOU NEED TO KNOW

Don't confuse the new millennium with the past decade. It won't be just more of the same. Ten years ago, for example, eBay, the Motley Fool, and Dell Computer didn't exist, and no Federal

Reserve chairman had ever warned about "irrational exuberance" in the stock market. Many individual investors focused more on real estate than on stocks, having witnessed home prices skyrocket throughout most of the 1980s and into the 1990s. In fact, *Business Week* reported in 1989 that the individual investor "has become as rare on Wall Street as a short-nosed sturgeon in the Hudson River."

Actually, fifty million Americans owned stocks a decade ago, either directly or through mutual funds. Now their numbers have almost doubled to over one hundred million, and the passion with which individual investors track the market has exploded. In 1990, there were 7,885 investment clubs. Today, there are more than 40,000. In 1990, daily NASDAQ trading volume averaged 91 million shares a day. By the end of the 1990s, an average of 1.4 billion shares were traded per day.

There's no question that the stock market has dished out its share of pain over the past few years, but many of the problems are of investors' own making. Investors thought short term. They panicked in bad times and sold good stocks for losses rather than holding them for the long term. Following hot tips from friends, they made decisions to invest thousands of dollars in companies they'd never heard of and hadn't researched. To succeed in the market, the first thing you need is common sense. You also need to make prudent, educated investment decisions rather than basing buying and selling decisions on hot tips and emotion. You also need the patience and persistence to hold on to good stocks through down times. And you need to be calculating and confident, drawing on the knowledge that no matter how bad things look, the market will ultimately move back up. The more you put into your buy and sell decisions, the more you'll get out of them.

Spend your life investing in small, emerging-growth stocks, and you'll no doubt endure years of volatility. But in the end, your returns will be far higher than they would have been with "safe, steady, secure" money market accounts or certificates of deposit. Depending on an investor's age, many investment advisers recommend that stocks constitute as much as 100 percent of an investor's portfolio because of their superior long-term track record over other types of investments. Extreme as it sounds, it's a strategy that will pay off very well over a lifetime.

MISTAKE 2

I Don't Need
an Investment Plan

*If you don't have a good plan, your investment
program will be like a ship without a rudder,
floating wherever the tide takes it.*

CMDR. E.F. RYE, U.S. NAVY

ACCORDING TO WEBSTER, A PLAN IS AN ORGANIZED WAY OF METHODI-
cally applying ideas and principles to make favorable events
happen. Think about it! If when you invested in the stock market,
you could consistently apply a set of ideas and principles that
would reward you with rates of return that would meet or exceed
your objectives, you'd have a winning game plan.

Some people think that if they're not wealthy, they don't need
to do any financial planning. That's a mistake. Stock market volatility, inflation, changing interest rates, unemployment, illness, and
hard times are all part of life. To do no financial planning or to allow others (like your broker or a financial adviser) to do your planning for you is to flirt with disaster. Always remember that no one
cares more about your financial well-being than you do.

You probably already do some financial planning, even if it's
only noting the bills you need to pay on the back of your pay-
check envelope. That's a start. But to be a successful investor, you
need to create a solid, well-thought-out investment plan. You also

need to write down your plan. Any plan you can keep in your head isn't much of a plan.

In this chapter, you'll learn how to create a plan that will work for you and where to find online worksheets to help you get started. I'll also show you how to compute your net worth, determine your investment objectives and financial goals, and access your investment risk tolerance level.

FOLLOW THE STEPS

Go into any Barnes and Noble bookstore or click on Amazon. com's Web site (www.amazon.com) and browse in their personal investment book sections. You'll find lots of books with numbers in their titles, such as *Ten Ways to Beat the Market, Nine Steps to Wealth, Twelve Steps to Financial Freedom,* and the list goes on. Why all of the numbers? Simple. Numbers imply a plan, a winning strategy, a system that takes you by the hand and leads you in an orderly way down the path to prosperity. To this end, we have put together eight rules for creating an investment plan that's right for you.

Rule 1: Get in the Game

Rule 2: Define Your Investment Goals and Objectives

Rule 3: Keep Your Investment Plan on Track

Rule 4: Know What You're Worth

Rule 5: Never Use "Should-Have-Done" Excuses

Rule 6: Never Count Your Money Until You Sell

Rule 7: Diversify Your Investments

Rule 8: Have a Minimum Loss Strategy

Rule 1: Get in the Game

If you want to get into the stock market game and become a winner, visit the Financial Center at www.financialcenter.com and click on the Savings icon. Then click the calculator titled "What will it take to become a millionaire?" Enter the required data and click Calculate. The results show how much you need to invest today to be a millionaire in the future.

As you'll see, if you save just a little money each month, you'll be surprised at how little you will have at the end of the year. You can't make big money in stocks by throwing nickels and dimes at the market. To reach your retirement years with a substantial nest egg, you need to invest substantial sums along the way. And the older you are when you begin, the more you will need to invest each year. For instance, to reach a goal of $1 million by age sixty-five (assuming an average annual return of 11 percent per year), a nineteen-year-old investor could invest just $1,000 a year. But a forty-year-old would have to invest nearly $10,000 a year to reach $1 million by retirement.

To invest wisely, you need to understand an investment's liquidity (how fast you can get your money), safety (will you get all your money back?), and the rate of return (how much will your money earn?). Often, investors expect too much too soon from their investments. One way to remove much of the risk and emotional turmoil of investing is to invest fixed amounts of money on a regular basis (e.g., monthly). This type of investing is called *dollar-cost averaging*. I'll talk more about it in Mistake #5.

Once you've selected, analyzed, and purchased securities, your work still isn't done. Managing your investment portfolio can help you squeeze profits from your investments and realize your financial goals. You need to keep current on what's happening in the market, study analytical techniques, and update your financial

---

Charles Schwab can help you develop a financial plan with his company's online calculators, tools, and advice. Go to Schwab's home page (www .schwab.com) and click Planning and then General Investing. The next screen shows financial tools that include a primer on the principles of investing, a general goal planner with an online savings calculator, and an asset allocation tool.

---

plan on a regular basis. The Internet provides several portfolio management tools, such as the ones offered on Morningstar's Web site at www.morningstar.com (see figure 2.1).

You can also calculate your investment returns with a pencil and paper. Start with the ending investment balance and subtract the beginning balance. Divide this number by the beginning balance and then multiply by 100 to determine your percentage return—or loss if it's a negative number. For example, suppose that you invest $10,000 in stocks on January 1, 2002, and on December 31, 2002, your account has a value of $12,175. The formula for calculating your return follows:

$$\text{Total Return} = [(\text{Ending Balance} - \text{Beginning Balance})/\text{Beginning Balance}] \times 100$$

Start your calculations with the ending balance and deduct the beginning balance:

$$\$12,175 - \$10,000 = \$2,175$$

Divide the result by the beginning balance:

$$\$2,175/\$10,000 = 0.2175$$

Multiply the result by 100 to calculate your percentage rate of return:

$$0.2175 \times 100 = 21.75 \text{ percent}$$

New Portfolio | Import Export | Combine Rename Delete | Print | Alerts | Updates | Definitions

Portfolios: **--rtinnonsportfolio** ⬍   Views: **--Snapshot** ⬍

⊙ X-Ray this Portfolio   Modify this portfolio ✏   Analyze this portfolio with these tools 📄 🔍 ➡

▲ Holding	Price ($)	Price Change ($)	Price Change (%)	Shares	Market Value ($)	Portfolio Weight (%)	Analyst Report	Morningstar Rating
AMO	23.520	0.120	0.51	100.000	2,352.00	9.32		★★★
ATT	—	0.000	—	50.000	0.00	0.00		
ATTWIN	—	0.000	—	50.000	0.00	0.00		
AWE	16.930	0.430	2.61	65.000	1,100.45	4.36	07-30-01	
AXP	39.960	0.110	0.28	40.000	1,598.40	6.34	07-31-01	
COMT	3.375	0.000	0.00	50.000	168.75	0.67		
COST	40.700	0.720	1.80	125.000	5,087.50	20.17	07-31-01	
DANA	—	0.000	—	125.000	0.00	0.00		
DCN	23.880	-0.720	-2.93	100.000	2,388.00	9.47	08-02-01	
LU	6.450	-0.060	-0.92	100.000	645.00	2.56	08-04-01	
VOD	19.210	-0.330	-1.69	200.000	3,842.00	15.23	08-08-01	
VZ	53.640	-0.290	-0.54	150.000	8,046.00	31.89	08-01-01	
XON	—	0.000	—	150.000	0.00	0.00		
rtinnonsportfolio			-0.21		25,228.10	100		

Data as of 08-13-2001 at 16:16

FIGURE 2.1 Morningstar Portfolio

Your return is 21.75 percent, or 22 percent. By anyone's standard, a return of 22 percent in one year is pretty good. This rate means that for each dollar you invested, you earned twenty-two cents.

Choosing the right investments is just one of many elements you need to consider when you enter the investment game. You also need to know the answers to the following questions:

1. Where do you stand? What are your present financial commitments, and what will they be in the future? Make sure you have emergency funds set aside to cover unexpected expenses, such as car repairs.
2. What are your financial goals? How much do you want to make over what period of time? How much risk can you tolerate? If you lost your entire investment, could you recover mentally and invest again?
3. How do you want to allocate your investments? What's the appropriate mix of investment types for your age (young adult, middle-aged, approaching retirement, retiree) and your circumstances (single, married, supporting children or older relatives)?

4. Are you in the game? Develop a regular investment game plan and stick to it regardless of market volatility.

Rule 2: Define Your Investment Goals and Objectives

Successful investing doesn't require a lot of effort or expertise. It just takes commitment and perseverance. The more you put into it, the more you'll get out of it. You don't have to follow the market every day and you don't have to take big risks. You just have to maintain an ongoing investment program. For most investors, success occurs over a long period of time.

The first step in financial planning involves setting objectives. What that really means is identifying the finish line. To reach that line, you need to set strategic and tactical goals that will get you there. Strategic goals are long term and tend to be general—for example, "I want to be a millionaire by the time I'm fifty." Tactical goals are short term and more specific—for example, "I want to save and invest $5,000 this year." Your financial plan should include both strategic and tactical goals. Write them down and check on your progress periodically. If your situation changes, update your goals to reflect the changes in your life.

"Everyone's goal," says Franklin Resource Fund manager Michael Price, "should be patience and risk avoidance, and then let time make you money. Our theme is slow and steady wins the race, and hence our logo is a turtle. Our newsletter is called *The Patient Investor* since patience is so important in successful stock market investing."

Most investors share a common goal. They want to make money investing in the market. Those who are successful establish investment plans that cover the essential money-making steps. First, they develop buying selection rules that help them pick the best stocks. They rely on stock charts to determine the right time to buy. Second, they develop a set of selling rules so that they know when to sell to make a profit and when to sell to avoid major losses. And finally, they have a specific method to tell them when the market averages are topping or falling, and subsequently, when to buy or sell.

How you achieve your financial goals is where your investment program enters the picture. Stop and evaluate your financial situation before you start investing. You want to be certain you're financially ready to be an investor. You don't want to pay penalties due to early withdrawals because you needed cash to cover unexpected expenses. Before investing, be sure that you have the following categories covered:

Monthly bills The goal is to be able to pay your monthly bills without relying on credit cards or future cash sources, such as bonuses.

Credit card debt If you use credit cards to pay for everyday expenses but can't pay your monthly card balances in full, you aren't ready to become an investor. You need to change your spending habits and pay off credit card debt before you begin investing.

Emergency fund Before investing, the first thing on your planning list should be to create an emergency fund. Unexpected expenses can include uninsured medical costs, property losses, and unemployment.

Insurance Make sure you have adequate insurance to cover disability, health, life, automobiles, and property.

Rule 3: Keep Your Investment Plan on Track

Many people want to jump into investing before they know where they are and where they're going financially. Investing always involves risk. Before you invest, you need to understand how this risk relates to your financial base. First, create a budget that includes a savings plan for emergencies, acquire all the insurance you need, and if you're not a homeowner, become one. It's one of the best investments you'll ever make. Then create a separate savings plan to fund your market investments. In the process, make sure you keep your independent retirement contributions (e.g., Tax Deferred Savings Plan, IRA, among others) on track.

Your investment decisions need to take into consideration your attitudes about risk. The amount of risk you can tolerate often depends on your knowledge of investments, your experience, and your personality. Each person has his or her own style and needs. Knowing exactly what your risk tolerance level is can help you select investments that are right for you. The Internet provides several sites that will help you get started, including the following.

Bank of America's Web site (www.bankamerica.com) offers a survey of twelve questions about your investment preferences. You enter your answers, and the online calculator suggests an investment strategy that suits your current needs and situation.

Frank Russell Company (www.russell.com) features a Comfort Quiz to help you allocate your investments in a mix that's right.

Rule 4: Know What You're Worth

The first step in getting where you want to go is figuring out where you are today. Although calculating your net worth may not be exciting, it's the starting line for your investment program. Later, you can compare your net worth to where you started to see how well you're doing.

One of the things that makes calculating net worth difficult is organizing all your personal finance data and sorting it into the right asset classes. Finding the data you need can be time-consuming. The following suggestions will help you organize your data into categories for calculating your net worth:

Liquid assets To find the value of your investments (bank accounts, certificates of deposit, money market accounts, stocks, bonds, mutual funds), refer to your most recent bank and brokerage statements.

Property assets For real estate assets, use your most recent property appraisal or check with a Realtor who knows your neighborhood. Be sure to include only your equity in the property (that is, subtract any mortgage balance due from the market value of the property).

Vehicles Remember to deduct depreciation from the original cost of the vehicle.

Jewelry, art, and collectibles Use your insurer's appraised value or your best estimate.

Saving and investing are different processes, although savings are often the source of funds for investing. Savings are funds that you put aside regularly. They usually earn a low rate of interest, but you can access them easily and immediately, and if you keep them in a bank or a savings and loan, the financial institution insures them. Investment funds are the monies you use to buy securities that can increase or decrease in value. These securities may pay interest or dividends, but you have no guarantee that they will increase in value or produce future income.

Other assets Use your best estimate of each asset's resale value.

Many financial planners will tell you that most people don't know their net worth. When their new clients make ballpark guesses as to what they are worth, they usually aren't even close. The Internet provides several online calculators that can assist you in determining your net worth. For example, the Altamira Resource Center Net Worth Calculator (www.altamira.com) both helps you calculate your current net worth and tracks changes over time. You can also determine your net worth with a pencil and paper by following the format in table 2.1.

After you have determined your net worth, test your financial fitness by visiting Quicken's Web site (www.quicken.com). Complete the questionnaire, which asks for your responses to a series of questions covering investments, debt management, and retirement planning. After you complete the questionnaire, you are provided with ideas that address your financial objectives, as well as self-improvement suggestions.

Rule 5: Never Use "Should-Have-Done" Excuses

Don't spend your time worrying about "should-have-dones" that you can't do anything about. "I should have sold" or "I should have bought" are two typical examples. Unless you've figured out how to build a time machine, get on with the future of your investment life.

For more information about the investment process and about bulletproofing your portfolio, check out Investor Home at www.investorhome.com.

TABLE 2.1 Figuring Your Net Worth

Property Assets		Liabilities	
Residence	$_____	Home mortgage	$_____
Real property	_____	Other mortgage	_____
Furnishings	_____	Bank loans	_____
Jewelry/art	_____	Auto loans	_____
Automobiles	_____	Charge accts	_____
Other assets	_____	Other debts	_____
		Total Liabilities	_____
Cash Assets		**Net Worth**	
Gov't bonds	$_____	Total assets	$_____
Municipal bonds	_____	Total liabilities	−_____
Corporate bonds	_____	Net worth	_____
Certificates	_____		
Equity Assets			
Real estate	$_____		
Stocks	_____		
Mutual funds	_____		
Annuities	_____		
Gold/silver	_____		
Other assets	_____		
Total Assets	_____		

Select investments that meet your financial goals and risk tolerance level. How much time do you have to invest? Do you want to be an active or a passive trader? Analyze your investment alternatives before you call your broker, to make sure you can explain clearly exactly why you're interested in a particular investment. Then sit back and listen to what the broker has to say before you make a decision. When you buy a stock, determine at what price you will either sell that stock for a profit or cut your losses so that you never have to use a "should-have-done" excuse again.

If you are using a "live" broker who seldom offers you viable advice, consider switching to an online brokerage firm to dramatically reduce your commission expenses. Avoid mutual funds that charge "front-end" loads. Monitor your portfolio and reevaluate your goals on a regular basis by using a "watch list" similar to that shown in figure 2.2. Like most watch lists that are available on the Internet, *SmartMoney* magazine's (www.smartmoney.com) watch list allows you to track the performance of up to thirty stocks that are in your portfolio or that you are considering for your portfolio.

Using your watch list, regularly check the performance of your investments so that you can make appropriate changes over time. Expect that changes in market conditions, new product introductions, and new technology will change how businesses operate. Use this information to gain an understanding of when to buy stocks for your portfolio—and when to sell stocks you own.

Rule 6: Never Count Your Money Until You Sell

How many times have you heard someone say, "Gosh, I made a fortune in the market today"? When you pressed them, though, chances are you discovered that the "fortune" was only a "paper gain" caused by the market being up. They didn't actually sell any of

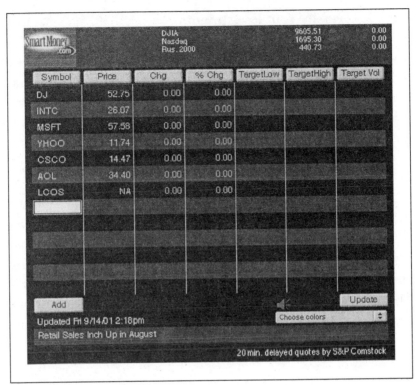

FIGURE 2.2 SmartMoney Watch List

their stock, so their purported gain was all fluff. You can't buy anything with fluff. If they had actually sold their stock at a profit, then their declaration about making money today would have been real.

It's of no value to enjoy several years of bull market gains only to have to give it all back when the inevitable bear market follows. And the bear market will take your money away much faster than the bull market gave it to you. As the old saying goes, "It's better to get off a faulty elevator on the way up rather than to ride it all the way to the bottom." Unfortunately, it takes some investors several years to learn this lesson the hard way. Your investment plan must include a sell strategy. Only count your dollars when you sell.

Rule 7: Diversify Your Investments

Each stock you buy should reflect the goals of your investment plan. How you choose to diversify your investments (e.g., mutual funds, stocks, bonds, and so on) depends on the following:

- Your required rate of return
- How much risk you can tolerate
- How long you can invest your capital
- Your personal tax liability
- Your need for quick access to cash

The Internet offers several sites that can assist you in developing diversification strategies. Check out brokerage firm Legg Mason's Web site (www.leggmason.com), which uses an online questionnaire to help point you in the right direction. Fidelity Investments (www.fidelity.com) also offers an asset allocation planner.

Rule 8: Have a Minimum Loss Strategy

The general market is represented by leading market indices such as the S&P 500, the Dow Jones industrial average, and the NASDAQ Composite. You need to carefully evaluate these indices so that when they top or turn down, you will know when to buy or sell. Seventy-five percent of stocks follow the market trend, regardless of how good you think they are. Growth stocks and lower quality companies usually get clobbered in a market downturn. They'll often drop two or three times the market average. Some will never rebound or will take years to rebound.

In the stock market game, the best offense is a great defense. You absolutely can't win unless you have a strong predetermined defense to protect yourself against large losses. If you invest in stocks, you are going to make mistakes in your selection and timing of purchases. These poor decisions will lead to losses, some of which can become significant. No matter how smart you may think you are or how good you believe your information or analysis is, you simply are not going to be right all the time.

As a general rule, cut your loss when a stock in your portfolio drops 7 or 8 percent below the price you paid. Make the sale automatic, with no vacillating. The fact that you are down 7 or 8 percent below your cost is the only reason you need to sell. Nothing else should have a bearing on the situation. Of course, nothing says you have to wait until a loss reaches 7 to 8 percent before you sell a stock. If you sense that the market or your stock isn't acting right, sell it. Don't think about it or wait a few more days to see what might happen.

By the same token, if a stock moves up into a good profit position beyond what you paid for it, raise your stop-loss position. Then, if the stock suddenly falls, you can still get out of it and make a profit.

THE LEAST YOU NEED TO KNOW

Determining what return you need requires having a clear understanding of where you are and where you desire to be in the coming years. This example shows the factors you need to consider when setting a ten-year goal. Suppose you're married, both you and your spouse have jobs that pay relatively well, you own a home (with a hefty thirty-year mortgage), you have $5,000 in an IRA, and you're vested in your employer's pension. You have two children; one is six years old and the other is seven. You expect that both children will want to go to college.

Your financial objectives for the next ten years are pretty clear: You need to raise the cash to send your children to college while covering your other obligations. What about the ten years after that? Do you want to retire early? How much cash will you need for a comfortable retirement? Will your investment strategies get you to your financial finish line? How much of your income should you invest?

If you want to start investing but are having trouble making ends meet, you may be due for a financial health checkup. Whatever your personal situation dictates, you can find investments that are tailor-made for your requirements. Determining how much money to invest is a big step in the right direction.

MISTAKE 3

I Accept Hot Stock Tips from Friends

If I had a buck for every piece of bad investment
advice I got from my buddies, I would be a
millionaire today.

JACK WASHBURN

INFORMATION AND OPINIONS ABOUT WHAT STOCKS TO BUY ARE AVAILABLE from a wide variety of sources. Not all of these sources are created equal. From your broker to your hair stylist to the buddies you play golf with, everyone has their own ideas and hot stock tips they're eager to share. Sharing makes them feel important. Unfortunately, most of them don't know what they're talking about. They're just trying to impress you with their grasp of the market or some secret channel into "inside" information.

Perhaps with the exception of your broker, most of these "sources" will be wrong 90 percent of the time when they recommend a stock for you to buy. Here's why. They probably got their "hot tip" from another buddy, and you can rest assured they haven't done any analysis of the stock they think you ought to buy. Test them by asking what their hot stock's earnings per share (EPS) are. When you get a blank stare, you'll have your answer. They probably won't even know what you're talking about, or they'll tell you, "It doesn't matter. Trust me. I just know this stock will take off!" Depend on the one person you can trust—yourself. Learn how to conduct your own investigation.

WATCH OUT FOR EXPERT RECOMMENDATIONS

Some investors rely on market pundits or their broker for stock tips and advice. Analysts are always touting stocks on TV and in business publications. Why? Because they want to sell their stock. Do you really think these people are going to say anything negative about something they're trying to sell? Be wary of advice from so-called experts in the newspapers, on radio, or on television. You usually don't know anything about their expertise or their motivations. By the time the average investor hears about a "hot" stock, the big institutions, such as mutual funds, have already made their move to take advantage of the situation.

On the surface, analysts' reports would seem like a good place to go for solid facts and advice on specific stocks that interest you. It's logical to assume the analysts have conducted extensive research and are in close contact with the companies they report on. However, take these reports with a grain of salt. Analysts rarely issue a "sell" rating and tend to rate any stock they review up rather than down. Although you can find lots of free analyst information on the Internet (figure 3.1), it's important to question the quality of the report and the motivation of the people behind the report. Have they been hired to promote the stock that you're interested in buying? To obtain a quality analysts' report, you may have to pay for it.

Be wary of merger rumors or any other rumors about what's "going to happen" to a company. Most of these rumors never become reality. Even if they do, the stock price could just as easily fall if the big traders decide to sell on the news.

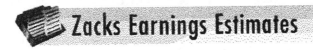

SOUTHWEST AIRLS CO (NYSE:LUV)

SOUTHWEST AIRLS CO - LUV

WALL STREET ESTIMATES

	MEAN	HIGH	LOW	NUMBER EST	MEAN CHG LAST MNTH ($)
FISC YR END 0112	0.97	1.03	0.84	13	0.00
FISC YR END 0212	1.15	1.27	1.08	6	0.01
QUARTER END 0103	0.17	0.20	0.16	11	0.00
QUARTER END 0106	0.28	0.31	0.26	8	0.00
NEXT 5 YR GRTH (%)	13.50	15.00	12.00	6	0.00

SOUTHWEST AIR   02/18/01
COMPANY VS INDUSTRY

---------- EPS GROWTH RATES --------
(CUR FY=0012)

	LAST 5 YRS ACTUAL (%)	CUR/LAST (%)	NXT/CUR (%)	NXT 5 YRS (%)	P/E ON CUR YR EPS
COMPANY	25.2	29.3	24.5	13.5	26.4
IND: TRANS-AIRLINE (T=287)	-8.1	-11.6	26.7	14.4	18.5
S & P 500	9.4	10.4	5.6	14.1	22.8
COMPANY/INDUSTRY	N/M	N/M	0.9	0.9	1.4
COMPANY/S&P	2.7	2.8	4.3	1.0	1.2

DISTRIBUTION OF EPS ESTIMATES
HISTOGRAM AS OF 02/18/01
SOUTHWEST AIR

FY1 - 0112	FY2 - 0212
13 ESTS.	6 ESTS.

FIGURE 3.1 Zacks Earnings Estimates

INVEST WITH YOUR EYES

Learn to invest with your eyes, not your ears. Depending on your ears means passively listening to opinions, which usually aren't worth much. On the other hand, facts that you can see with your eyes have value. There is no substitute for your own hard work and judgment to gather the facts on a stock before you invest. Learn the facts about the company's products and prospects. Study its stock performance on the charts and analyze fundamental data. In particular, review the key data elements such as sustained earnings that separate the winners from the losers.

You can get free information and facts about stocks from a wide array of sources. Your best bet for finding great investment opportunities in the stock market is to rely on two unbiased sources: the market itself and the financial performance of the companies in that market. The best stocks, especially the ones that make consistent, long-term advances, share key characteristics. Their earnings and sales growth far exceed those of their competition, they have superior profit margins, and they offer an attractive return on equity. Institutional investors are also buying the stock at a rapid rate.

Your most reliable sources for specific stock information are Web sites that feature databases and chart services. They're in the

---

George Burns once said, "Too bad the only people who know how to invest in the stock market are too busy driving cabs and cutting hair." Unless your cab driver works the area around Wall Street, he probably shouldn't be your first source of investment advice. In most cases, by the time a hot tip makes it deep into the general public—to your barber, your butcher, or your taxicab driver—the game's over for that stock. As they say on Wall Street, "What everyone knows isn't worth knowing."

business of providing facts, not random opinions. You can tap into these databases to find stocks that are consistently reporting stellar financial performance (one of the hallmarks of a winning stock). One of the best Internet sources for obtaining this information is *SmartMoney* magazine's Web site, at www.smartmoney .com. More comprehensive databases and charting services are available on the Web for a fee.

INTERNET CHAT ROOMS

The heart and lungs are vital organs, but on their own, they are lifeless. Like the human body, investing is a complex system. Think of each aspect of your investment plan as part of a living system. The entire system must be healthy for you to win. If you receive investment advice from one of your friends, check it out. Picking the right stocks is crucial. If you choose to rely on advice from others and ignore the market, you will end up taking big losses. By the same token, if you follow the market without regard to specific stocks, you will never beat the market.

Internet chat rooms and bulletin boards are filled with "hot" investment tips. Question everything you read in these environments. Ask who's posting the message and why. It can often be impossible to find out. Is it an overeager junior investor who thinks he knows more than he does or a desperate investor trying to get the price of her stock back up so that she can sell it to some other sucker? There will be some nuggets of good information out there, but distinguishing the real gold from the fools gold isn't easy. If you think you've found gold, confirm it through your chart and database resources.

WATCH OUT FOR POPULARITY

There's a good way to tell when a bull market rally is about to run out of gas. Whenever *Time* or *Newsweek* runs a cover story on stocks, that's a good sign the market is about to peak, and the next big correction is just around the corner.

The popularity rule applies to mutual funds as well. Fidelity's Magellan Fund, one of the world's biggest funds, has seen its performance decline as its popularity increased. In the fund's early years, when its assets were less than a billion dollars, its performance was outstanding. The fund beat the market by 20 to 30 percentage points per year in the late 1970s and early 1980s.

But as the fund ballooned with additional investment dollars to assets of over $40 billion, its performance began to decline. Its three-year performance through 1996 was substantially worse than the S&P 500 index, although things improved in 1997. The next time you hear a rash of hot tips about a certain stock or sector, consider it a sign of imminent danger, and make a point of looking elsewhere for your next investment.

COMPOUNDING:
A FRIEND YOU CAN TRUST

Think of compounding as the precious gem in your portfolio. Stocks can crack under the weight of bad news, and the bond market is easily tarnished by interest rates. Inflation drags down the return on cash while compounding just keeps on producing. Seemingly small contributions invested over long periods of time can grow to astonishing amounts as a result of compounding.

To figure out exactly what compounding can do for you, there are several Web sites you can use. Three sites that I recommend are www.calcbuilder .com, Vanguard Group's site at www.vanguard.com, and Charles Schwab's site at www.schwab.com.

Compounding and time counter the short-term ups and downs of investment returns. Compounding should be a fundamental part of your investment strategy. Compounding coupled with where you allocate your investment are two keys to accumulating substantial wealth. For investors in their twenties, the impact of compounding is profound. If you stash away $125 a month into your employer's 401(k) plan or in growth-oriented stocks, you'll have in excess of $2 million when you retire.

Here's a simple example of how compounding can work for you. Let's say you're making $60,000 a year and saving 5 percent of your income, or $250 a month, at an annual return of 13 percent. In twenty-five years you would accumulate about $600,000. If you increased your annual savings rate to 6 percent, you would add $100,000 to your portfolio.

Table 3.1 shows what you sacrifice by putting off investing for the future by even one year. The result of delaying for five years is even more surprising. The power of compounding is shown clearly in table 3.2, where even a small investment almost doubles in ten years.

TABLE 3.1 The Cost of Waiting
(Investing $1 a day at 12 percent)

Begin Saving	Total Savings at 65	Cost of Waiting
Age 25	$296,500	0
Age 26	264,400	32,100
Age 30	116,900	147,540

TABLE 3.2 The Rewards of Discipline
(Investing $100 a month at 12 percent)

10 Years	20 Years	40 years
$22,400	$92,000	$979,300

THE LEAST YOU NEED TO KNOW

Never accept a stock tip from a friend or from an Internet investment chat room unless you first check it out. Chances are the source knows less about what's happening in the market than you do. Expert advice from stock analysts can also be biased, especially if the analysts are being paid to promote a particular stock.

I Don't Analyze the Stocks I Buy

I want to buy stocks that no one else knows about, and I want to sell them after everyone discovers them.

JOHN MARKESE

A WINNING RACE CAR HAS A LOT OF THINGS GOING FOR IT. IT HAS A potent engine, a lightning fast pit crew, and an expert driver. If one of these elements fails during a race, you'll lose the race. Stocks need the same sort of synergy to rise to the top. A stock may have a fabulous earnings-per-share (EPS) ratio, but if it lacks a healthy base of institutional investors, it won't go very far. Flat sales growth might cast doubt on strong current profits. If the market is in a downtrend, the stock will likely fall. It is vital to analyze any stock you are thinking of buying. Don't settle for a stock with only one or two winning characteristics. Pick stocks that have all the elements to ensure you'll cross the financial finish line.

If you're not prepared to perform a technical analysis on a stock you're considering buying, how can you know what you're really purchasing? Buying without knowledge substantially increases your investment risk. Technical analysis is the process you go through to understand the volatile, unpredictable, and often mysterious characteristics of a stock so that you can make an informed investment decision. If you don't do it, then, quite frankly, you're a fool. It doesn't take all that much time to qualify a stock.

In this chapter, I'll show you how professionals conduct time-efficient technical analyses. The tools are available on the Internet. You'll learn how the forces of supply and demand play on a stock's price and how to determine what a stock's price strengths and weaknesses are. I'll also show you how to access "free" Internet screening tools to quickly determine when it's time to buy or sell a stock.

GREAT STOCKS START WITH GREAT FUNDAMENTALS

Put your feet up on the desk for a moment, lean back in your chair, and think about some of the greatest stocks in the decade of the nineties—stocks such as Microsoft, Cisco, AOL, Yahoo!, and Circuit City. What did they all have in common? They all had super fundamentals, such as sales and earnings that were growing consistently year after year. They all had good margins, high returns on equity, and price/earnings ratios that were not in the stratosphere. They were also the leaders in fast-growing industries that Wall Street was behind. As you consider your investment options, keep in mind that industry leaders are the stocks that will produce the largest gains over time.

Look for companies whose earnings have grown at least 20 to 25 percent every quarter over at least the past two years. Demand the same for sales growth. Although you can use a slew of ratios to gauge a company's performance, the basics don't go away. Companies still have to sell something at a profit. And a healthy profit is virtually impossible without strong sales. A company's sales figures show you whether there is a demand for its products or services and, more important, whether that demand is increasing. If you want to invest in companies that are the best in their industry, sales figures will help you find them.

Look for quarterly sales that have increased at least 25 percent over the past three to six quarters. An ideal company will have accelerating sales growth, with each quarterly percentage increase in sales larger than the previous quarter's. Pay special attention to companies with significant earnings increases over the past six to twelve quarters. Indeed, sales growth is one of the best ways to identify companies that are truly on the move.

It All Starts with Sales

Sales figures are a key measure of a company's strength or lack of it. Perhaps no other piece of financial information reflects growth better than sales, the money that comes into a company from products sold or services rendered. If a company is run efficiently, sales growth essentially drives earnings growth. Companies basically have two ways to increase earnings. They can either increase sales or reduce expenses—or ideally they can do both. Although a well-managed company controls expenses, healthy sales are the main engine for growth.

Demand is driven by a number of factors, including increasing numbers of customers, customers increasing their purchase volume, introduction of new products, expansion into new markets, and the improvement of existing products. The top-performing companies show consistent double- or triple-digit sales growth. It's even better when the growth rate percentage increases quarter after quarter. Such acceleration is the hallmark of quality growth companies and reflects a well-managed organization.

Think of sales growth as the foundation under your house: if it's loose or crumbling, it's not as stable as one with all the structural elements in place. When you find a company that is increasing its sales, that tells you demand for the company's products is increasing. That means its sales growth is structurally sound and the company is capable of increasing earnings to boost its stock price.

Sales numbers can sometimes mask problems at companies. Companies may rely on just a handful of customers and losing any of them may spell big trouble. Other companies rely heavily on overseas markets, putting them at risk of bad economies or political strife abroad. Also, fluctuations in foreign exchange rates can seriously dilute sales figures. Some companies, such as pharmaceuticals, get the bulk of their sales from just a few flagship products. If sales in these items falter, it could mean trouble for overall sales.

With retailers, additions of new stores increase the sales figures, even if sales at existing stores slow down. That's why retailers report total sales as well as average-store sales, to provide an apples-to-apples comparison. Another pitfall to watch for occurs when companies include sales that haven't actually taken place. Orders that won't be shipped or paid for until weeks or months later sometimes are added to the sales total to inflate results.

GRADING A STOCK: A SUMMARY

Here's a summary of the important points to consider when you analyze a stock:

Industry Is the company in a growing industry with strong long-term potential?

Position within the industry Does the company have a strong niche position within its industry?

Product line Is the company expanding its product line?
Is it spending a good share of its revenue on research and
development? Do its key products have solid long-term
potential?

Profit margin The higher a stock's profit margin relative to
the industry's profit margin, the more attractive the stock.
A high, or growth, profit margin is an indication that a company might still be in the early stage of its growth curve.

Relative strength Is the company one of the leaders in its
market and its industry?

Management ownership What share of the company's
stock does management own? Management ownership of a
significant share of the stock is a strong indication that
management believes in the company.

Looking Beyond the Bottom Line

Sometimes you have to look beyond a company's bottom line to determine whether you want to own its stock. If you don't like a company, don't buy its stock—no matter how healthy its earnings. Many
investors decline to own the most profitable stocks on the New York
Stock Exchange. Philip Morris has led the market in total shareholder
return for the past sixty years. But because it's the world's leading cig-
arette producer, some investors refuse to buy its stock.

Other investors have had other socially responsible reasons
for steering away from certain stocks. Teetotalers sometimes avoid
the stock of brewers such as Anheuser-Busch. On the other hand,
a lot of Bud drinkers own the stock because they love the beer.

Environmentalists often refuse to buy stocks of companies that are notorious for polluting the environment. Pacifists typically decline to invest in the stocks of defense contractors.

Of course, you don't need a reason of conscience not to buy a specific stock. You might decide against investing in a retailer because you don't like its stores, or in a restaurant because you don't like its food. McDonald's stock has been riding high for years, but I've never been interested in owning it because the expression "Big Mac" has an unpleasant meaning to my digestive system. You might choose not to invest in a manufacturer because you don't like its products. My friend refuses to buy Microsoft stock because she owns an Apple computer and has always considered Microsoft a competitor. Personal preference should be a part of the stock selection process. It's your money. Invest it in the stocks of companies you like after you have thoroughly checked them out. *Individual Investor* magazine offers an excellent Web site (www. individualinvestor.com) for checking out stocks.

What Can You Learn from Analysts' Reports?

If you want to broaden your search for investment advice beyond investment newsletters and personal finance columnists, where can you turn? Some investors like to read through brokerage company research reports to see how professional stock market analysts view a stock. Research reports are available to investors through their brokerage firm or through the company that is the subject of the report. Many companies will send you free copies of analysts' reports that discuss their stock—or at least they'll send you the reports that paint their stock in the best light. Unfortunately, they are not likely to send the negative reports, so you're never quite sure if you're getting the full story.

After years of reading analysts' reports, I've discovered that an analyst's guess is liable to be as good—or as bad—as anybody else's. I've read many a glowing report for a stock that was headed for disaster. Just the same, it's probably worth reading analysts' reports to get a broader view of a stock and its prospects. But like newsletters and investment columns, analysts' reports are far from gospel.

Some Internet services, such as VectorVest (www.vectorvest .com), (see figure 4.1), track stocks and include analysts' evaluations in their stock reports. America Online and Prodigy's Strategic

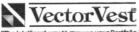

VectorVest®

"The intelligent way to manage your Portfolio."

VectorVest Free Stock Analysis:

Get Stock Info

Welcome to VectorVest

The key to intelligent investing lies In knowing what your stocks are really worth, how safe they are and when to buy, sell or hold. VectorVest advocates buying safe, undervalued stocks rising in price.

VectorVest ProGraphics is the only service that:

Click here to Order your Four Video Set!

- Analyzes, ranks, and graphs over 7000 stocks each day for Value, Safety and Timing.

- Gives Buy, Sell, Hold recommendations and a Stop-Price on each stock,every day.

- Combines the insight of fundamental valuation with the power of technical analysis

- Uses a Market Timing System that has NEVER FAILED!

"I've tried nearly every software program in the business...AIQ, Super Charts, you name it. VectorVest ProGraphics is absolutely the best. I don't use or need anything else."

-Edward J. Conrad
Private Investor
Naples, Florida

"VectorVest ProGraphics users will find stocks of good value before the crowd finds them."
"...you'll be choosing from a cross-section of stocks that includes hundreds of young, relatively unknown companies, new issues, and a comprehensive list of the country's fastest-growing companies."

-Stocks & Commodities Magazine
Seattle, Washington

FIGURE 4.1 VectorVest

Investor section both include analysts' evaluations in their stock reports. They show how many analysts rate the stock a "strong buy," a "buy," a "hold," a "sell," or a "strong sell."

But even those "buy-hold-sell" ratings are less objective than you might expect, because analysts are discouraged from giving a stock a "sell" rating. Company officers naturally hate sell ratings, and often complain bitterly to brokerage companies who list their stock as a "sell." They also tend to become less cooperative with analysts who publish negative reports, making it more difficult for them to research the company. For that reason, analysts rarely issue sell ratings. The worst rating most analysts are likely to give a stock is a "hold," which has now become almost the equivalent of a "sell." This has compromised the entire rating system and makes it difficult to trust any analyst who speaks well of every stock.

What Can You Learn from Financial Newsletters?

For many years, Mark Hulbert has published a monthly newsletter called the *Hulbert Financial Digest*, which rates the performance of all the leading investment newsletters. Hulbert's research suggests that their guesses are liable to be as good—or as bad—as anybody else's.

About 80 percent of the newsletters don't beat the market over long periods of time. That record may sound dismal, but it is no worse than the results of other branches of the financial advisory industry. On the bright side, that means 20 percent of newsletters do beat the market. But as Hulbert is quick to caution, the important factor is whether the 20 percent that beat the market in the past will be the same 20 percent that will beat it in the future. "If there is no such correlation, then it doesn't help us to know that 20 percent will beat the market in the future because it is only randomly related to how they have done in the past," explains Hulbert.

So the real question is whether there is any correlation between predicting past and future performance. The answer is "yes," although you have to look at performance over a long period of time before you find such a correlation. If you look at performance over one year or less, there is no correlation. Basically one year is statistical noise. So picking a performer on the basis of one year is just like flipping a coin. But over a five- or a ten-year time period, there is a statistical correlation. By betting with the top performers of the past decade and following them through the next decade, you have a chance of beating the odds. There are no guarantees, of course, but you'll dramatically increase your odds of success by going with the long-term winners.

For many years, Louis Navellier's *MPT Review* has been one of the top-ranked newsletters in the country, but the typical investor would not be able to follow his recommendations. Navellier's buy and sell lists feature several hundred stocks each month, and most of the stocks on the sell list just appeared on the buy list a month or two earlier. Although Navellier has established a strong performance record with his newsletter, it has little practical application for the typical investor, who simply can't afford the time or cost to trade hundreds of stocks each month.

If you're shopping for a good newsletter, consider buying the *Hulbert Financial Digest*, which will steer you to the newsletters that have rated the highest over the past few years. (For a one-year subscription, send $59 to *Hulbert Financial Digest*, 316 Commerce St., Alexandria, VA 22314.) Hulbert has several suggestions for investors interested in selecting a newsletter. He recommends that you read through several different newsletters to get a feel for the type of advice they offer. Look for several key factors:

Risk level How risky are the newsletter's recommendations? You may find that a letter has done very well over the past several years but that its portfolio has been fully margined. You may decide that approach is just not for you.

Tone A lot of apologizing is a giveaway the newsletter is more interested in protecting its ego than in making you money.

Follow-up Does the newsletter tell you not only what to buy but when to sell?

Approach Are you comfortable with the newsletter's philosophy and its writing style, or do you find its approach irritating, egotistical, or obnoxious?

Ultimately, you want to choose the newsletter that has the most relevance to your investment situation. You also want one with a good long-term track record.

What Can You Learn from Annual Reports?

Before you invest in a new stock, review the company's annual report. Focus on substance, not sizzle. Don't be swayed by dazzling artwork, flowery praise, or bold predictions.

Entire books have been written on how to read annual reports. Some investors like to study every detail of a report's financial section, combing through the balance sheet, the cash flow figures, and the footnotes in search of any undiscovered nuggets that could help them decide whether the company is destined for stellar performance. In truth, that effort probably won't yield anything that the analysts on Wall Street haven't already discovered months before, but it may be worth your effort for your own peace of mind.

Typically, you can get a very good indication of a company's success within the first two or three pages of its annual report, based on what the company chooses to feature up front. The deeper you have to page into a report to find anything about the company's financial results, the worse those results are likely to be. If the returns have been stellar, you can rest assured the company will put that information right up front.

If a company is doing well, it will nearly always publish three graphs in the front of its annual report: one showing sales revenue growth over the past few years, another showing net income growth, and a third illustrating earnings per share growth. Invariably, those three graphs will show steady growth during the years featured. If these graphs aren't present, it probably means recent results have been disappointing. Companies in this position often substitute other graphs showing meaningless numbers, such as the growth in number of employees, assets, inventory, or anything the corporate PR people can come up with to imply some type of positive growth. But if the graphs don't display revenue, net income, and earnings, everything else is likely little more than a cover-up.

THE LEAST YOU NEED TO KNOW

If you are not prepared to conduct a functional and technical analysis of a stock you're thinking of buying, then don't buy it. Be on the lookout for winning stocks that can historically demonstrate great fundamentals, such as solid earnings growth and stellar sales performance. Read these companies' annual reports and search for the key information you need to make a buying decision. Check what the stock analysts are saying, but temper their advice with the results of your own research before accepting their recommendations.

MISTAKE 5

I Bet with the Bulls and Wonder Why I Get Gored

Sometimes the best investments are the ones you don't make.

DONALD TRUMP

WHEN INVESTORS WITH MONEY TO PUT TO WORK SEE OTHERS MAKING windfall profits from a high-flying bull, they're tempted to do just about anything to join the party. But don't buy the first sweet deal you see. There are thousands of stocks and funds to choose from. Take your time and check out your options.

In this chapter, I'll show you what you can do to manage stock market risk in a bull market. Let's begin by first looking at the history of the bull markets.

1982 It all started in 1982 when the current, amazing bull market was born. The Dow bottomed at 1,163 on August 8. Two months later it was up 10 percent.

1984 Another year when interest rates were rising. The Dow bottomed at 1,086 in late July, before surging 14 percent in roughly four weeks.

1986 The Dow bottomed at 1,763 on August 1, before rebounding more than 8 percent by September 4.

1988 From late August to October, the Dow jumped nearly 10 percent.

1989 After hitting 2,440 on June 30, the Dow soared more than 14 percent by October.

1994 After falling for the final two weeks of June, the Dow staged a 9 percent rally by mid-September.

1996 Investors worried when the Dow corrected to 5,346 on July 23. However, by the end of the year, it was up to 6,560, a ferocious 23 percent move.

1998 The Dow's descent culminates with a more than five-hundred-point plunge on August 31, to 7,539. By November 23, though, it was back up to 9,374, a 24 percent rally.

1999 The bull continued to race through 1999, easily topping the "magic" 10,000 Dow barrier.

2000 As we gently stepped into the new millennium, almost everybody expected the bull to continue charging up the hill. The NASDAQ soared to over 5,000 in the early months of the year until April, when the first bear caught up with the bull and knocked the NASDAQ down 20 percent. By the end of the year, the NASDAQ had fallen to less than half its fifty-two-week high.

2001 Both the NASDAQ and the Dow remained sluggish throughout the year as the U.S. economy took a tumble that many thought would pull the country into the double whammies of recession and inflation. Although it didn't happen, stellar stock like Cisco dropped close to its fifty-two-week low.

The moral of this history lesson is to stay loose, be flexible, and use dollar-cost averaging, especially if you are a mutual fund investor, when investing in a bull market. In many respects, a bull market is like a supercharged engine in a drag racer. It can thunder past any passenger car, but the chances of the dragster's motor blowing up are very high.

Stocks also travel at different speeds. High-growth stocks have the muscle to double or triple in price in a short span of time, leaving the major market averages in the dust. But when the market tanks, these stocks typically sink faster than they rallied. In the nineties, tech stocks were the darlings of Wall Street and generated the biggest returns. During the bear market that followed, leading techs, such as Dell Computer, lost 60 percent of their value.

WHAT'S DOLLAR-COST AVERAGING?

Dollar-cost averaging is an investment strategy that ensures that an investor automatically buys more shares of a stock when its price is down and fewer shares when its price is up. The approach takes advantage of the volatility of the market to even out the fluctuations in a stock's price over time. You dollar-cost average by investing the same dollar amount at regular intervals (e.g., monthly). The approach is also commonly used to purchase mutual fund shares on a regular basis.

For example, let's say that you invest $100 a month automatically in shares of a mutual fund that holds a broad selection of stocks in the overall market. When the market is high and the mutual fund's shares are trading at, say, $25, your $100 buys four shares. When the market is down and fund shares are trading at, say, $20 a share, your $100 buys five shares. So you buy more shares when stocks are low and fewer when stocks are high.

You can implement a dollar-cost averaging program with companies that offer direct stock purchase plans or with mutual funds that offer automatic investment programs. Many of these plans will automatically deduct a set amount from your checking account at a regular interval you specify. Most of the Fortune 500 companies offer direct stock purchase plans to individual investors. Here's how these plans work. Let's say you want to open a dollar-cost averaging account with IBM; you contact IBM's investor relations department and authorize a deduction of $300 a month from your checking account to purchase whatever number of shares or partial shares $300 will buy on your behalf. You'll have to sign an authorization form to make all this happen. When it does, you will start accumulating IBM stock every month until you submit written notice to stop the process.

You may ask: Why waste time reading earnings reports, tracking PE ratios, following the market, and agonizing over when to buy and when to sell if dollar cost averaging is that simple and that reliable? If it takes so little effort, why doesn't everyone do it? The reason is few people know about dollar-cost averaging or how to get started in the program.

To compare dollar-cost averaging with buying a set number of shares, let's look at an example. Let's say you chose to buy 100 shares of XYZ Corporation on the fifteenth day of every month for four consecutive months (table 5.1). Assume that the share prices were as shown on the fifteenth of each month. If you divide the total amount you paid ($22,000) by the number of shares you purchased (400), you find that your average price is $55 per share.

Now let's examine what happens when, rather than buying a set number of shares each month, you invest a set amount of dollars

TABLE 5.1 Purchasing a Set Number of Shares

Date	Price per Share	Shares	Cost
January 15	$30	100	$3,000
February 15	50	100	5,000
March 15	100	100	10,000
April 15	40	100	4,000
		Total: 400	$22,000
			Average price per share: $55.00

each month (table 5.2). If you were to invest the same amount of money as in the previous example over four months, you would invest $5,500 on the fifteenth of each month. Your results: You would purchase 486 shares (actually, 485.833, but I've rounded things off for simplicity) with a total investment of $22,000. By dividing $22,000 by 486, you arrive at an average price of $45.27 per share. This is a savings of $9.73 per share from the $55 per share in the previous example. You purchased more shares with the same investment dollars.

TABLE 5.2 Investing a Set Number of Dollars

Date	Price per Share	Shares	Cost
January 15	$30	183	$5,500
February 15	50	110	5,500
March 15	100	55	5,500
April 15	40	138	5,500
		Total: 486	$22,000
			Average price per share: $45.27

You can see that when prices are low, you can buy more shares. Conversely, when prices are high, you buy fewer shares. Over time, because of the ups and downs of market prices, you should accumulate more shares than if you had purchased the same stock using the set-number-of-shares approach. And if your stock pays dividends, you will have more shares on which you can earn dividends.

WELCOME TO THE TWENTY-FIRST CENTURY

Did you or one of your friends get gored by the bull as the market slid through 2000 and into 2001? The message of the new millennium may have been unpleasant, but at least it was easy to read: The U.S. economy is slowing down. It's not reversing, not stopping. It's still growing, just not so fast. This is the reality. Investors can face it now or face it later—but it's generally better to face it sooner. Federal Reserve chairman Alan Greenspan raised interest rates, and this is the rest of the story.

As Warren Buffett likes to say, your problems will not improve with age. How big a problem do we have? It depends on what you own. If Wall Street continues to respond as poorly to quarterly earnings warnings from major corporations as it did in 2000, investors are in for some bad times. The landscape darkened for investors when many companies cautioned that they wouldn't hit profit estimates.

What Caused the Carnage?

As the third quarter's end approached in 2000, company after company realized there was just no way they could make their earnings estimates. And Wall Street was merciless in its response. Here were firms admitting their profits wouldn't meet expectations for a sin-

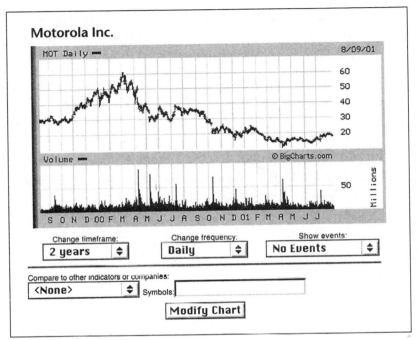

FIGURE 5.1 Motorola

gle quarter, and their stocks were being taken down in some cases by 50 percent or more overnight. Look what happened to "bell-wether" Motorola in the first half of 2001 (figure 5.1).

At the same time that Motorola was having problems, Wall Street really seemed to snap in late September 2000 when Intel announced its third-quarter earnings problem. Its stock dropped 22 percent in a day and drifted lower for days after. When Kodak announced similar news, it got similarly hammered, dropping 25 percent in a day, to a five-year low. In the quarter's final five weeks, 60 U.S. companies issued advisories that profits would be better than expected and 332 announced they'd be worse. All of this raises two important questions: Why did so many companies get into trouble and what could you have done to avoid getting gored?

The first question has many answers—and all of them make you wonder why Wall Street was so surprised by the shortfall epidemic of 2000. Oil prices were the highest they had been in decades, and that can mean trouble, especially with winter approaching, even in an information-based economy. It's a very serious problem for any company that is dependent on petroleum-based chemicals or is a heavy user of transportation.

The euro was so weak at the time that some thought it was doomed. The effect on U.S. companies was the familiar double whammy: prices of U.S.-made products go up in euros, reducing demand, and euro earnings get translated into fewer dollars. In addition, we were finally seeing evidence that the tight labor market at home was leading to higher employment costs.

Putting these facts together, is it not surprising that a lot of companies got into earnings trouble? Yet analysts who follow stocks were blindsided when Kodak issued its third-quarter warning. It explained that July and August had been particularly strong, and it had been counting on a strong September. Instead, the month had been ho-hum, for reasons the company couldn't figure out other than just a broadscale weakening in the economy.

The story was the same at Priceline, whose stock plunged 42 percent the day it warned of third-quarter trouble. A slow September destroyed its estimates despite a great July and August. Enlarge that picture and you have an image of an economy that was still growing, but no longer at extraordinary rates. The slowest the U.S. economy had grown in the preceding four quarters was at a zippy 4.8 percent annual pace, and the fastest was an almost incredible 8.3 percent (in 1999's fourth quarter). When that kind of growth slows to 3 or 4 percent a year, most economists will claim we're healthy as a horse, just not roaring like a Formula One car.

The apparent end to supergrowth helps to answer the second question: Why were investors so wrathful at being disappointed?

You can understand why a stock with a towering price–earnings (PE) ratio gets pummeled when earnings so much as quiver, which was Intel's situation. It was trading at a multiple of 55, nosebleed territory for a huge, capital-intensive manufacturer, and its third-quarter warning knocked that ratio down to 35. But most of the household-name stocks that got clobbered in late 2000 weren't Intels. In fact, many were already scorned, trading at pitiful discount prices, yet they got kicked some more. Alcoa tumbled from a PE of 19 to one of 14, and DuPont went from 16 to 13. Rockwell International was trading at a measly 12 and still got squashed to a multiple of 8. Why was the punishment so severe?

Investors believed that, in many cases, this missed quarter would not be the end of the story. High raw-material prices, a weak euro, and wage pressures are not short-term problems. Add the prospect of a general economic slowdown and the outlook turned even less rosy. The general opinion was that we could be looking at many quarters of earnings below the estimates on which the prewarning stock prices were built. What's more, investors were plainly jittery. They knew the S&P 500 multiple had about doubled in the preceding five years, to historically unheard-of levels, but how long could that last? They had also been expecting an economic slowdown and finally saw evidence it was arriving. With most equities in the hands of institutions, no fund manager wanted to be holding a slowdown casualty at end-of-quarter evaluation time, so there was a stampede to abandon any company showing weakness.

Where Do We Go from Here?

This brings us to question three: What should investors do now? Naturally, you'll want to screen anything you own (or are thinking of buying) for exposure to oil prices, the euro, and labor costs.

With those major threats, it's easy to see why big, old-economy companies were the first victims, but they won't be the last (look at Priceline). You'll also want to check any analyst earnings estimates and ask whether they still seem reasonable in a less-than-turbocharged economy.

For example, until Kodak declared trouble, some analysts expected 2000 earnings to be up as much as 14.5 percent from a year earlier and to keep rising from there. Was that expectation realistic? Just as important, watch for signals of how much the economy will slow and for how long. Yes, that means making some educated guesses. But the rewards will go to those who discern the subtler economic changes to come. Those signs—unlike the spate of earnings warnings we've experienced—won't be the kind that hit you over the head.

THE LEAST YOU NEED TO KNOW

It's easy to get complacent in a bull market. Everything you buy seems to go up after you buy it and you're able to brag to your friends about how well you're doing. Always keep in mind that you are just a small frog playing in a very big pond. A single negative announcement from a company whose stock you own can instantly wipe out all your profits and throw you into a loss position. Don't let the bull gore you.

MISTAKE 6

I Never Sell My Losers—
and That's All I Have Left

*Selling your winners and holding losers is
like cutting your flowers and watering
your weeds.*

BILL O'NEIL

TWO THOUGHTS CROSS MOST INVESTORS' MINDS WHEN THEY PLUNGE
into the stock market. They want to either make a big profit
or avoid a huge loss. Achieving either objective has a lot to do
with how well you build your position. Let's face it, we all have a
tendency to dwell on our successes and keep quiet about our fail-
ures. The following story illustrates this point.

A friend of mine (let's call her Jill) jumped into the market and
bought six stocks that her brother-in-law, who knew less about the
market than she did, told her were "hot stocks" to buy. After a couple of months, three of the stocks were up and three were down.

Jill promptly sold the winners and bragged to anyone who
would listen about the killing she had made in the market. She
kept the three losers in the hopes that they too would go up some
day and used the profits from her winners to buy three more "hot
stocks" that a friend recommended. Two went up. She promptly
sold them, bragging again to her friends about how well she was

doing in the market, and kept the loser. And, as Paul Harvey used to say, "You know the rest of the story!"

By repeating this process, Jill ended up with a portfolio filled with losers. If she had done the opposite and sold her losers, she would have built up a portfolio of winners. At the very least she could have taken the tax break against her gains when she dumped the losers. Your ultimate investment goal should be to build a great portfolio of winning stocks and funds. You don't do that by selling your winners. Cut your losses by selling your losers, replace them with winners, and let your winners run. I'll show you how to do that in this chapter.

WHY INVESTORS RESIST SELLING

Many investors are reluctant to sell a stock that has declined because they're convinced it will recover and take off. After all, now that the stock has fallen 8 percent, it has to bounce back, right? Wrong. Wall Street is littered with stocks that may take years to regain their former glory. Every 50 percent crash in the price of a stock starts out as a small 8 percent loss. There's no sure way to tell the difference. Even well-known stocks may continue to fall, your investment shrinking with their share price. Goodyear Tire and Rubber, J. C. Penney, Xerox, Lucent, and Philip Morris are all big-cap stocks that have lost two-thirds of their value in recent years.

No one likes to sell a losing stock. It means admitting you made a mistake. But everyone commits errors, even the best professional investors. The goal is to learn from your miscues and to keep losses as small as possible. When a stock falls by 8 to 10 percent from your buy point, sell it. You don't need any other reason for your decision. The stock's slide is reason enough.

CUT YOUR LOSSES SHORT

A selling strategy that keeps losses small is a lot like buying an insurance policy. You may feel foolish selling a stock for a loss and downright embarrassed if it recovers. But the idea is to protect yourself from a devastating loss. Once you've sold, your capital is safe. Limiting your losses makes it relatively easy to bounce back. An 8 percent loss on a stock needs only an 8.5 percent gain on the next purchase to break even (the extra half point covers brokerage fees). But a 25 percent loss requires a 33 percent gain. And, you'll need a 100 percent winner to repair the damage of a 50 percent loser.

If you don't stop the bleeding in your portfolio quickly, small price declines can hemorrhage into massive losses. That is especially true if you are investing in a bad market. You should always, without exception, sell any stock that falls 8 to 10 percent below your buy point. As long as you hold it, you're losing money. The stock for whatever reason isn't working. You don't need any other reason to pull the plug.

Limiting your losses to 8 to 10 percent is cheap protection when you consider how many mighty corporations like Microsoft have plunged 50 to 70 percent or more in the past. The 8 to 10 percent sell rule is in our opinion a maximum. You may choose a lower percentage that's more suitable to your tolerance—or lack of it—for risk.

DON'T FIGHT THE FORCE

Never buy a stock on the way down. Always sell on the way up. Momentum is one of the strongest forces of the stock market. When stocks catch fire, they can climb far beyond reasonable levels. And when they drop, they can also drop beyond all common reason or expectations. The historical chart of Amazon.com in figure 6.1 illustrates my point. The stock peaked early in the year 2000 at $50 a share. If you had bought it and then sold it somewhere near the peak, you would have been in good shape. But look what would have happened if you had held it when it started to drift down in March. It continued to tumble throughout the remainder of the year. At mid-year, shares were selling for $12, a whopping 76 percent decrease in value in less than twelve months.

Of course, there's always another side to every decision. When you sell a stock on the way up, hoping to time your move at or very near the peak, you risk missing out on even greater growth. Imagine investors who sold their Wal-Mart stock in 1969 after it

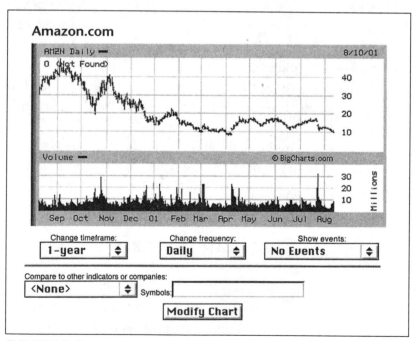

FIGURE 6.1 Amazon.com

had enjoyed a nice run-up. If they had held on to the stock instead, $1,000 worth of Wal-Mart stock would have grown to more than $1 million twenty-five years later. As Peter Lynch once said, "Never jump off a winning racehorse or stock."

The same is true of trying to catch a stock at or very near its bottom, just before it turns around. When you buy a stock on its way down, you could be in for a long, unexpected drop.

CREATING STOCK CHECKLISTS

It's a good idea to make up a separate checklist for each stock you buy and to keep them in a notebook or on your computer. Over time these checklists create an extremely useful record that reveals recurring patterns of selling strengths and weaknesses. Here are the items to record.

1. Stock purchase date
2. Price paid per share and number of shares
3. Target sell price
4. Target sell date
5. Events or changes that should cause the stock to go up or down
6. Stop-loss order entered? At what price?
7. Dow Jones Industrial Average (DJIA) and NASDAQ on date of stock purchase
8. Stock sell price and date

You should create a checklist for each stock in your portfolio that provides you with instant access to key information about that stock.

THE HOLD OR SELL QUESTIONNAIRE: WHAT TO ASK YOURSELF

As we've said, the when-to-sell part of the investment process is just as important as the when-to-buy side of the equation. The questions that follow are designed to help you fine-tune your selling strategies. Your answers will help you decide whether to sell or hold. Use the same set of questions to review each stock in your portfolio, to consistently evaluate all your holdings. The following questions were adapted from a training session originally developed for brokers and have proven useful for individual investors as well. Photocopy the questions for reference when you talk to a broker or other adviser about selling a stock.

1. Are you currently more or less excited about this stock than you were when you first bought it?
2. Has the expected story (i.e., good news) for this stock played out yet? If not, is there still a chance the story will play out? If yes, did the stock go up on the news? If the stock went up, did it reach your price objective?
3. What is the stock's price now? How much has it gone up or down since you bought it?
4. What is expected to happen fundamentally with this stock? If you had the money, would you buy more shares today?
5. Where do you expect the price of this stock to go over the next eight weeks—up or down and how much? Why?
6. What is the revised estimated annualized percent return for this stock? Does it still meet your short- and long-term expectations?
7. What is the downside price risk from the current price if nothing happens?

8. Is the risk/reward balance favorable from the current price?
9. Where are the DJIA and the NASDAQ now? How are the market averages affecting the price of this stock?
10. Have there been negative surprises from this company or its industry since you purchased the stock?
11. Since purchase, did you ever almost decide to sell, only to hold on for a little longer? Did you set or revise either a mental or an actual stop-loss price?
12. With your current knowledge, would you buy this stock again right now at today's price?
13. Have you identified any significantly better opportunities for purchase right now than this stock?

It's a good idea to write down your responses to these questions for two reasons. Written answers reinforce the discipline of thinking through the exercise in detail. Written answers also give you an archival record that you can use for later reference, comparison, and learning. How often should you go through this exercise for each stock you hold? In my opinion, the answer is at least once a week.

Use of this questionnaire will not automatically make every position profitable. It will, though, help to impose closure on situations that are not working out as expected. It will also generate urgency by reinforcing the time value of money. A decision to hold should be every bit as active as a decision to buy or to sell. The only thing missing is the need to pick up the telephone and call your broker or go online to execute your trade.

As you review each of your stocks, it's advisable to create a tickler file. If you decide to hold a stock after reviewing it closely, file its page to review again at a predetermined date.

THE LEAST YOU NEED TO KNOW

To be a successful investor, you need not only buy stocks at the right time, but sell them at the right time, too. Until a stock is sold, the outcome is only a temporary paper result. A handsome profit can melt away in a moment until you close out your position. Use the questionnaire as a reminder, a guide, and a prompting tool to sharpen your sale-execution decision-making skills. Formalize your stock review process using the tips provided in this chapter. Write down everything so you can track both where you've been and where you are going. And do it on a regular basis.

I Stop My Winners Before They Cross the Finish Line

Never jump off a fast-moving train or a winning racehorse.

PETER LYNCH

EVEN THE MIGHTY PETER LYNCH, ONCE MANAGER OF FIDELITY'S MAGELlan Fund, admits that plenty of his investments have failed. He'll also tell you that far worse can happen. "As long as you're not leveraged, and you should never borrow to buy stocks, all you can lose is what you've invested. But if you get out of a stock too soon, you can miss out on big multiples of appreciation," says Lynch.

That lesson was driven home in the late eighties when Lynch sold Magellan's position in Toys "R" Us, which had returned a lot of money to the fund. Lynch recalls, "I bought the stock early, before there was really any competition in toy retailing. When I saw Milton Petrie buying up 20 percent of the company, I figured that the stock would back off because that was probably all that Petrie would buy. So I sold Magellan's position and guess what happened? The stock went up four-fold over the next twelve months." The mistake that Lynch made was ignoring the stock's fundamental values. If it's a growth company, not just a cyclical stock, stick with it.

FIRST, FIND THE WINNERS

Winning stocks go through three stages: discovery, accumulation, and distribution. Recognizing the stages helps you identify the winners.

At the discovery stage, the big institutions (mutual funds and other major investors) ferret out the best new companies at the forefront of dynamic industries. Early on, top-rated funds spotted technology companies such as Cisco Systems, Dell Computer, and EMC Corporation.

When they find great new companies, the big institutions start building positions in them. This is the accumulation stage. These heavy hitters can't buy all the shares they want at the drop of a hat. They have to buy thousands of shares day after day, month after month, to build their position. After a series of bases and advances, the stock becomes well known to the general public. The CEO shows up on the covers of business magazines, while analysts tout the stock on TV. Ordinary investors go into a buying spree because everybody knows the stock is going up. Of course, by the time it's obvious to everyone, there's usually something wrong. Mutual funds may recognize that the company faces slower growth or more competition down the road. So they begin selling out, which again takes a long time. This is the distribution stage.

How many times have you concluded a stock's best days are behind it, only to watch it soar as you stand on the sidelines? In reality, the stocks that are doing best tend to keep doing well, while those that are slumping likely will continue to do poorly. Why? The great companies manifest their strength through superior performance in terms of earnings, sales, profit margins, and even stock performance.

A study of the greatest stock market winners found that all-star stocks had, on average, outperformed 87 percent of the market before they began their most dramatic price advances. In other words, they were already in leadership positions. This concept is contrary to the popular bargain-hunting mentality, but it is based on historical facts. You can draw a rough parallel to the real estate market. Homes that are structurally sound and have all the amenities will sell for higher prices and appreciate more over time than those that are structurally inferior. In both markets, you get what you pay for.

USE RELATIVE PRICE STRENGTH TO SPOT FUTURE WINNERS

If you want to find next year's winning stocks, look at today's better-performing stocks. Remember, the biggest winning stocks historically have been, on average, in the top 13 percent of stocks at the time they began their major advances. To help you identify today's leaders, *Investor's Business Daily* developed the Relative Price Strength, or RS, rating. This rating shows where the price performance of each stock falls relative to other stocks. It helps you compare stocks and identify the strongest. Each stock is rated on a scale of 1 to 99, with 99 representing the top 1 percent in terms of price movement over the previous twelve months. An RS rating of 85 means that a stock is outperforming 85 percent of all stocks in terms of price performance. An RS rating of 25 means the stock is being outperformed by 75 percent of the market and should be avoided.

A good starting point for selecting winning stocks is to identify stocks with the highest RS rating in an industry group that's leading the overall market. You can find every stock's Relative Price Strength rating in the *Investor's Business Daily* newspaper, which is available at most locations where you would also find the *Wall Street Journal*.

WATCH FOR THE BREAKOUT

Champion thoroughbreds burst out of the gate in their race for the finish line. But it takes more than a good start to win the race. Market-leading stocks are much the same way. They should burst out of a sound price base where the price of the stock hasn't changed more than 2 percentage points over five or more trading days in heavy volume. If you buy one of these stocks, don't even think about relaxing after the stock breaks out of its base. The first days and weeks after a breakout are critical. Many stocks will pull back a day or two after a breakout. This is normal as long as they don't crash back into their bases. Affiliated Computer Services offers a classic example of a company that broke out of a solid base (figure 7.1). Notice how the stock formed a relatively flat base from

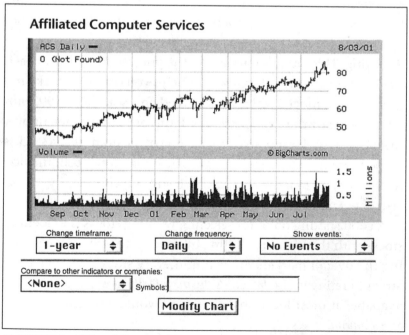

FIGURE 7.1 Affiliated Computer Services Breakout Graph

September to October 2000 and then took off on a rapid acceleration. The price of the stock jumped from $45 to $85 over the next six months.

ADD TO YOUR WINNERS

You can also manage a winning stock by buying more shares as the price of the stock rises. That may sound imprudent, but what works on Wall Street doesn't always seem comfortable at first. Executed properly, averaging up in price leverages your gains and minimizes potential losses.

Here's how this approach works: First, decide how large a dollar position you want in a quality stock. Then invest, say, half that amount just as the stock breaks out of a sound price base in heavy trading volume. Then look to add smaller dollar amounts at yet higher prices. Buying up means you're buying a stock that's working its way up the price ladder. It's a confirmation your first purchase was sound.

RIDE THE UPTRENDS

If a stock's RS line—its relative strength rating—stays on an uptrend, that's positive. It shows the stock is keeping ahead of the overall market and confirms the stock's uptrend. If a stock's relative strength line fails to follow along with a new high in its price, that's a warning signal. This shows the overall market is moving up faster than the stock. This may signal the stock is weakening, even though the stock's price may not reflect it immediately. An RS line that starts drifting lower over a period of time, even if the stock price remains steady, indicates the stock is weakening. This also shows the stock is slipping in comparison with the rest of the market.

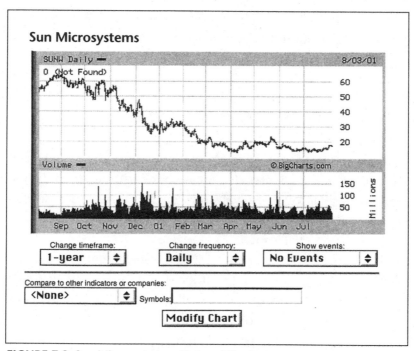

Sun Microsystems

FIGURE 7.2 Sun Microsystems—Uptrend Stock

The chart for Sun Microsystems (figure 7.2) dramatically illustrates how quickly a stock can decline. The stock was enjoying a nice uptrend in the early fall of 2000; then the stock's relative strength started to drift lower over the next five months. In that relatively short period of time, Sun's stock dropped from $65 to less than $20 a share.

AVOID LOW-PRICED SUBSTITUTES

Another common temptation among investors is to seek out stocks that resemble the industry leaders in that they offer similar products or services, but are trading at lower prices than the leaders. You're usually better off sticking with the leader of the industry, even if its share price is higher. Take the chip-making industry. Intel has dominated the field, sending its stock up about 485 percent from 1996 through 1999. Advanced Micro Devices, a maker of Intel-clone chips, went up only about 55 percent in the same time span. This is not a rare example, for any industry. Stick with the leading stocks in a leading industry group.

SELL YOUR WINNERS NEAR THE TOP

A winner always exerts some sort of pressure over its rivals. With stocks, that special edge can take many forms. A winner might be the first company to go to market with a much-needed product or service. Its sales and profits surge, taking the stock price along for the ride. The same is true for management shake-ups, in which old ways of doing business are swept aside to make room for new, more profitable methods. Or a company may benefit from a big industry shift. In the case of the chip makers, a boom in personal electronics and Asia's economic rebound joined forces with breakthroughs in chip manufacturing methods that lowered costs and increased speed.

Whatever form these changes take, they can generate profits for astute investors. For many air travelers, takeoff is the most nerve-rattling part of the trip. Once it's over, they can sit back and enjoy the ride. Investors face a similar dilemma with stocks. When a stock shoots up after a breakout, it may be tempting to sell it and take a quick profit. But you'll often receive a bigger reward if you hold on. That initial jump could signal the start of a long advance.

Pay special attention to stocks that score a 20 percent gain in just a few weeks after taking off. If a stock breaks out of a solid base and rises 20 percent from its pivot point in less than eight weeks, you should hold the stock at least eight weeks total. For example, if you buy a stock June 1 and by June 14 it rises 20 percent, you'd want to hold onto the stock until at least July 27. Large gains need time to develop. Eight weeks gives you a good idea of whether you've latched on to a potential big winner.

Always be on the lookout for a fresh face. Once in a while you may come across a stock with a good-looking base and strong fundamentals—only you've never heard of the company and don't know exactly what it does. That should pique your interest. By finding winning stocks before they become widely known, you can get in on the ground floor.

REVIEW YOUR PAST TRADES

All investors make mistakes, but not all learn from them. Reviewing your past trades is critical to improving your stock market prowess. These reviews help you spot your weaknesses. Identifying a problem is half the work of solving it. Keep a spreadsheet listing the stocks you've purchased, along with the dates and prices at which you bought and sold them. Other columns might contain the stock's Relative Price Strength, earnings per share, accumulation/distribution, and other ratings at the time of purchase and sale. Allow sufficient time to pass so that you can be objective about the results. Then analyze your winners and your losers.

THE LEAST YOU NEED TO KNOW

No investor should pick stocks based on a single factor. You must weigh the full picture, including a company's earnings, industry group performance, institutional sponsorship, and chart patterns.

The Relative Price Strength rating measures a stock's price moves over the past twelve months compared with all other stocks. Because the better-performing stocks tend to go even higher, while the lagging stocks tend to lag even more, look for stocks with RS ratings of 80 or higher. If a stock's relative strength line is moving in a strong uptrend, that helps to confirm its upward price momentum.

MISTAKE 8

I Buy Stocks Without Knowing What They're Worth

*Everything comes to the man who hustles while
others stand around waiting and watching.*

THOMAS A. EDISON

*I*F ANYONE DOUBTS THE SCHIZOPHRENIC NATURE OF HOW STOCKS ARE VAL-
ued, go back to New Year's Day of 2000 when America Online
(AOL) announced that it would buy Time Warner (TWX). Early in
January, the price of both stocks soared. After all, a phenomenal
upstart was acquiring a proven provider of information and entertainment. Slow-moving Time Warner was getting hitched to one
of the fastest growing tech companies on the market. It had to be
a marriage made in heaven.

But the market suddenly began taking back much of its applause
along with the gains it had awarded the two stocks. When analysts
took a second look, they decided that AOL was saddling itself with a
slow-growing media behemoth and Time Warner's healthy cash flow
would be drained to prop up AOL's slim profit margins. Investors
threw up their hands, unsure how to value such an odd couple.
When the merger was finally approved in January 2001, the stock
values of the two companies began to return to their normal levels.

In today's wild roller-coaster market, how can you determine
what a stock is really worth? Fortunately, several excellent services

available on the Internet have done the job for you—and most of them are free. I'll show you where to find them and how to use them in this chapter.

WHAT'S A STOCK WORTH?

If you spend enough time at cocktail parties or backyard barbecues, you'll eventually run into someone boasting about their latest "bargain" stock or the hot company they managed to pick up "cheap." And as the ice melts in your glass, they'll probably ramble on about their superior stock-picking skills and all the winners they've found in the past. There's nothing more boring than somebody else's stories of buying stocks cheap. However, learning to spot bargains is the essence of successful investing.

Some investors make the mistake of thinking that a low stock price means that a company is inexpensive. For instance, if Microsoft is selling for $78 a share and IBM is selling for $212, then Microsoft must be the cheaper stock, right? Not necessarily. Those were real prices in early May 1999, and at the time, Microsoft's total market value was $404 billion compared with IBM at $195 billion. The difference was Microsoft had some five billion shares outstanding, while IBM had about a fifth that many. Share price is total market value divided by shares outstanding. And since the number of shares is largely arbitrary, so is the stock price.

Understanding Market Valuation

The crucial consideration is why the market thought Microsoft was worth $404 billion while it assigned IBM a value of just $195 billion. Investors value stocks based on one question: If I put my money into this company, what are the chances I'll get a better return than if I invest it in something else? It's a matter of risk versus reward. The safest investment is a U.S. Treasury bond because its return is guaranteed by the "full faith and credit" of the federal government. The determination of a stock's value starts there. How much more will it return than a Treasury bond and at what risk?

When you buy a stock, your return depends on the company's stream of earnings over time, which is hardly guaranteed. The more reliable that stream, and the more quickly it grows, the more investors will be willing to pay for the stock of the company. The average electric utility has reliable earnings, but historically utilities haven't grown very fast, so they have tended to be pretty sleepy stocks. Microsoft's earnings, on the other hand, have been both steady and fast-growing, which is why there are more than a few secretaries in Redmond, Washington, who count their net worth in millions.

Comparing Stocks

In order to evaluate companies against each other and themselves, investors long ago developed a measure called the price–earnings, or PE, ratio. You calculate the PE ratio by dividing a company's price per share by its earnings per share. If a company has a PE of 20 to 1, for instance, that means investors are paying $20 for every $1 of earnings. If the PE is 18 to 1, they're willing to pay only $18 for that same $1 of earnings. Most people use only the first number in the ratio when referring to a company's PE.

PE ratios fluctuate with investor perceptions of companies. That's why two companies with the same earnings per share (EPS) may have different multiples. If Company A and Company B each earn $1 a share, but Company A's stock is trading for $20 and

Company B's is trading for just $18, the market is making a judgment on the future earnings prospects of these two companies. Investors think Company A's earnings are poised to grow more quickly based on any number of factors, such as its financial health, competitive position, management style, and industry leadership. Consequently, they're willing to pay $2 more for Company A's stock than for Company B's stock.

WHAT'S A "CHEAP" STOCK?

To identify a stock that's "cheap," you have to look at that stock's behavior over time. Most established companies trade up and down in a range depending on how investors are weighing their earnings prospects. Sometimes disappointing news, such as a lackluster quarter or a poor earnings report, can depress a stock's price. Conversely, good news can spark a flood of investor interest.

This ebb and flow is reflected in the PE ratio, which can be compared both to a company's historical stock price range and to that of other companies in its industry. For example, Ford Motor Company typically trades at a wide discount to the S&P 500 average multiple because the auto industry is notoriously cyclical. But because Ford has been a more reliable earner in recent years than General Motors, it usually trades at a slight premium to its larger rival. If Ford strays downward out of its normal range because it has a bad quarter and investors sour on the stock temporarily, you might be able to buy it for a smaller earnings multiple than usual. In other words, the stock could be considered a bargain.

The object of investing, obviously, is to buy low and sell high. And as you can see, that often means looking for stocks that are temporarily out of favor. If you buy stocks near the top of their range, the danger is they will reverse course and tumble downward. If you buy near the bottom or when the stock is cheap relative to its true potential, you can enjoy the full ride back up. The art of investing is deciding when to strike—and before everybody else does.

RESOURCES FOR RESEARCHING
A STOCK'S VALUE

Taking the time to conduct research to determine the value of any stock you're considering will reward you richly. Your investment returns will be directly proportional to the quality of the companies you buy. Fortunately, there is more information available than you can use. Peter Lynch wrote in *One Up on Wall Street,* "I can't imagine anything that's useful to know that the amateur investor can't find out. All the pertinent facts are just waiting to be picked up." And yet, there are people who say they can't invest because they don't know where to get information. I submit that it is now more difficult to avoid investment information than to get what you need. Information is everywhere—from your library to the magazine rack at the grocery store to the Internet.

Even though it's an electronic world these days, there are lots of traditional publications that form the backbone of individual investment research. It's nice to curl up with your favorite investment magazine, peruse the paper over a cup of coffee, or receive a newsletter targeted to your situation. This section will introduce you to all forms of printed publications.

Magazines

The first money you spend on investment research should go toward a magazine subscription. These magazines are cheap, come packed with helpful how-to articles, and many offer excellent investment advice. Here are several top magazines to consider.

Never buy a stock if its valuation makes you uneasy. Instead, find an alternative investment with a more attractive value. Screening programs available at various Web sites let you specify your own valuation criteria. The screening program then searches databases for stocks that meet your search parameters. The free screener at Hoover's Online (hbn.hoovers.com/search/forms/stockscreener) has over seven thousand stocks in its database.

SmartMoney This magazine is described by its publisher as the "*Wall Street Journal Magazine* of Personal Investing," and it's excellent. It's not a tabloid, like many investment magazines; it's printed on quality magazine stock. *SmartMoney* runs articles on every aspect of investing but does a particularly good job with mutual funds and stocks. The editors hold themselves accountable for their stock picks and are always striving to improve their methods. By following their progress, you can improve your own skills as they improve theirs. For subscription information, call 800-444-4204 or visit the Web site at www.smartmoney.com.

Worth Columnists, including Peter Lynch, are second to none, and *Worth's* regular features are dynamite. For instance, it runs a global-investing section that highlights returns in every major country in the world and comments on specific regions. It also shows stocks that successful mutual funds are buying and their reasons for doing so. Another section picks the brains of newsletter editors for hot tips. The magazine reveals stock measurements that aren't widely used, such as price-to-sales and quality-of-earnings ratios. Finally, its periodic mutual fund surveys are among the best available. For subscription information, call 800-777-1851.

Kiplinger's This magazine has a broader scope than either *SmartMoney* or *Worth*. Instead of focusing only on investing, *Kiplinger's* moves into other issues of personal finance, such as credit card spending, loans, college tuition, and vacation planning. The other magazines touch on these subjects, too, but not as often as *Kiplinger's*. The magazine's real claim to fame is its mutual fund surveys. With clear graphics and easily digested tables, the magazine leads the industry year after year. Its columns are nothing to sneeze at, either. For subscription information, call 800-544-0155.

Money This magazine does an excellent job of keeping its readers informed about what's happening in the mutual fund market. *Money* periodically reports on the top funds to invest in by sectors. Feature articles include profiles of average investors with an emphasis on what they did right to get ahead. For subscription information, visit the Web site at www.money.com.

Newspapers

Just about every newspaper includes stock tables. Your local newspaper probably provides the latest numbers. But there are times when you need more than quote or volume information. Those extras are only available in a top-notch financial newspaper.

Wall Street Journal (WSJ) This is certainly the Big Kahuna among investment newspapers, although its authority isn't as unquestioned as it once was. Everybody who's anybody glances at the *WSJ* from time to time and so should you. The front page contains top news summaries in a section called "What's News." A quick skim of the summaries will alert you to items of interest. The heart of the paper is section C, "Money & Investing." That's where you can see how the Dow is performing, what interest rates are doing, whether the dollar is falling or rising against foreign currencies, where commodities are headed, and a slew of other information. For subsscription information, call 800-778-0840 or visit the Web site at www.wsj.com.

Investor's Business Daily (IBD) This great financial newspaper is the result of founder William O'Neil's frustrations in trying to find what he considered was the most important information in determining the value of a stock. When he couldn't find that information anywhere, he decided to publish it himself. Thus was born *Investor's Business Daily*.

IBD covers news in an executive news summary on the left side of the front page. The summary contains key national and international news items in single-paragraph form. The right side of the front page covers important news stories in depth. Inside the front page is a feature called "To Make a Long Story Short," and it does exactly that. There you'll find around a hundred and fifty news items you can review in a glance. The streamlined front page combined with long stories made short gives you twice as many news items in a page and a half as you'll find in twenty pages of other publications.

IBD publishes four measurements of a stock's value that you won't find anywhere else: earnings-per-share rank for the past five years, Relative Price Strength rank for the past twelve months, accumulation/distribution rating for the past three months, and a daily percentage change in trading volume. Here's a brief description of *IBD*'s four measurements:

> ***Earnings-Per-Share Rank*** This measurement compares the earnings growth of all companies and expresses it as a ranking from 1 to 99, with 99 being the highest. By looking at this one simple number, you can see how IBM's earnings growth stacks up against Microsoft's, Hewlett Packard's,

Hamburger Hamlet's, and Gillette's. To compile the ranking, *IBD* takes each company's earnings per share for the two most recent quarters and computes the percentage change from the same two quarters the previous year. That result is combined and averaged with each company's five-year earnings growth record. The resulting figures are compared, and a ranking from 1 to 99 is assigned to each company. Thus, a company with an EPS rank of 95 has earnings growth in the top 5 percent of all companies in the tables.

Relative Price Strength Rank This measurement looks at a stock's price performance over the latest twelve-month period. That's it. It doesn't look at stories, earnings, or price ratios. It simply reports the hard numbers and answers the question, How did this stock perform compared with all the others? *IBD* updates the numbers daily, compares all stocks with each other, and ranks them from 1 to 99, with 99 being the best. That means a company with a Relative Price Strength of 90 outperformed 90 percent of all other stocks in the past year.

Accumulation/Distribution Rating This measurement looks at whether a stock is being heavily bought or sold by comparing its daily price and volume. Each stock receives a letter grade A through E, with A being the best. An A grade means the stock is under heavy accumulation, or being bought frequently. An E grade means the stock is under heavy distribution, or being sold frequently. The purpose of this measurement is to convey the direction that the price is likely to head as a result of trading trends. In other words, is the trend one of accumulation, where the price should rise as a result of high demand, or is the trend one of distribution, where the price should fall as a result of low demand?

Volume Percent Change *IBD* calculates the average daily trading volume of each company's stock during the past fifty trading days. Then it compares each day's trading volume to the fifty-day average and prints the difference as a percentage.

For subscription information, call 800-831-2525 or visit the Web site at www.investors.com.

Barron's If you don't subscribe to the *Wall Street Journal*, you might consider *Barron's*. Either way you're dealing with Dow Jones & Company, which owns both papers. *Barron's* is easier to read in restaurants and on airplanes. If you hate bending and folding the pages of standard-size newspapers to finish the article you've started, you will like *Barron's*. You just turn its pages like a magazine.

In the center of *Barron's* you'll find "Market Week," the best part of the paper. It shows vital signs of the economy, the week's biggest winners and losers from each exchange, and superbly designed stock and fund tables. Unlike the typical abutting columns of other papers, *Barron's* prints tables with white space between different pieces of information. Though the tables don't contain data as complete as *IBD*'s, they display the most recent and past earnings of all stocks. The mutual fund tables show performance for the past week, year-to-date, and three years.

Finally, "Market Laboratory" will give you plenty to think about for the next week as you ponder how every relevant index performed, how much volume the markets moved, what the economic indicators are saying, and so on. For subscription information, call 800-277-4136 or visit the Web site at www.barrons.com.

Newsletters

A good newsletter is a trusty friend that accompanies you through good times and bad. Investment newsletters make or break their relationship with their readers based on one measurement: how well they perform. Never subscribe to a newsletter without first seeing a sample copy. The *Oxbridge Directory of Newsletters* at your local library (research desk) lists thousands of newsletters by category. A quicker review alternative is on the Web. Point your browser to www.yahoo.com and search on "newsletters." Call any newsletters that interest you and request a sample copy. Here are eight newsletters to consider.

Dick Davis Digest The strangest thing about the *Dick Davis Digest* is that there's no Dick Davis listed on the masthead. Beyond that interesting aside, the publication is chock-full of information. Companies covered in each issue are listed alphabetically on the first page, making it easy for you to spot the latest news about stocks you own or are watching. The stories assemble expert information from other newsletters into one convenient source. For subscription information, call 800-654-1514.

John Dessauer's Investor's World This is a good general-purpose publication. Based in Zurich, John Dessauer is a former Citicorp investment officer. His rambling letters discuss global investment issues and contain stock recommendations within the narrative. Much of his writing teaches investment lessons through stories of his childhood, family vacations, and discussions with friends. You won't find detailed charts or model portfolios here. For further information, call 301-424-3700.

Louis Navellier's MPT Review (MPT) Even the title makes this publication look serious, and it is. *MPT* prints performance numbers on hot stocks. It is one of the top-performing newsletters around, listing hundreds of volatile growth stocks from which to choose. It groups them into several different model portfolios that you choose based on how much money you have to invest and how aggressive you want to be. For subscription information, call 800-454-1395.

NeatSheet This is my stock newsletter. It lists stocks to watch and tracks my own portfolio. The *NeatSheet* is published for people who do not have a lot of time to research and monitor stocks. It fits on the front and back of one sheet of paper and reports just the facts on specific companies. Subscribers also receive a straight-shooting annual report. For subscription information, call 800-339-5671 or visit the Web site at www.neatmoney.com.

Louis Rukeyser's Wall Street This is one of the best investment newsletters around. *Louis Rukeyser's Wall Street* is a good balance between Dessauer's conversational letters and the hard data contained in other newsletters. It's conversational enough to keep your attention and gives you some meat to chew on. The publication hosts guest experts each month, prints interviews, profiles companies, and answers subscribers' questions. It doesn't provide enough content for serious researchers, but it's a great rag for beginners. For subscription information, call 800-892-9702.

Outlook Published weekly by Standard & Poor's, the *Outlook* is one of the most widely read investment newsletters. S&P analysts provide clear market commentary, stock updates, stock screens based on S&P's STARS rankings and Fair Value rankings that show the top-performing stocks of the week, and investment recommendations. You can find the *Outlook* in a three-ring binder at most public libraries. Just ask for it at the reference desk. For further information, call 800-852-1641.

Outstanding Investor Digest This is a collection of the best ideas from the most successful investors. Warren Buffett writes, "I'd advise you to subscribe to *Outstanding Investor Digest*. I read each issue religiously. Anyone interested in investing who doesn't subscribe is making a big mistake." That's about as much endorsement as any publication should ever need. For subscription information, call 212-777-3330.

Red Chip Review The *Red Chip Review* is a comprehensive small-cap investment publication. It covers around three hundred stocks with market caps under $750 million. Each stock receives a two-page information summary including almost everything you'd want to know about the company, including the investor-relations phone number in case you want to learn more. For subscription information, call 800-733-2447 or visit the Web site at www.redchip.com.

Value Line Investment Survey Value Line publishes the premier stock-research tool, the *Value Line Investment Survey*, which covers around seventeen hundred companies. Almost everything you could want to know about each company is condensed on a single page.

First published by Arnold Bernhard during the Great Depression, *Value Line* boasts more than one hundred thousand subscribers today. If you count the number of people who look at its reports at libraries or review photocopies from brokers, *Value Line*'s readers number in the millions. The company's analysts have learned a thing or two about stock research over the past seven decades. For subscription information, call 800-634-3583.

Standard & Poor's Stock Guide *Standard & Poor's Stock Guide* is a professional publication similar in spirit to *Value Line*. It lists vital information about each stock in a single row spanning two pages. You'll find a description of the company's business, its stock-price range over several time periods, its dividend yield, PE ratio, five-year earnings-per-share growth, annualized total returns, current position, long-term debt, and earnings for the past five years. The guide is considerably smaller than the *Value Line Investment Survey*, but it contains everything in a single softbound volume that's updated monthly. For subscription information, call 800-221-5277.

Annual Reports

Before you invest in any company, review the company's annual report, which you can request from corporate headquarters. It contains projections about the company's future, financial statements, press releases, analyst reports, and general information. For many small companies that interest you, the annual report will form the bulk of your research. The *Value Line Investment Survey* and *Standard & Poor's Stock Guide* don't cover most small companies. The whole idea of investing in small companies is discovering them first. If Value Line and Standard & Poor's and everybody else already know about them, there wouldn't be anything to discover.

To get a company's investment package, call the company. You might get the phone number from *Value Line*, a magazine article, the Internet, or directory assistance. On the Web, try typing www.name of company.com to find the company's site. For instance, you'll find IBM at www.ibm.com and Ford at www.Ford .com. The company site should contain investor information and contact information. At the very least, it should provide a phone number. When you call, ask to speak with the investor-relations department. The switchboard operator or service representative might ask if you need an investor's packet and simply take your address on the spot.

How do you go about interpreting an annual report? Sometimes, if you're researching new companies, the annual report will look more like a student term paper, which is okay. The money the company saves on fancy printing can be put toward something that will earn a profit. In the beginning of the report, you'll be greeted with a letter from the chief executive officer. Next, you'll page through photos of company headquarters, lots of pictures of happy customers, and other public relations stuff. Then you'll find the important stuff, the company's financial position. Here's some of the information you will encounter.

Assets Assets are divided into current and long-term. Current assets are things like money in the bank and uncollected invoices. Long-term assets are things like buildings. Notes and accounts receivable are money that the company is owed by customers for their goods and services. The rest of the asset section shows things like marketable securities, inventory, plant and property, and other things the company owns.

Liabilities Liabilities are also divided into current and long-term. Current liabilities are due within a year, while long-term liabilities are due further in the future. The liabilities section is pretty straightforward. Taxes are what the company owes to the IRS. Debt is bad from an investor's perspective. You want to see as little debt on the balance sheet as possible. As Peter Lynch points out, a company can't go bankrupt if it doesn't owe any money.

Stockholders' Equity Stockholders' equity is the difference between assets and liabilities. It consists of outstanding shares of stock and other things such as retained earnings and unrealized gains. Added to liabilities, stockholders' equity causes the balance sheet to balance.

Income Statement An income statement shows the company's earnings and expenses. It's where you can figure the all-important profit margin—the difference between what a company earns and what it spends.

THE LEAST YOU NEED TO KNOW

Make sure you know or at least have a fair idea of what a stock is worth before you buy it. At a minimum, you should know what its price–earnings ratio is and how the price of the stock has held up over the past year. Financial magazines, newspapers, and some newsletters are an excellent source for finding this and more information that will help you establish the value of a stock. Review a company's annual report to see what it has to say about itself. In the end, if you feel comfortable with what you have to pay for a stock, buy it.

MISTAKE 9

I Don't Understand
or Follow
Economic Indicators

*If all the economists in the world were laid end
to end, they would not reach a conclusion.*

GEORGE BERNARD SHAW

I T DOESN'T SEEM POSSIBLE THAT AS RECENTLY AS THE EARLY 1990s, ONLY one of the fifty largest companies in the Standard & Poor's (S&P) 500-stock index came from the tech sector. That company was IBM. Yet by the end of the 1990s, almost a third of S&P's 500 companies were tech companies. Companies like Yahoo! and Dell didn't even exist when the 1990s began. If you were following the economic indicators back then and had invested $1,000 in Dell when it started up in 1992, you would be a multimillionaire today.

Stunning market shifts such as these reflect the radical transformations that are taking place in the U.S. economy. These transformations will continue for a variety of economic reasons. If you are going to invest in the stock market, you need to have a basic understanding of how key economic indicators affect the market and how to interpret them so that you can buy the right stocks.

THE KEY TO PRICE:
SUPPLY AND DEMAND

The economic laws of supply and demand affect the health of the stock market, driving it up or down, depending on the economic cycle we're in. Unfortunately, economic gurus do everything they can to make economic theory as complicated as possible. However, if you peel away all the charts and graphs, economics is really quite simple to understand. If someone wants to sell something and others want to buy it, the agreement they reach is the equilibrium point, or the price. If demand rises faster than supply, buyers bid up the scarce resource and prices rise. If there's too much supply, prices fall.

Let's take a look at the petroleum industry, which is expert at playing the economic game. If demand for gasoline remains constant and the seller can produce gasoline at the same cost, the price of gasoline will stay where it is. A price balance between buyers and sellers has been reached. But suppose there's a sudden boom in the popularity of gas-guzzling sport utility vehicles (SUVs).

Suddenly, SUV owners start demanding more gas for their guzzlers. As they bid up the same amount of supply, the price of gasoline rises. If the petroleum industry can't or won't increase production to meet the new demand, the price of gasoline rises dramatically, as we saw in 2001. Now imagine what happens if oil prices spike overnight because of tensions in the Middle East. Or what happens if OPEC decides, for whatever reason, to reduce its production of crude oil. The price of gasoline goes up even further.

When we're talking about stocks, things get much more complicated. Any number of supply or demand factors can upset a stock's price. These supply and demand relationships are what drive the market. When you add millions of them together and throw in government and foreign activities, you get what's known as aggregate supply (the amount the economy is willing to produce) and aggregate demand (the amount the economy is willing to consume). If you have more buyers of a stock than sellers, the stock's price generally goes up. Conversely, if you have more sellers than buyers, the price drops.

Money is the lubricant in all of this because it's the universally accepted medium of exchange. Without money, you'd have to rely on a barter system to buy and sell products and services. So the government issues bills and coins that are backed by the U.S. Treasury. With the exception of gold and silver currency, which has intrinsic value, money is really only worth what it will buy.

WHERE DOES INFLATION FIT IN?

What a dollar will buy fluctuates all the time. If the price of a new home rises 20 percent, the value of your money relative to housing drops 20 percent. If it costs 15 percent more to buy a gallon of gas, a dollar relative to gas purchases is worth 15 percent less. This is what we call inflation, or the erosion of money's purchasing power brought on by a period of steadily rising prices.

Inflation does not occur just because there's a spike in the price of gasoline or housing. While changes in the pattern of supply and demand often result in higher prices for individual goods, individual price increases don't necessarily trigger inflation across the broad economy. Inflation doesn't occur unless many prices increase simultaneously, eroding the general purchasing power of each dollar bill you hold.

For example, if prices rise 3 percent, but you get a 3 percent raise, inflation wouldn't matter much, would it? That's basically what's been happening for the past decade. Inflation has been chugging along at about 3 percent, but the economy has adjusted for the difference. There is tacit agreement between employers and employees that annual raises will grow in line with inflation. If nominal income goes up at least 3 percent and prices go up 3 percent too, what difference does it make?

Unfortunately, inflation can't be counted on to remain so predictable. Once it gets going, it can erode the purchasing power of your money much more quickly than the economy can adjust to it. You can handle a 10 percent inflation rate if you get a 10 percent raise. But what if you don't? And what about those bonds you have in your retirement account, the ones returning a mere 6 percent? With inflation running at 10 percent, your real rate of return would be minus 4 percent.

Inflation is ghostly and hard to pin down. Even the best economists are never quite sure where it's coming from. What is insidious is that it travels like a disease through the economy. University of Washington economics professor Paul Heyne says in his book *The Economic Way of Thinking*, "Economic systems transmit viruses. A setback or unexpected bit of good fortune in one sector of the economy generates setbacks or good fortune for other sectors. Pretty soon, a relatively minor event is having a broad aggregate effect."

The threat is an inflationary spiral that begets strong consumer spending, which, in turn, puts upward pressure on prices. That spurs employees to demand cost-of-living increases, which their employers pay for by raising prices further still. Maybe some of that money gets invested in the rising stocks of those prospering companies, creating even more wealth and more disposable income. The cycle builds until it breaks. Prices can go up only so far before they start to destroy prosperity.

HOW INTEREST RATES
AFFECT THE ECONOMY

Inflation leads to higher interest rates, which are enormously dis-
ruptive for businesses. Not only do they boost borrowing costs,
but they also slow the economy by limiting demand, and that's
bad for stock prices. With all this in mind, you can begin to see
why Wall Street gets very upset when there's the slightest threat of
inflation. As prices increase, it becomes more expensive for companies to do business. The added costs put downward pressure on
corporate earnings, which tends to reduce what investors are willing to pay for the stock.

Preventing inflation has become the job of the Federal Reserve
Board (the Fed). Why? Because the central bank controls the nation's money supply, the amount of actual currency available to
pay for the nation's output of goods and services. Since money
greases the cogs of the economy, restricting its flow can slow down
the economy. Conversely, increasing the money flow speeds up
things. If we are in an inflationary period and the Fed wants to control it, the Fed raises interest rates to reduce the supply of money.
Consumers have less to spend, so they purchase fewer goods and
services. This effectively reduces prices.

Unfortunately, moving money in and out of the economy is not
easy or efficient. The most important thing to know about interest
rates is that when the Fed raises them, it tends to limit the money
supply and slows the economy. When the Fed lowers interest rates,
the money flow increases and the economy tends to speed up.
Consequently, if the Fed fears inflation, it will work to "tighten," or
raise interest rates. If it fears recession, it will lower rates.

In hindsight, it's easy to see how things can go woefully wrong
with the economy. During wars, aggregate prices usually rise as

governments increase spending on war materials. The Vietnam War in the late 1960s and early 1970s was no exception. The increased military expenditures pushed the economy to its capacity and then over it when President Lyndon Johnson refused to pay for the expenditures with tax increases. Instead, he borrowed money, which increased the money supply, and was largely responsible for the inflationary period we encountered in the early 1970s.

At the same time, several external cost factors really got the inflation ball rolling. The Organization of Petroleum Exporting Countries (OPEC) aggravated the situation by drastically slashing oil production in response to the Arab–Israeli conflict. Supply shortages sent oil prices soaring and triggered back-to-back oil shocks in 1974–75 and 1979–80. Adding salt to the wound, weather-related crop damages caused food prices to surge, and raw material prices exploded due to growing worldwide demand. Between 1972 and 1974, U.S. inflation leapt from 3.2 percent to 11 percent and it reached 13.5 percent in 1980.

The Fed's decision to let too much money into the economy fueled inflation until it was out of control. The problem was there was no political will for the tough medicine it would take to bring the economy under control. Prices were so high in the mid-1970s that personal consumption began to decline, eroding aggregate demand. Businesses cut back on production, laying off workers and driving up the unemployment rate.

Normally, such conditions would bring inflation to a halt as recession took hold. At the time, however, the Nixon Administration was more worried about the political implications of a recession than about the inflation crisis. More money was injected into the system in an attempt to jump-start the stagnating economy. That merely drove prices higher and made the pain worse.

The term for this unusual and unpleasant combination of low growth and high inflation is *stagflation*.

The spiral wasn't broken until the Carter Administration's Fed Chairman Paul Volcker spent 1979 and 1980 engineering a recession by driving interest rates from 6 percent to a 20 percent range. Fortunately, OPEC increased oil production at the same time and the United States learned how to conserve. Rising mortgage rates tempered consumer and business borrowing. Wages dropped back to sustainable levels and prices fell.

It seems as if all the Federal Reserve has to do is utter the word "imbalance" and stocks topple like dominoes. Sure, the market usually corrects itself a couple of days later after destroying billions of dollars in market value. But when the Fed starts raising interest rates, the result will be turmoil and uncertainty in the market.

THE NEW ECONOMY: DO NEW RULES APPLY?

While complacency is never wise, a growing number of economists believe that so much has changed in the U.S. economy since the 1980s and 1990s that the old rules don't apply anymore. Increased competition in a global marketplace has forced U.S. companies to become more efficient. The revolutionary technical and communications advances have given them the tools to do so. That means the economy can produce more goods and services at lower costs. If the additional output for which there is more than enough demand generates fatter corporate revenues, employers can absorb higher wages or costs without raising prices, and the price of their stocks can continue to go up.

Many companies have succeeded in muting demands for wage hikes by establishing incentive pay and profit sharing plans, which aren't necessarily inflationary since they're tied to productivity. Moreover, the prices of computers and communications equipment are declining so rapidly that businesses have more incentive to replace old equipment with cheaper new substitutes to increase their productivity. And increased competition in a global market also makes it hard for companies to increase prices.

There is no denying the fact that a more efficient economy has changed the inflation model. However, some skeptics still worry that the strong economy will ultimately create imbalances. They believe a shrinking pool of available workers is bound to lead to wage inflation, regardless of impressive productivity gains. The wealth effect created by a booming stock market, which itself feeds off a benign inflation environment, can create spending pressures on the economy. For that reason, the Fed strives to preempt potential inflation rather than react to pricing pressures after they have already appeared. Since the Fed's monetary tools work slowly, policymakers can't afford to wait until inflation rears its head.

KNOWING WHEN TO INVEST

If you understand economic cycles and know the effects they have on stocks, you will significantly improve your odds of making money in the market. Certain types of investments tend to do better during specific stages of the economy. You wouldn't want to make all your buying decisions based on economic cycles, but you'll improve your investment performance by shifting the weighting of your portfolio as the economy shifts. There are five phases to a typical economic cycle: recession, recovery, early upswing, late upswing, and economic slowdown. It's important to understand each one, as well as the types of investments that tend to perform best in each phase.

Recession

Recession is characterized by falling production, peaking inflation, and weakened consumer confidence. Recessions are usually a good time to buy cyclical stocks, such as automakers, paper companies, and other heavy manufacturers. Their earnings may look anemic and their stock prices may be floundering, but they are among the first stocks to take off when the economy turns around. Long-term bonds are also a good bet in a recession because the government tends to lower interest rates to help spur the economy. As interest rates go down, bond prices go up.

Recovery

Stimulatory economic policies, falling inflation, and increasing consumer confidence mark the recovery phase of the economic cycle. Recovery is a good time to buy stocks and long-term bonds. Smaller emerging growth stocks often do especially well during a recovery, and cyclical stocks should still have some growth left. Real estate is also a good investment during recovery periods.

Early Upswing

In the early upswing, the recovery period is past, confidence is up, and the economy is gaining some momentum. This is the healthiest period of the cycle, in a sense, because economic growth can

continue without any signs of overheating or sharply higher inflation. Consumers are prepared to borrow and spend more. Businesses facing increased capacity use begin investing in capital
equipment. Unemployment falls, but inflation may pick up.
Higher operating levels allow many businesses to cut unit costs
and increase profit margins. The early upswing stage can last for
several years, and the stock market should remain strong through
this phase. Real estate should continue to do well. Unload any
cyclical stocks that you own; their growth is probably over.

Late Upswing

The economic boom is in full swing in the late upswing phase.
Manufacturing capacity nears a peak, prompting an investment
rally as unemployment continues to fall. Real estate prices move
up, prompting a construction boom. Inflation picks up as wages
increase in the wake of labor shortages. With interest rates rising,
bonds and bank stocks become less attractive, which could cause a
lull in the stock market.

Economic Slowdown

As the economic slowdown phase appears, the economy begins to
decline. Short-term interest rates move up sharply, peaking as consumer confidence drops. The slowdown is exacerbated by inventory corrections as companies, fearing recession, try to reduce
their inventory levels. Manufacturing capacity begins to drop
while wages continue to rise, resulting in increased inflation. Stock
prices may fall significantly.

Ultimately, despite economic ups and downs, you need only to trust yourself. Become confident in your own investment decisions based on your personal experience and knowledge of the economic indicators. Don't chase hot trends and don't panic every time a market expert predicts a fall in stock prices. Develop your own strategies and your own system for playing the market. In the end, there is one fact on which all the experts agree: Over time, the market always moves up.

THE LEAST YOU NEED TO KNOW

Since stocks were invented, stock analysts have attempted to come up with economic formulas that would tell them when a bull or a bear is in the neighborhood. They've studied charts of the market's ups and downs for decades, looking for telltale patterns in the wiggles of the trend lines. Back in 1920, for example, Leonard Ayre, a vice president at the Cleveland Trust Company, noticed a telling connection between changes in interest rates and stock prices. He discovered that when interest rates went up, stock prices generally fell, and vice versa. Over the next several decades, countless other economic events that might affect the stock market were identified and analyzed in detail by economists.

To be a successful investor, it's vital that you have a basic understanding of how certain economic events affect the stock market. Armed with that information, you can immediately take evasive action if the market is going down, or jump right in if the market is going up.

MISTAKE

I Think
Global Investing Means
Buying Stock in Taco Bell!

*If you ignore the international market, you'll miss
out on getting in on a big piece of the action.*

KRISTI GROTE

A<small>S WE TURNED THE CORNER INTO THE NEW MILLENNIUM THERE WAS A</small>
growing consensus that the overseas stock markets were
poised to outperform the U.S. markets. Asia was rebounding and
even Japan was coming out of a long financial slump. The U.S.
market had climbed so fast in the 1990s, with the Standard &
Poor's (S&P) 500-stock index appreciating 316 percent, that it had
left the rest of the world's stocks comparatively undervalued.

To help you take advantage of depressed overseas stock prices,
there are now 1,700 international mutual funds that actively invest in multinational companies. Compare this with the 120 that
existed in 1990. If you're interested in diversifying your investments, you should definitely consider adding an international
component to your portfolio. The consensus is that you should
have between 10 and 20 percent of your holdings in the international market. I'll provide you with guidelines for assessing investment opportunities abroad in this chapter.

WHY YOU SHOULD CONSIDER INTERNATIONAL INVESTMENTS

Many of today's developing nations are enjoying strong increases in personal income as they begin to discover excellent markets for their goods and services among wealthier nations. American-style investor protection, the policing of foreign stock exchanges, use of standardized accounting practices, and public disclosure are making foreign markets more attractive for international investors.

These factors and others make for good odds that many foreign stock markets will outperform U.S. equities. Globalization may also benefit U.S. markets through an increase in foreign-capital investments in the U.S. markets as well. One of the easiest and least risky ways to benefit from the potential world boom is by owning foreign stock through mutual funds that invest in small, fast-growing firms based in other nations.

The Numbers Are Changing

Patient investors have the potential to benefit from the long, gradual strengthening of global economic performance. They are the ones who will make the money. Although many investors believe that the investing world doesn't extend beyond the U.S. borders, the facts point in the opposite direction. Over three quarters of the world's companies are listed on foreign stock exchanges. Non-U.S. companies already account for over 60 percent of the world's stock market, and their share is expected to exceed 70 percent in less than ten years.

The fact is that a plethora of investment opportunities exist outside the United States and many of these investments have

---

Investors in overseas markets must have a high tolerance for volatility and risk, eschewing market timing in favor of calm, committed ownership of quality stocks and equity mutual funds through up and down cycles. Both currency fluctuations and political instability are more prevalent in international markets. It's important to take the long view when investing overseas.

---

turned in stellar results over the years. One reason is the fast-growing economies in many foreign countries. For example, the Gross Domestic Products (GDPs) of over sixteen countries have grown faster than the U.S. GDP in the past two years. Economic activity in developing countries is, on average, growing at rates well above those seen in developed countries.

To ignore such economic growth is to ignore the investment opportunities that often accompany such growth. Even if you don't buy the diversification benefits of investing abroad, it still makes sense to include select foreign investments in your portfolio. In many cases, their growth opportunities exceed those of many U.S.–based corporations.

WHY FOREIGN STOCKS WILL INCREASE IN VALUE

In addition to fast-growing foreign economies, several other factors point to higher stock prices abroad in the coming years.

Values Relative to U.S. Stocks International stocks as a group have badly lagged behind U.S. equities in the past few years. This underperformance has created excellent values in many international markets relative to U.S. equities. But value doesn't always equal immediate price rises. Patience and a long-term focus are necessary when investing overseas.

Fall of Communism The fall of Communism has led to a world-wide shift toward free markets. Countries are seeing the wisdom of shifting the control of corporations from the government to the private sector. Of course, adjustments to new economic systems don't occur overnight and many countries will see their fortunes worsen before they improve under free markets. Still, over the long term, the shift toward more capitalistic societies will be positive for investors in foreign equities.

Global Competition The increasing cost-consciousness of U.S. companies and the continued paring of corporate fat have not gone unnoticed overseas. U.S. companies have become even more formidable competitors in the global marketplace. Foreign companies now understand that in order to be successful in the global markets, they have to cut costs, shed losing operations, and improve productivity. These measures should help company profitability and thus foreign stock prices.

Increased Flow of U.S. Pension Dollars According to the *Wall Street Journal*, U.S. pension funds have increased their international holdings over the past five years at a 30 percent average annual rate. U.S. pension funds could have 14 percent of their total assets in non–U.S. investments within the next five years, up from 11 percent in 2001.

Changing Attitudes Many countries are making slow but steady progress in changing investors' attitudes toward their stocks. For example, changing regulations should fuel greater equity participation in countries such as Japan. Investments by U.S. pension funds is helping to change individual investor attitudes.

Global Merger Activity U.S. investors have reaped the benefits of the explosive merger activity that has occurred in U.S. markets in recent years. As global markets develop, this merger activity will expand beyond our own borders. International merger activity is already taking place in such areas as utilities, steel, health care, and financial services. It will likely be commonplace in every industry sector in the next couple of years. International mergers could accelerate even more if the attractive valuations of international companies relative to U.S. companies persist and U.S. companies find it cheaper to buy than build abroad.

WHAT TO WATCH OUT FOR

Although overseas investing offers plenty of pluses for investors, several pitfalls await the unwary. One of the biggest potential problems is currency fluctuations, which can impact the performance of international investments. When local currencies weaken against the U.S. dollar, foreign investment returns suffer. Conversely, owning shares in a country whose stock market is rising and whose currency is strengthening against the dollar gives your portfolio a double-powered boost.

One of the common arguments against investing overseas is that individual investors do not have the necessary expertise to make informed foreign investment choices. Other considerations include accounting standards that are rarely uniform and that can hinder fundamental analysis of foreign companies, the tax consequences of buying foreign securities, and the ability of individual investors to obtain timely financial information.

Although these are important concerns, they should not prevent you from considering investing overseas. As far as obtaining

---

The Internet is a rich source of information on foreign companies. Three especially useful Web sites are www.bankofny.com, www.jpmorgan.com, and www.globalinvestor.com.

---

financial information on most foreign companies, annual and quarterly reports are readily available by contacting the company's U.S. agent. *Value Line* and *Standard & Poor's Stock Guide* provide ample coverage of international firms.

A final potential pitfall in international investing is the political and/or economic instability of many foreign countries. Volatile political and economic systems can create major shocks, such as rampant inflation, oppressive regulations, and currency devaluations—none of which bodes well for stock prices. For that reason, investors should diversify their foreign investments across a number of regions, especially when investing in emerging countries.

WHAT FOREIGN MARKETS ARE BEST FOR YOU?

Europe and Latin America stand out as solid investments over the next couple of years. Europe remains the safest bet for investors. It is benefiting from many of the same factors that have fueled corporate profits in the U.S., such as restructuring and cost cutting. The environment for investing is improving with the development of the European Common Market and increased merger activities. Eastern Europe may be more difficult to analyze. Countries such as Poland seem well ahead of the curve compared with certain regions of the former Soviet Union.

Latin America has always promised big things, but ill-advised economic policies have short-circuited companies in this region. Still, certain Latin American countries offer good potential. Mexico is dramatically raising its standard of living, and the emerging middle class is helping consumer-oriented firms grow significantly. Chile is another up-and-coming country with lots of exciting opportunities.

Aggressive investors might do well to check out the Asia/Pacific Rim countries. In the past, news coming from this region has been bad. Japan's financial markets have been stuck in low gear and other Pacific Rim countries have been experiencing difficult economic times. Over the long term, the Pacific Rim offers perhaps the biggest challenge for more aggressive investors. Many believe that China may hold the biggest investment opportunities, but investors who pursue this avenue will need plenty of patience.

INTERNATIONAL VERSUS GLOBAL MUTUAL FUNDS

Many investment advisers believe that mutual funds represent the safest way for individual investors to venture into foreign markets. There are two types of funds: international funds (which invest solely in the stock of non U.S. companies) and global funds (which may invest in large U.S. multinational companies as well as foreign stocks). These funds have professional managers who have special expertise in navigating international investment waters. Funds provide investors with the necessary diversification for investing in potentially volatile markets and also take care of the tax problems that can arise when investing overseas.

A well-diversified international mutual fund offers an excellent way to invest overseas, providing its expenses are not too high and you don't have the inclination to pick individual stocks. However, it's important to recognize that not all international funds are alike. Some focus exclusively on a specific country, while others target a particular region. Some international funds focus on bond investments, while others may hold both bonds and stocks. Other international funds focus on small-capitalization foreign companies, which can increase not only the fund's potential return but also its risk.

If you already have ample U.S. stock exposure, a global fund with large U.S. holdings may not be the best choice. Also, an international fund that claims to be diversified across the world, but in reality has 40 percent of its assets in the Pacific Rim, may not be the wisest pick. If you decide to use one or more funds to add foreign-stock exposure to your portfolio, make absolutely sure you understand the investment objectives and holdings of each fund before you buy it.

Morningstar estimates that the average annual expense ratio of an international equity fund is roughly 1.9 percent. In other words, for every $50,000 in the typical international equity fund, an investor pays $950 per year in "carrying fees." And fees are only part of the costs. Another downside of international mutual funds—as with any mutual fund—is the unwanted tax liability created every time the fund manager distributes capital gains to fund holders.

CLOSED-END INTERNATIONAL FUNDS

Closed-end funds are similar to open-end mutual funds in that they let you invest in a basket of stocks selected and managed by an investment company. However, there are major differences between an open- and a closed-end fund. Open-end funds continually sell new shares to the public and redeem shares at the fund's net asset value, which is the market value of the firm's portfolio, minus short-term liabilities. Closed-end funds sell only a certain

Most major no-load fund families offer international funds. Two funds to consider are the T. Rowe Price International Stock Fund (800-638-5660), a diversified international fund, and the Acorn International Fund (800-922-6769), an international small-cap fund.

number of shares at the initial public offering, just like a stock. Once the shares are sold, the fund is "closed" and new money is not accepted. To invest in a closed-end fund, you buy shares of the fund just as you would buy shares of a company's stock.

Closed-end funds trade on the stock exchanges; open-end funds do not. Because closed-end funds are publicly traded, their prices are set by supply and demand among various investors, just like common stocks. Unlike open-end funds, which always redeem shares at the net asset value, closed-end mutual funds may trade above or below their net asset value. These premiums or discounts can sometimes be quite large. How do you know if a closed-end fund is trading at a discount or a premium? The *Wall Street Journal* and *Barron's* regularly provide this information.

A number of closed-end funds focus on international investments. These funds include both international bond and international stock funds. Merely because an international closed-end fund trades at a discount does not make it a good investment. It is important to evaluate whether the fund meets your investment objective, follows an investment strategy that makes sense to you, and fits with the rest of your portfolio. This last factor is crucial. If your only international investment is a closed-end fund, for example, it probably isn't a good idea to buy a single-country, closed-end fund.

Closed-end funds charge expenses, and these expenses can be rather high. One rule of thumb is to avoid investing in closed-end funds where the discount is not at least ten times the fund's annual expenses. A closed-end fund with annual expenses of 1.5

percent should trade at a discount of at least 15 percent for you to consider it.

Keep in mind that the disparity between an international closed-end fund's price and its net asset value may result from the difficulty of pricing fund investments that do not trade frequently. Also consider that prices used to establish a fund's net asset value are estimates of the true value of each of its investments. This may be especially true of international closed-end funds that invest in bonds.

Never buy any closed-end fund at the initial public offering (IPO). Most closed-end funds perform poorly immediately following the IPO. You'll probably dodge a bullet or two by waiting and taking a fresh look at the fund six months or so after it is issued. Although most closed-end funds must be purchased through a broker, a small but growing number of funds are allowing investors to purchase shares directly.

AMERICAN DEPOSITORY RECEIPTS (ADRS)

One of the easiest ways to invest in specific overseas companies is via American depository receipts (ADRs), which are securities that trade on U.S. exchanges and represent ownership in shares of foreign companies. ADRs are issued by U.S. banks against the actual shares of foreign companies held in trust by a corresponding institution overseas. Often, ADRs are not issued on a share-for-share basis. Instead, one ADR may be the equivalent of five or ten of the company's ordinary shares.

ADRs have become increasingly popular in recent years. According to the Bank of New York, trading volume in ADRs in 1997 reached 15 billion shares, a 23 percent increase over 1996. The 1997 dollar value was $555 billion, a 53 percent increase over 1996. In 2001, there were over 1600 ADRs traded on U.S. exchanges.

One reason for the growing popularity of ADRs is convenience. Investors can buy and sell ADRs just like they buy and sell securities of any U.S. company. Prices of ADRs are quoted in U.S. dollars and ADRs pay dividends in U.S. dollars. Some investors who buy well-known foreign companies, such as Sony or Royal Dutch Petroleum, don't even know they are actually buying ADRs rather than common stock. That's because the difference between a stock and an ADR is transparent to the investor.

The Bank of New York now offers an index that tracks the performance of ADRs. Called the Bank of New York ADR Index, it consists of 431 companies from thirty-six countries. It comprises a composite index and four regional indices: the Europe ADR Index, the Asia ADR Index, the Latin America ADR Index, and the Emerging Market ADR Index. For more information regarding the Bank of New York's ADR Index, visit the bank's Web site at www .bankofny.com/adr.

How to Buy ADRs

Traditionally, investors purchased ADRs through a stockbroker; now you can bypass the broker and invest directly in a growing number of ADRs. More than one hundred fifty foreign companies offer direct-purchase programs through which individual investors can purchase ADRs directly from the companies' U.S. agents.

You purchase these ADRs in the same way as you would shares of U.S. companies offering direct-purchase plans. You call a toll-free phone number to request a plan prospectus and enrollment information; you fill out the form and return it with a check for the number of shares you want to purchase. The minimum initial investment in all ADR direct-purchase plans is $250. Once you have made your initial investment, you can make subsequent purchases directly through a payroll or checking account deduction plan. The plans make it easy even for investors with limited funds to buy quality ADRs and build a diversified international stock portfolio over time.

THE LEAST YOU NEED KNOW

Just a few years ago, many financial pundits were sounding a death knell for international investments. They had abandoned the belief that an increasingly integrated world economy would raise living standards for all peoples, with special benefit for Americans invested abroad. At the time, emerging stock markets from Asia to Russia to Brazil were in shambles. Fortunately, over the past few years, we have seen a broad recovery in the world economy. Foreign stock markets as a group have delivered higher total returns than many U.S equities. All in all, globalization is alive and well and there are several good reasons for participating in this phenomenon.

More than 95 percent of the world's population lives outside the United States. The global dispersal of technology can dramatically boost manufacturing productivity in developing nations, which will lead to higher economic growth rates. Europe and Japan will continue to deregulate their industries to make them more competitive.

MISTAKE 11

I Think My Broker Knows Everything

A broker's guess is liable to be as good as anyone else's.

WILL ROGERS

SOME INVESTORS ENJOY READING THE RESEARCH REPORTS BROKERAGE companies routinely send to their clients. These reports reveal how the broker's analysts view the market and where they think specific stocks are going. Unfortunately, brokerages seldom send you negative reports, so you're never sure if you're getting the full story. After spending a great deal of time reading these reports, I've discovered a couple of things. By the time you get them, the information is obsolete. Second, as Will Rogers notes in the quote that introduces this chapter, these analysts' guesses are likely to be just about as good as anybody else's.

Unfortunately, most stockbrokers parrot the information that's published by their firm's research department. In most cases, you're better off conducting your own research and buying stock through either a discount broker or an online brokerage service like Ameritrade or E*Trade. You'll save a bundle on commissions using either and may end up with a better portfolio in the long run.

Woody Allen once said, "A stockbroker is someone who invests your money until it is all gone." It's important to remember that nobody cares more about your money than you do. Protect it at all times.

ARE YOU BROKER DEPENDENT?

Of course, it's important that you determine how much support you really need from a broker. Your answers to several questions will help you identify your "broker dependency" quotient. Do you shamelessly beg stock tips from strangers? Or are you a lone wolf who'd rather chew off a paw than ask for advice? I've constructed a quick quiz to point you toward the type of broker you should consider: full-service, discount, or online. When you've answered the questions, total the points to the right of your choices to determine your final score.

THE BROKER DEPENDENCY QUIZ

1. When you invest in the stock market, you're:
   Generally pessimistic. I expect the worst and usually get it.   (3)
   Somewhat optimistic. I don't know what to expect but hope
   for the best.   (2)
   Generally optimistic. I expect the best.   (1)
2. How willing are you to share your investment strategies with others?
   Very willing. In fact, I share my approaches with others every
   chance I get.   (3)
   Not very willing. I reveal my strategies only if I'm backed into
   a corner.   (2)
   Not at all. I keep most of my investment strategies to myself.   (1)
3. How emotional are you about the investments you make?
   Overly emotional.   (3)
   Somewhat emotional.   (2)
   Not very emotional.   (1)

4. How would your friends describe you when you're about to make a tough investment decision?

   Friendly and relaxed.   (3)

   Cool and calm.   (2)

   Mean and irritable.   (1)

5. If you're lost in a city, do you:

   Immediately stop for directions.   (3)

   Consult a map, then try to find your own way.   (2)

   Drive around until you run out of gas.   (1)

6. How communicative are you?

   I don't make decisions without consulting someone.   (3)

   I may consult with someone, but I make most decisions myself.   (2)

   I make most decisions on my own.   (1)

7. Do you consider yourself:

   An arts person.   (3)

   A renaissance person.   (2)

   A quantitative person.   (1)

8. Which leadership profile best describes you?

   Lineman: Just tell me who to go out there and hit.   (3)

   Quarterback: I want some control over the outcome of the game.   (2)

   Coach: I want to call every play.   (1)

9. Which of these statements sounds most like you?

   Tell me what to do.   (3)

   I have an idea I'd like to discuss.   (2)

   I know what I want, so get out of my way.   (1)

How Did You Score?

22–27 You depend on others for advice. You would probably be better off with a full-service broker.

14–21 You're not overly confident. Avail yourself of the services that a good discount broker can provide.

9–13 You're self-reliant. Station yourself in front of a computer and point-and-click your way to stock ownership with an online brokerage service.

SELECTING THE RIGHT BROKER

No one goes it alone in the world of investing. There is a burgeoning brokerage industry out there dedicated to making investing easier for all of us. The type of brokerage you use depends on the degree of assistance you need, as we just discussed. For all the negative press about brokerage firms, the truth is that most experienced brokers do a fairly good job of managing their clients' money. But not all good brokers work well with all investors.

Selecting the right investment adviser can be a challenge. A broker who's right for your friend may not be right for you. You need a broker who is in tune with your investment style, your investment objectives, your threshold for risk, and your personality. If you need the counsel of a full-service broker, search until you find one who is ideally suited to your needs. Your broker becomes a vital element in your investment program's potential for success, offering both direction and encouragement along the way.

With just a modest effort, you can find the right broker. Unfortunately, many investors do a poor job of selecting a broker. In fact, many never even meet their broker. Here's how a typical investor selects a broker.

Joe or Josephine Investor is at home watching TV, a cool drink in one hand, a bag of potato chips in the other, when the phone rings. The voice on the other end of the line says, "Good evening. I'm John Doe of ABC Investments. If I could come up with an investment opportunity for you with the potential to grow 30 to 40 percent over the next year, would you be interested?"

If Joe or Josie says yes, the broker promises to get back to them in the near future and hangs up. About two weeks later, the broker calls back: "Hello again. This is John Doe of ABC Investments. As you'll recall, we talked a couple of weeks ago and you said you'd be interested in an investment with the potential to grow 30 to 40 percent. Well, you'll be happy to know that I've found a great one for you." The broker explains the investment and gets the order. Joe or Josie is hooked. He or she is now the client of a broker they've never met and know absolutely nothing about.

The right way to select a broker is to take a proactive approach. Start by identifying two or three broker prospects through referrals from friends or by attending investment seminars sponsored by brokers. Meet with your prospects in their offices and ask the following questions:

- What types of investors do you work with the most?
- What is your investment approach?
- What types of investment products do you specialize in?
- How long have you been a broker?
- What kind of experience do you have?

Rather than asking the broker what type of service he or she will give you, set your own agenda. Outline the type of service you require. If you want the broker to call you once a week, or once a month, get the broker to agree to your terms in advance. If the broker answers all your questions to your satisfaction, that's a start. Also make sure that you have rapport with and a good feeling about this person—because your goal is to develop a long-term working relationship with him or her. Take one final step: Call the National Association of Securities Dealers' hot line (800-289-9999)

You may not want the most experienced brokers in the firm, because most of them already have hundreds of clients. You also don't want brand-new brokers who will make all of their mistakes with your money. The ideal broker should have at least five years' experience making some mistakes with other people's money. Look for someone with the investment experience and the enthusiasm to help you meet your investment goals.

to find out if the broker has ever been the subject of disciplinary action. Only after a broker has passed all your tests should you sign on as a client.

WHAT TO EXPECT FROM YOUR BROKER

A big part of a broker's job is to provide you with information you can use to manage your investments and to meet your investment objectives. You have a right to understand exactly what your money is invested in. The North American Securities Administrators Association recently issued an "Investor Bill of Rights" to help consumers steer clear of trouble. The document states that you have the right to ask for and receive information from a brokerage firm about the work history and background of your broker and the brokerage firm itself. In addition, you have the right to:

- Receive account statements that are easy to understand and are accurate.
- Withdraw your money in a timely manner and receive information about any restrictions on access to your money.
- Discuss account problems with the branch manager or compliance department of the firm and receive prompt attention and fair consideration of your concerns.
- Receive complete information about commissions, service charges, maintenance fees, redemption fees, and penalties.
- Receive enough information from your broker to understand the terms and conditions of transactions you make.

All good brokerage firms adhere to these investor rights. If you believe your brokerage firm has breached any of these rights, immediately transfer your business to another firm. If your broker talks in circles or talks over your head about investment products he or she is trying to sell you, find a new broker. A broker's job is to simplify your life, not complicate it. It's a service he or she is paid handsomely to perform.

If you experience any of the following, seriously consider firing your broker.

Unsolved operational problems If your statement contains mistakes (for example, charges were mistakenly added or there is a cash balance error), you should expect your broker to solve those problems, no questions asked. You don't want a broker who lets problems fester.

Lack of rapport If you don't feel comfortable dealing with your broker, if he or she has trouble answering your questions or helping you shape a solid investment portfolio, or if you simply don't like or don't trust the individual, move on. You need a broker with whom you can have a compatible, trusting relationship.

Poor performance This, of course, is the bottom line. Even if your broker is the nicest person you've ever met, if she or he isn't making you money, you need to look elsewhere. But be fair. Don't expect every pick to go up. No broker can deliver 100 percent of the time.

Some brokers are more interested in their own commissions than they are in your investment returns. Brokerage firms may have special products they push their brokers to sell. Often these are prepackaged portfolios of stocks and bonds that come with a good sales pitch and a fat commission to encourage the brokers to

---

Brokers cannot make false or misleading promises about investments they're trying to sell you. For instance, if a broker claims that a stock or mutual fund is guaranteed to produce a specific rate of return, that is misrepresentation. Brokers can guarantee the return of some government bonds and insured certificates of deposit, but they cannot guarantee the performance of stocks or mutual funds.

---

push them. Or the company may have large positions in certain stocks it wants to unload, so managers may offer brokers extra incentives to push those stocks.

Watch out for those types of investments and the brokers who try to sell them to you. You want a broker who recommends investments that fit your investment objectives, preferably good quality stocks or mutual funds that you can hold for the long term. If your broker seems to be more interested in her own returns than she is in yours, it may be time to take your business elsewhere.

SmartMoney magazine offers a broker ranking service on its Web site (www.smartmoney.com). You can view how it ranks brokers in each of these three categories: brokers for do-it-yourselfers, for delegators, and for navigators (see figure 11.1).

DON'T GET CHURNED

Just because there's a lot of activity in your account doesn't mean you're making money. All it really means is that your broker is making money. Churning, or the practice of trading excessively in a client's account to generate commissions, is the most common violation brokers make. Churning occurs thousands of times a day and most investors don't even realize it's happening.

Broker Ratings

Broker Rankings

The categories in this ranking are weighted for Do-It-Yourselfers, who run the gamut from zippy traders to convenience-seeking one-stop financial shoppers.

We covered the spectrum by attaching the heaviest weights to Commissions and Fees and to Services. Number in ( ) indicates rank in category.

Also see our Broker Selector for Do-It-Yourselfers.

To see broker rankings for other types of investors, go to Delegators and Navigators.

In This Section

- The Do-It-Yourselfer
- The Delegator
- The Navigator

Also See

- Methodology
How we conducted this survey

- Broker Meter
See how fast your broker's site is.

Broker Rankings

Firms	Commissions & Fees[1]	Ease & Accuracy of Trades	Services	Investment Products[3]	Stock Research	Mutual Funds	Stays Out of Trouble
	Cost of Trades / Fees Score	Failure Rate / Trading Score	Services / Statement Scores	No. of Online Products	Research Score	No Load Funds / Top Perfprm Funds	Damages Awarded per Account
1. TD Waterhouse	$48 / 4 (5)	0.28% / 7 (4)	7 / 13 (4)	12 (4)	12.5 (12)	1,760 / 999 (4)	$0.00 (10)
2. Muriel Siebert	60 / 6 (3)	0.78 / 6.5 (8)	4 / 12 (12)	10 (11)	17 (2)	1,677 / 979 (5)	0 (15)
3. Charles Schwab	120 / 4 (23)	0.84 / 7.5 (2)	6 / 9 (10)	17 (2)	17 (2)	1,809 / 805 (9)	0.14 (12)
4. DLJdirect	80 / 4 (14)	0.77 / 7 (9)	6 / 10 (8)	14 (7)	15 (6)	1,500 / 914 (7)	0.02 (7)
5. National Discount Brokers	59 / 3 (12)	3.61 / 6.5 (7)	4 / 15 (7)	9 (16)	15 (6)	1,947 / 1,070 (3)	0.54 (20)
6. Fidelity	100 / 3 (24)	2.84 / 7.5 (3)	7 / 12 (5)	14 (3)	15 (6)	1,498 / 917 (8)	0.05 (8)
7. E*Trade	60 / 1 (19)	1.69 / 7 (1)	6 / 7 (11)	20 (1)	13 (10)	746 / 495	0.06 (12)

FIGURE 11.1 *SmartMoney* Broker Rankings

How can a broker churn an account without the client realizing it? Here's how. The broker buys a stock for your account. A couple of weeks later, when the broker realizes that he needs to generate a commission to meet his firm's sales quota, he calls you to present one of three possible scenarios. He might say, "That stock we bought a couple of weeks ago has gone up, so why don't we sell it, take our profit, and move into another stock that looks more promising right now." Or he might say, "That stock we bought two weeks ago has gone down, so let's get out of it and reinvest in another stock that looks more promising right now." Finally, he might say, "That stock we bought a couple of weeks ago hasn't moved. Let's sell it and buy something that looks more promising."

Whatever the circumstances, whether the stock has gone up, stayed the same, or gone down, the broker can find a reason for you to sell the stock and buy another, generating two commissions. You don't want a broker who is constantly urging you to turn over your portfolio. Tell your broker you want him or her to recommend good quality companies that you can hold for the long term. If the broker continues to try to churn your account, find a new broker. You may also want to report your experiences to the brokerage company's compliance officer or to the Securities and Exchange Commission.

BYPASSING BROKER FEES WITH DRIPS

One way to get more return from your investment dollars is to cut out the middleman, the broker. More than a thousand U.S. companies sell their stock directly to shareholders with no commission. These are called direct-purchase plans. If the company's stock pays dividends, most of these plans also let you automatically reinvest the dividends in additional shares. Your broker will never tell you about these direct-purchase plans or about dividend reinvestment plans—or DRIPs, for short.

While some companies set modest limits for cash contributions to direct-purchase or DRIP plans, other companies have liberal contribution policies. American Home Products allows shareholders to invest more than $100,000 a year in its commission-free program. To find out if a company you're interested in offers a direct-purchase or a DRIP program, call its investor relations office.

THE LEAST YOU NEED TO KNOW

John F. Kennedy once said, "How could I have been so mistaken as to have trusted the experts?" It's no secret the experts are often wrong in projecting the future of the stock market. As one investment newsletter writer recently put it, "It's too early to know what lies ahead." Of course it is, but by the time we do know, it will be too late to do anything about it. Opportunity will have passed us by.

The experts do the best they can to provide direction and insights into the market. Mistakes are inevitable. No one gets it right all the time. But some brokers seem to have a better handle on it than others.

If you find a broker who consistently makes good recommendations, stay with that individual. However, don't expect miracles. Brokers are only human. To get the most from a broker, you need an open mind and a healthy degree of skepticism. Before you act on anyone's advice, weigh the facts, study the data, and consider your alternatives. Then base your decision on your own analysis—taking into account your broker's advice. After all, it's your money at stake.

MISTAKE

I Believe Only the Weak Invest in Mutual Funds

*If you don't have time to get intractably involved
in the online investment process, then mutual
funds can be your best friend.*

KORI BOWERS

MUTUAL FUNDS HAVE BECOME FAST FOOD FOR INVESTORS WHO DON'T have the time to track individual stock investments. Funds are easy to get into and feature diversification, giving you exposure to a plethora of stocks (and, depending on the fund, bonds) without the hassle of pouring over stock tables and thumbing through annual reports. Ignoring the option of investing in mutual funds means missing out on an excellent opportunity to diversify your portfolio.

Finding a good fund can be frustrating, though, because there are over eight thousand funds to choose from. That's nearly four times the number of stocks on the New York Stock Exchange. And, despite a professional management team, diversification, and finely tuned trading strategies, the vast majority of funds have lagged behind the stock market over the past ten years. Fortunately, a few exceptions rise above the crowd. In this chapter, I'll show you how to easily find and evaluate premier funds.

HOW FUNDS EVOLVED

The snowballing popularity of mutual funds today belies their long history in America. The idea of pooled investment assets dates back to nineteenth-century England, where such pools were called "investment trusts." The concept migrated to the United States in the 1920s. Prosperous industrialists in New York, Boston, and Philadelphia found these "unit trusts" to be a convenient way to invest. The capital in these trusts helped finance farm mortgage companies and railroads. Some of the early funds required investors to commit their money for a specified time.

The stock market crash of 1929 drained most of these funds of their assets. Many fund organizations folded, along with other financial intermediaries. However, the basic structure of the mutual fund survived, and over the years, the financial services industry has honed funds into a highly flexible and liquid instrument. As America recovered from the Depression, the industry and regulators introduced wide-ranging safety measures that culminated in the Investment Company Act of 1940. The legislation gave the federal Securities and Exchange Commission (SEC) the authority to oversee investment companies that offer funds to the public. Under SEC rules, firms wishing to set up mutual funds must register as investment companies and follow strict guidelines. Fund executives with access to investment company securities must be bonded.

Fund managers must provide key information about risk and about their compensation for managing fund assets. This information is provided in the prospectuses that funds must send to investors before accepting their money. Funds are also required to keep shareholders informed of what's going on. They're required to send out shareholder reports twice a year disclosing the fund's investment strategy, recent performance, and the percentage it has invested in securities. These reports also give an accounting of expenses and explain how the fund's net worth was calculated at the end of the latest period. Many fund groups also send out periodic newsletters covering the market and investment strategies.

The various rules covering mutual funds tightly control how funds conduct their business, but they give managers great freedom in how to invest your money. Although the bonding that funds carry protects you from fraud, nothing will save you if the manager makes poor investment decisions. Because funds run the gamut of investment choices, it's important to read prospectuses and other materials carefully to make sure you know what kind of risks fund management is taking with your money.

THE ADVANTAGES OF MUTUAL FUNDS

There's no question, investing in individual stocks can be a lot of work. If you've tried it and don't enjoy it, a different approach to stock market investing might serve you better. Instead of trying to maintain your own portfolio of winning stocks, invest in winning mutual funds. Mutual funds enable you to participate in the stock market without the trouble of tracking the market, researching new stocks, and making all the buying and selling decisions yourself.

When you invest in a mutual fund, you become part owner of a portfolio of dozens or hundreds of different stocks. Worries about the volatility of a single stock are less because your investment is spread across several stocks and industries. Additional advantages of mutual fund ownership include:

Professional management A professional portfolio manager makes all the decisions about which stocks to buy and sell, as well as the other day-to-day responsibilities of stock ownership, leaving you free to do other things, such as sharpen your golf game, climb the nearest mountain, or just take care of all your other responsibilities.

Low fees About half of the eight thousand mutual funds on the market are known as "no-load funds" because you pay no fee to buy or sell fund shares. You are assessed a small annual management fee of about 1 to 2 percent of your holdings to cover fund expenses. "Load" funds charge a front-end fee ranging from about 3 to 8 percent when you buy the fund. Some also charge a "back-end" fee when you sell. In most cases, buy no-load funds. Studies show that no-load funds perform just as well as load funds, so why not save on fees?

Variety You can invest in a wide variety of stocks and bonds through mutual funds. There are funds that specialize in small stocks, large stocks, specialty sectors, high-yielding stocks, and international stocks. You'll also find a whole range of bond funds as well as balanced funds, which include both stocks and bonds in their portfolios. You can have a strong position in nearly every type of stock, both foreign and domestic, just by buying a handful of mutual funds.

WHO INVESTS IN MUTUAL FUNDS?

More than 30 million U.S. households have invested in mutual funds either directly or through retirement plans at work. The migration to funds can be traced in large part to demographics: aging baby boomers who have kids on their way to college and retire-

---

The fund industry has gone a bit crazy recently with market segmentation funds that invest in select portions of the market, attempting to attract customers. Between 1993 and 2001, the number of funds grew from twenty-six hundred to more than eight thousand.

---

ment on their horizon. And, just as the boomers drove fashion and pop music when they were in their teens, and car and home sales when they were in their twenties and thirties, they now have the investment community falling all over itself to meet their financial needs. Mutual fund companies offer a smorgasbord of products at a variety of prices. This vast selection of financial products is capturing an ever-greater share of our savings dollars.

The reason you should start investing now is that you'll need more money than your parents to maintain today's standard of living when you retire. Social Security is widely predicted to encounter financial problems unless it's reformed. So far, the system has worked because retirees have been supported by an ever-greater number of workers paying Social Security taxes. When the system was set up in 1934, the average life expectancy was sixty for men and sixty-three for women. Fewer than half of eligible Americans were expected to reach retirement age and to receive payments from the system.

But when the boomers start retiring, they can be expected to live another seventeen years on average. At that point, there won't be enough new workers to pay for their Social Security benefits. In 1935, forty-two workers supported one retiree on Social Security. By 2025, the ratio is expected to drop to just two workers for each retiree. In other words, we all face the real threat of outliving our retirement savings unless we do something now. Investing in mutual funds for retirement can reduce that concern.

A fund's NAV is its *net asset value* of the per-share value of the fund's portfolio. For example, a fund with $100 million in assets and with five million shareholders would have a NAV value of $20 per share. The NAV on a given day is the price you pay to acquire one share of a fund on that day.

Investors have also flocked to mutual funds in recent years due to a lack of alternatives. Lower interest rates have made bank certificates of deposit and other short-term investments less attractive, and real estate in many parts of the country has not appreciated the way it once did. That's not to say that mutual funds are risk-free. Just as with individual stocks, most funds are affected by fluctuations in the market. However, there's good reason to believe that funds, and particularly diversified U.S. stock funds, will continue to deliver in the years ahead.

Many corporations are offering employees the chance to invest in mutual funds through retirement savings plans. One reason is the relatively low cost of mutual fund investing. By pooling the assets of many people, funds achieve economies of scale that cut their cost of investing. They benefit, for example, from price breaks that brokers and traders give for large accounts. Moreover, a fund group's fixed costs are about the same whether it has $10 million or $10 billion under management.

THE POWER OF COMPOUNDING

We've talked about the power of compounding before, but it's an important factor in mutual fund investing. Investors who did nothing more than put $10,000 in Fidelity's Magellan Fund in 1985 saw their investment grow to $50,000 by 1995. That's an

average annual return of 17 percent. The Schroder Micro Cap fund
(figure 12.1) averaged more than a 100 percent annual return for
its investors over three years. Unfortunately, the fund is now
closed to new investors.

Not all funds have done as well as Magellan and Schroder, but
they all generate returns in two ways: via current income (dividends and/or interest) and via capital appreciation (the increase in

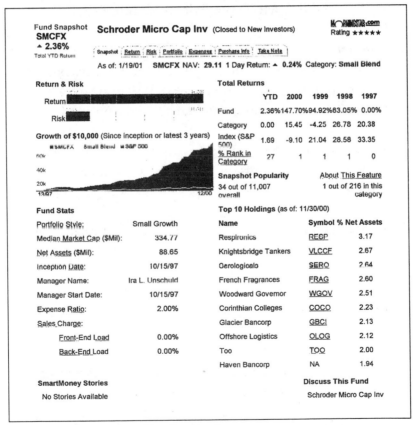

FIGURE 12.1 Schroder Micro Cap Fund

value of the stocks or bonds the fund owns). Bonds held by a mutual fund pay interest into the portfolio, increasing assets. In addition, if interest rates fall, the value of the bonds may increase, which also increases fund assets. Likewise, dividends from the stocks a fund holds are paid into the portfolio, or the stocks in the fund may rise in price. Dividend and interest payments collected by the fund are used to buy additional securities.

ONLINE MUTUAL FUND RESOURCES

To learn more about the funds investment companies offer, check out fund company Web sites, such as www.Fidelity.com, www.Vanguard.com, and www.Troweprice.com. Here are five excellent sites offering general information that are also worth a visit:

www.aaii.com Sponsored by the American Association of Individual Investors, this site offers advice on funds and portfolios.

www.mfea.com This site is sponsored by the Mutual Fund Education Alliance, the trade association for no-load fund sponsors.

www.investorama.com This extensive, well-organized site lists fund-related web links.

www.morningstar.com This is one of the best sites for finding all kinds of information about mutual funds.

www.maxfunds.com This site specializes in news and statistics on small and little-known funds.

HOW TO FIND WINNING FUNDS

If you build a portfolio of strong mutual funds, you should enjoy excellent returns over time. With the more than eight thousand mutual funds on the market, the most difficult aspect of mutual fund investing is deciding which funds are best. Among the wide range of books and magazines that rate mutual funds, check out *The 100 Best Mutual Funds to Own in America* (Dearborn Financial Publishing). *Money, Forbes, Barron's, Consumer Reports,* and *Bloomberg Personal Finance* are among the magazines that publish periodic mutual fund ratings. Most should be available at your library.

Regardless of which sources you use, there are several key factors you should consider in deciding which funds are right for you:

Five-year track record Rarely do the best funds lead the market every year. It's a mistake to choose a fund based on its performance over just one year. Instead, compare fund performances over a three- to five-year period. Look for funds that have been top performers in their categories over three to five years and that have done well relative to the market year in and year out.

Same fund manager The success of any mutual fund is a reflection of its manager's skills. Before you buy a fund based on its great performance, be sure the manager who established that record is still managing the fund. If that manager has moved on, so, probably, should you.

Fees All other factors being equal, select the fund with the lowest fees. There are plenty of great no-load funds from which to choose. Choose no-load funds over similarly performing load funds.

BIG IS NOT NECESSARILY BETTER

With a little research, you can accumulate a portfolio of all-star funds managed by some of the ablest managers in the investment business. The more successful a fund becomes, though, the faster its assets grow. It not only grows from within through its savvy investments, it also grows from without—through the inevitable flood of new investors attracted to the fund's sterling track record. Once lean and mean, many popular funds quickly become obese and are no longer able to maneuver lightly through the market. That's why many funds close their doors to new investors after their assets reach a certain level.

Oversized funds face several drawbacks, not the least of which is a dwindling universe of investment choices. First, to maintain proper diversification, funds limit their holdings of any individual security to at most 2 to 5 percent of their portfolio. Second, to ensure adequate liquidity should they wish to sell shares, funds are usually unwilling to hold positions representing more than 5 to 10 percent of a firm's outstanding shares.

Together, these constraints sharply limit the number of companies in which large funds can invest. A fund with $1 billion in assets and a 2 percent maximum holding in any individual stock could invest in about 2,650 stocks if the fund is willing to hold 10 percent of a company's capitalization and in 1,825 stocks if it sets the limit at 5 percent. But for a fund that has grown to $20 billion in assets, the comparable numbers are 352 and 176 companies, respectively. In other words, growing from $1 billion to $20 billion in assets can reduce the number of securities a fund can purchase by as much as 90 percent.

Trading is another casualty of size. Moving substantial blocks of securities tends to move market prices. Large funds are able to take on a substantial position in a stock only at a premium to the going market price, and to liquidate that position only at a discount to it. What does that mean for mutual fund investors? Look for funds with stellar track records, but favor funds with smaller, more manageable asset bases. There are plenty of good funds with solid track records that have asset bases under $1 billion.

HOW TO GET STARTED IN FUNDS

There are several ways to buy mutual funds. Most no-load funds and some load funds can be purchased directly from the fund group. For example, you can buy all of Fidelity's funds directly through Fidelity. When you call the fund group, the representative takes your name and address and sends you an application along with a prospectus for the fund you're interested in. Toll-free phone numbers for groups with more than two funds are listed in the mutual fund tables in *Investor's Business Daily*. Other publishers of fund group directories include:

- The Investment Company Institute (202-326-5872)
- The 100 Percent No-Load Mutual Fund Council (call 212-768-2477, fax 212-768- 2476, or visit the Web site at http://networth.galt.com/council)
- The Mutual Fund Education Alliance (816-471-1454)

Many of the load funds are sold through brokers, who charge a commission. Load structures vary. With some front-end loads, the investor pays 1 to 5 percent of the amount invested. For example, if the broker is charging 5 percent and you invest $2,000 in a load fund, you would pay $100 in commission to purchase the fund.

Types of Funds

Over the years, as fund groups have grown in number, they have expanded their offerings to include funds with more and more specialized investment universes. This section presents just a few examples of the categories available to mutual fund investors.

Sector Funds Sector funds do what their name implies: they restrict their investments to a particular segment, or sector, of the economy. For example, a fund such as Northern Technology buys only tech companies for its portfolio. Munder NetNet limits its universe even further by holding only Internet-related tech stocks. Fidelity has a whole stable of sector funds, from Fidelity Select Insurance to Fidelity Select Automotive. The idea is to give investors vehicles for emphasizing specific industries or sectors whenever they think those industries or sectors might heat up.

Blend Funds These funds vary across the board. Their only commonality is that they invest in more than one type of stock, bond, or both. They might invest in both high-growth tech stocks and cheaply priced automotive companies. The Vanguard 500 Index fund invests in every company in the S&P 500 and could therefore qualify as a blend. The nature of blend funds makes them difficult to classify in terms of risk.

Value Funds Value funds like to invest in companies that the market has overlooked. They search for stocks that have become

---

Although growth funds tend to be flashy and often dominate the market, value funds have a better long-term record. Since the late 1920s, value stocks have gained an average of 13 percent compared with 10 percent for growth stocks.

"undervalued," those that are priced low relative to their earnings potential. Sometimes these value stocks are facing short-term problems that fund managers believe will eventually be resolved.

Growth Funds As their name implies, growth funds tend to look for the fastest growing companies on the market. Growth managers are willing to take more risk and to pay a premium for their stocks in an effort to build a portfolio of companies with above-average momentum or price appreciation.

Micro-Cap Funds Micro-cap funds look for companies with market values below $250 million. These companies tend to be either startups or companies about to exploit new markets. With stocks this small, the risk is extremely high, but the growth potential is exceptional.

Mid-Cap Funds These funds invest in stocks in the middle of the capital value range, those with market capitalizations of between $1 and $6 billion. The stocks at the lower end of this range are likely to exhibit the growth characteristics of smaller companies and therefore add some volatility to these funds.

Small-Cap Funds Small-cap funds focus on companies with market values below $1 billion. Their degree of volatility often depends on the aggressiveness of their manager. Aggressive small-cap managers buy hot growth companies and assume high risks in hopes of high rewards. More conservative managers look for companies that have been beaten down temporarily. Small-cap value funds aren't as risky as small-cap hot-growth funds, but they can still be volatile.

Index Funds For many investors, index funds are by far the easiest, most effective way to go. These funds simply buy all the stocks or bonds in a chosen market index with the goal of matching that index's performance. Common indexes include the S&P 500, which contains widely held (generally larger-capitalization) stocks; the Wilshire 5000, which represents the entire U.S. market; and the Russell 2000, which represents small-cap stocks. There are also international index funds. If your goal is long-term growth without the need for too much oversight, these workhorse funds are your best solution.

THE LEAST YOU NEED TO KNOW

Mutual funds offer you a convenient way to diversify the investments in you portfolio. Look for funds that have performed well over the past several years and that fit the risk level you're comfortable with. When you buy a fund, watch over its performance just as you would an individual stock. If it doesn't perform to your expectations, get rid of it.

MISTAKE

I Don't Read Stock Charts

If you start with the fundamentals and finish with the graphs, you'll qualify winners every time.

BILL O'NEIL

T HE BEST STOCKS HAVE GREAT FUNDAMENTALS. THIS IS THE PLACE TO start in researching a stock. Search for companies with superior earnings and growth. They should also have top-notch profit margins and a good return on equity. Is the company a leader in a fast-growing industry? The firms that are gobbling up market share are likely to keep delivering the best results year after year.

If the fundamentals of a company look good, that's a great start. But before you buy any stock, make sure you also examine its graphs. How has the stock performed over the past six months, one year, and five years? Some stocks may be extended and could be due for a pullback, while others may be lagging the market. But the big winners are already outperforming most other stocks. The time to buy is just as a strong stock resumes its uptrend after it has gone through a consolidation period.

If all of this sounds complicated, it isn't. In this chapter, I'll show you how easy it is to interpret a stock's chart so that you can properly time your buying and selling opportunities.

WHERE TO GET STOCK CHARTS

The best way for investors to calibrate their state of mind about a stock against the market's thinking about it is to rely on the stock's chart. A chart shows you the price movement history of a stock. A mere couple of inches on a chart provide a motion picture of a stock's movement over whatever period of time you select. Fortunately, several excellent charting services are available on the Internet at little or no cost. *Money* magazine's Web site (www.money .com) offers free charting services. Most stock charts, including money.com, are updated at least every fifteen minutes during market hours. Both CompuServe and its parent company, America Online, offer stock charting services to their customers.

You don't need any expertise in charting techniques to spot whether a stock is on a downtrend or whether its price has overcome negative momentum and is on an uptrend. Only rarely will you be tempted to say, "I'm not sure. It seems to be right at the point of reversing." If that's the situation you find, look at the stock's chart again in a week to see where it's headed. As you can see from figure 13.1, which was printed from *Money* magazine's on-line financial page, Dell Computer Corporation offers a classic example of a great stock that has gone through some great and not-so-great times.

As Dell entered the new millennium in 2000, its stock slid from $45 a share to $20 a share in just four months, for a 55 percent loss in value. Then it climbed back up in February of 2001, when the tech stocks were generally on a bullish run, hitting a high of $30 a share. However, as the end of March approached, investors feared that most of the tech stocks were overvalued, and Dell lost $10 a share over the next two months. The company successfully recovered most of its loss in May, but when personal

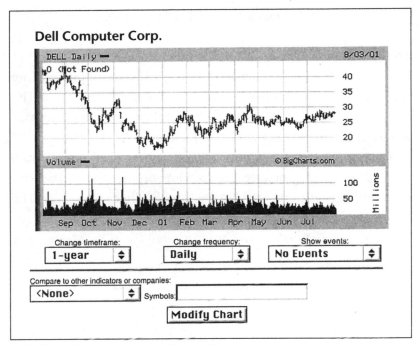

FIGURE 13.1 Dell Computer Corporation

computer sales began to soften toward the end of summer, Dell stock plummeted, hitting the low-$20 range in January. If you had not been following Dell's stock chart, you could easily have lost over 50 percent of your investment in the company over this twelve-month period.

When you look at a stock chart, focus entirely on the reality of the data. Avoid what expert investors call "analysis paralysis," waiting for just a little more news or technical confirmation. The market keeps moving no matter what you decide. There will never be an unchallenged answer or a point of total certainty. Investors need to exercise discipline, evaluate a stock's chart, and make a buy or sell decision based on what they see.

KEY PARTS OF A STOCK CHART

The price and volume movements shown in a stock's chart reflect demand for that stock. They are especially helpful in pinpointing the exact time to buy a stock or when to sell it. Wall Street lives by the phrase "timing is everything." The ability to use charts to your advantage is a major aspect of the stock selection process.

Typically, a stock chart consists of vertical bars that plot the stock's price range for a day or a week (depending on the type of chart you use), and a short horizontal bar that marks the closing price. The two-month chart for Dell in figure 13.1 shows how another price bar is added each subsequent day to document the stock's trend over

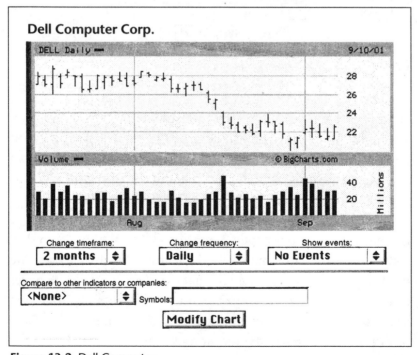

Figure 13.2 Dell Computer

time. Notice the corresponding vertical lines underneath the price bars. These are volume lines, representing the number of shares traded for the day or week. Volume indicates supply and demand, and how strong a trend is or how likely it is to continue.

The most helpful charts span six to twelve months of trading activity. You can miss the big picture if you use charts showing shorter time periods.

READING A STOCK CHART

There is a natural tendency to fall victim to excitement and buy a stock when it is hot. Only disciplined investors consistently refuse to buy stocks on rumors or excited rallies. Instead, they demonstrate self-discipline by placing a buy limit below the market price prevailing at the time they first decide to purchase a stock.

Buying too high on a burst of excitement is a sure way to lose money in the stock market. Even greater damage can result from holding on to a position because of unjustified optimism. What makes it difficult for investors to abandon their position is that declining stocks occasionally do rally. These occasional bursts of countertrend strength in weak stocks do their diehard owners more harm than good.

Knowing how to interpret a stock chart can help you buy and sell at the most opportune times. Generally, a falling stock price accompanied by abnormally heavy trading volume is a bad sign, because it usually indicates that big institutional investors are selling large blocks of shares. If volume is less than normal, however, falling prices aren't necessarily bad news. The low volume may mean that the selling is not significant and may be drying up.

The six-month chart for NVR, Inc., in figure 13.3 offers an excellent example of how to interpret a stock chart. If you look at how

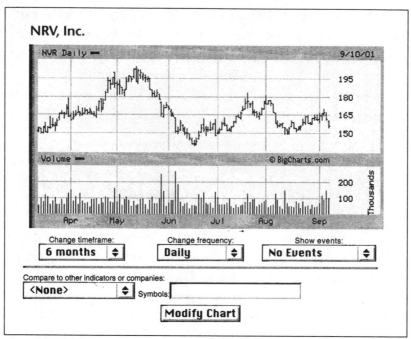

FIGURE 13.3 NVR, Inc.

NVR was performing in August and September, you probably would have wanted to own some of its stock during that period. The stock price was consistently above its moving average as it trended upward. In early October, however, the stock dipped just below its moving average, which is why the down (sell) arrows appeared. However, notice how NVR rebounded nicely. After hugging its moving average line for a couple of weeks, the stock took off in mid-October. It peaked in mid-November, when the down (sell) arrow appeared.

Most investors probably had positive feelings toward NVR when it reached its four-month peak in mid-May, before the profit-taking sell-off. It took approximately three months for NVR to recover from that sell-off and begin another uptrend in early June. It's important to keep in mind that even uptrending stocks have their good days and their bad days, as this example shows.

ANALYZING CORPORATE EARNINGS REPORTS

Even if you had time to sift through endless earnings reports, that's not a very efficient way to identify companies announcing superior earnings. And how can you tell the difference between a one-hit wonder and a potential stock market winner when you are looking at raw earnings numbers for thousands of companies reporting their earnings each quarter? Instead, look at a stock's price–earnings (PE) ratio, which compares its price to its annual earnings per share. For example, a stock quoted at $50 a share with annual earnings of $5 per share has a PE ratio of 10. In other words, the stock is selling at 10 times its annual earnings.

Conventional wisdom says stocks with higher PE ratios are overpriced and should be avoided. But the truth is that the best stocks often have high—some would say ridiculous—PE ratios when they start their big climbs. And they continue having high PEs throughout their advances. Several studies prove that a company's percentage gain in earnings per share over the year-earlier period has a great impact on the company's stock price.

Companies report their earnings every three months. Most business and financial publications provide these numbers as they are announced. *Investor's Business Daily* publishes a comprehensive list separating companies posting earnings gains from those reporting lower results. To save investors time, the list is arranged from highest to lowest (or negative) percentage gains in earnings. The number of companies in each category helps you get an overall idea of the market's trend.

Be wary of corporate announcements of "record" earnings. A company could be growing earnings at just 2 or 3 percent and still have its best-ever quarter. You don't just want earnings to be better than the year before. You want to see remarkable gains.

The last part of the earnings picture is estimates, or the earnings Wall Street analysts expect the company to report in the coming quarters or year. Look for estimates that represent positive indications of growth. But remember, estimates are just that—educated guesses. They are no substitute for a track record of past performance.

RECOGNIZING FALSE SIGNALS

Not only does daily price and volume action in the market renew investors' hope in stocks that have been slipping, but positive fundamental news has the same effect. Fundamental analysis looks at a company's financial statistics—its balance sheet and income statements. A reasonably good quarterly earnings report or an optimistic brokerage recommendation generates optimism in the heart of most investors. As a stockowner, it may be difficult to be entirely objective. Every positive wiggle in your stock's price, every time the quote holds steady against a thirty-five-point drop in the Dow, and every piece of good news is a source of positive psychological feedback.

However, if the dominant price path of the stock is downward, these false signals should be viewed as uninvited distractions from the truth rather than as rays of hope. Investors must separate the facts of the situation from the fiction. They must discriminate the truth about the company and its industry from rumor and hope. Guard against optimism based on false signals.

USING BASES TO SPOT WINNERS

You can get a good idea how far your car can go just by glancing at its fuel gauge. You can do the same with a stock by looking at its chart. Before hopping in, check how many bases a stock has formed. A base has formed when the price of a stock remains relatively flat for at least a week. If a great stock has logged one or two bases, it may have lots of mileage left for gains. But a stock with three or four bases could be running on empty. The greater the number of bases, the higher the risk.

Few stocks have the specs to build four bases during a bull market. Many Internet service provider and software stocks that took off in 1999 and early 2000 went up so fast they flamed out in one huge climax run after only their first or second base. Bases are like staircases when you review a stock's chart. They'll hit a certain price range on their chart, stay there for a while, and then move "up the stairs" to the next higher price. Counting bases can be tricky. Don't count a 15 to 20 percent decline as a base if it lasts six weeks or less. It could be a normal pullback or an indication that a stock is about to move "up the stairs."

The best stocks tend to launch rallies with little fanfare. They form a firm base in a bear market while most stocks are getting clawed. Then they break out to new highs just when the market begins to rise, but most investors are still nursing their wounds or aren't willing to get back in.

If your stock declines and then rebounds, note your personal optimism level. Keep a notebook where you write down the stock's price and your feelings about it. Then decide whether the new facts truly justify a revival of optimism. Bear in mind that when a declining stock rallies back to a higher price level, it feels better to the owner than when the stock fell to that same price earlier. The rally creates hope, while the earlier move produced fear. Note the emotional difference, even though the stock price is the same.

Statistically, most market participants in one cycle are around when the drama repeats itself in the next cycle. Incredibly, a majority again fall prey to the same mistakes they made in the first cycle. Most such mistakes have to do, not with fundamentals, but with investors' emotional reactions to news and price volatility. So it pays to remain emotionally clear-headed.

All speculative markets move from one extreme to the other. For example, in a recession, the U.S. economy might show a 3 to 5 percent drop in real gross national product (GNP). Corporate earnings may slide 20 or 25 percent. But the major stock averages might fall 30 to 40 percent in a year, as if economic life were about to disintegrate.

In this scenario, some individual stocks fall 80 to 90 percent. Other companies go out of business and their stock certificates become expensive wallpaper. What takes hold of investors when this kind of extreme market movement occurs is crowd psychology, a total loss of self-control. What investors should instead hold on to is a high awareness of the patterns in a stock's chart. The reason is simple. A stock's degree of recent success or failure has a powerful influence on its subsequent market moves. Success enables more success, to a point at which inhibitions disappear. Investors suffer when they let faulty, irrational, or incomplete evaluation of the graphic performance of a stock over time rule their actions.

THE LEAST YOU NEED TO KNOW

Examining a stock's chart can often tell you where that stock has been over a period of time. That information may not make itself clear when you do a fundamental analysis of the same stock. Don't allow yourself to get sucked into exciting short-term uptrends. The true measure of a great stock is how well it has done over time, as the market rode its own up- and downtrends.

I Don't Believe Online Trading Makes Cents

Online traders are the Zorros of the Internet.

ZORRO

YOU'VE PROBABLY HEARD STORIES ABOUT COMPUTER NERDS WHO ARM themselves with cheap personal computers and make a killing day-trading stocks online. But not all online traders are day-traders. Could trading online be your ticket to greater financial rewards? In this chapter, I encourage you to explore the many advantages that online trading can offer. I'll show you how easy it is to make a trade for less than $10. Compared with paying a broker $100 or more for the same trade, that's a whopping 90 percent savings.

ONLINE TRADING EXPLODES

Although online trading is a relatively recent phenomenon, its impact on the brokerage industry has been revolutionary. December 1997 was a watershed for the brokerage industry. Charles Schwab and Company reported that 50 percent of its retail commission trading for the month was done online and that Internet brokerage sales accounted for 41 percent of its total sales.

Schwab is not the only brokerage firm benefiting from investors making online trades. Investor interest in online trading has also caused rapid growth in the number of brokerage firms going online. In 1997, there were fifteen. A year later, there were over sixty. According to a Piper Jaffray report, industry-wide online trading in 2001 accounted for an estimated 38 percent of all retail trading, more than double the 1998 level. Today, more than one hundred fifty firms offer online trading.

As usually happens when companies race to enter a new market, consumers are benefiting from lower prices. Online trading commissions have fallen from an average trade price of $35 in 1996 to less than $10 today.

WHY ONLINE TRADING IS POPULAR

What is it about online trading that has attracted so many investors? Obviously, low commissions are a major attraction, but price doesn't completely explain the allure. There's a high degree of independence and freedom that comes with the ability to turn on your computer and make a trade. No broker calls or passes judgment on your decisions. You can buy or sell any security you wish. In an age when more and more investors feel comfortable calling their own investment shots, online trading gives them the power to trade instantaneously on their own terms, without a broker.

For many people, the days of calling a stockbroker for investment advice have gone the way of the ticker-tape machine. Instead, they simply log on to one of the growing number of brokerage sites and, for a modest fee, buy and sell stocks with a click of the mouse. They also track their portfolios, transfer funds, and conduct investment research online.

Lots of Upside, Little Downside

Over 35 percent of the daily trading volume on the New York Stock Exchange and NASDAQ is driven by online traders. Investment industry officials say the advantages of online trading, which include value, convenience, and speed, far outweigh the disadvantages. On the downside, some investors neglect to conduct adequate research before making online trades. And for an unfortunate few, clicking on the button that concludes a trade provides an adrenaline rush that is hard to resist.

However, a recent survey conducted for Fidelity Investments found that four out of five online traders closely follow all of their investments. "Our online clients are, by and large, buy-and-hold investors, and they're self-directed," said Robert Blunt, vice president and manager of Fidelity's Scottsdale, Arizona, branch. Blunt noted that "80 percent of Fidelity's customers use the Internet. It's more than just trading. You can check your accounts, transfer funds, and conduct research. You have access to your account twenty-four hours a day, seven days a week."

WHO TRADES ONLINE?

The investors who are best suited to online trading are those most comfortable making their own investment decisions. They are willing and able to conduct their own research on stocks. Investors who rely on full-service brokers to select investments for them and who are willing to pay for that advice should probably avoid online trading. When you trade online, no broker calls to suggest a hot stock or a strong-performing mutual fund for you to buy. Online brokerage firms are for hands-on investors.

Many online brokerage firms discourage day-trading, the practice of buying and selling stocks rapidly, sometimes within a matter of minutes, to turn quick profits. Some of them, including Vanguard, don't let their customers order initial public offerings (IPOs) over the Internet when they're first issued. They argue that investors who chase IPOs in an effort to get in on the ground floor of a stock often end up paying more than the stock is worth.

Online trading shouldn't be used for rapid-fire investing. The newfound freedom and power of investing online can sometimes cause Internet investors to become overly aggressive and lose sight of basic investment concepts. Trading online is no reason to change your investment strategy.

WHERE'S THE ONLINE BROKERAGE INDUSTRY GOING?

There's no denying that online trading has been a boon in providing low-cost and easy access to the financial markets for millions of investors. However, online trading is a double-edged sword to full-service brokerage firms. On the one hand, cheap online trading has the potential to turn individual investors into trading machines who buy and sell stocks many times a week. These customers generate small but repeated commissions—good news for online trading companies such as E*Trade and Ameritrade.

Until recently, such full-service firms as Merrill Lynch were absent from the online trading list. Is that because Merrill Lynch couldn't figure out the technology? Of course not. It's because the firm has a huge network of brokers earning top commissions. However, as Merrill Lynch has started to push its online trading program, it has simultaneously attracted more accounts to its full-service brokers as well.

Profile of an Online Trader

Age: Thirty percent of online traders are under thirty-five years of age, with 57 percent under forty-five. Full-service traders are twice as likely to be fifty-five and older (25 percent) as online traders (14 percent).

Education: Fifty-nine percent of online traders have college degrees compared with 49 percent of full-service traders.

Gender: Sixty-seven percent of online traders are men; full-service traders are divided almost equally between women (51 percent) and men (49 percent).

Source: *SmartMoney* magazine, February 2001

Schwab's experience has been particularly telling. The company still accepts telephone orders for a fee. But it encourages online trading by telling its customers that it's a cheaper way to trade.

In the future, all brokers will offer online trading if they want to stay in business. Over time, online commissions are projected to go even lower. In fact, there is talk of rebates, where brokers pay customers for doing trades. How can brokers afford to charge $8 a trade, $0 a trade, or even to pay for a trade?

Brokerage firms make money by lending stock held in their accounts and from the interest they earn on margin loans. Brokers also earn interest on cash balances held in accounts. Another source of revenue is what's called "payment for order flow." This payment is, in effect, a kickback to brokers for steering trades to certain market makers.

Also, many investors who use online systems pay rates considerably higher than $8 a trade when they buy stock options, like call and put options. Commissions on these investments are higher than commissions to buy and sell stocks. The upshot is that, for large accounts, the time may come when investors are paid to trade.

SELECTING AN ONLINE BROKER

Online investors want a lot from online brokers: they demand fast downloads, instant trade executions, and great customer service, all at a cheap trading price. When considering an online broker, it's important to look beyond commissions. Get answers to questions like these from your candidates:

- *What research services do you offer?* Many online brokers make a plethora of stock research tools and quote services available. The better the tools, the more you're likely to pay in trade fees.
- *What investments can I buy online?* Some online brokers don't allow you to buy certain types of investments, such as mutual funds, online.
- *How good is your customer support?* Send a few E-mails to the company and see how quickly and competently the firm responds to your queries.
- *What fees other than commissions do you charge?* Check for hidden fees. Some online brokers charge a startup fee to open an account or an administrative charge per trade.

How do you find a good online broker? Fortunately, the Web provides sites that compare the prices and services of online brokers to help you select one that's right for you. A good place to start is at www.internetinvesting.com. Paul Shread launched this site a few years ago. He lists online brokers in two categories: brokers suitable for garden-variety online investors and brokers suitable for day-traders. The site is a good starting point for novices in either kind of investing. Shread summarizes commission expenses, account minimums, and special features offered by online brokers. He also provides links to helpful books and Web sites about investing on the Internet.

Money magazine routinely rates online brokers on such criteria as commissions, availability of real-time quotes, research links, account information, technology support, fees, and product availability. An example of its online brokers' scorecard is shown in figure 14.1.

★ SCORECARD THE ONLINE RANKINGS

Company website (www.)	Telephone (800)	Ease of use	Customer service	System responsiveness	Products and tools	Cost	Overall ranking
Fidelity fidelity.com	544-7272	★★★★★	★★★★★	★★	★★★★½	★★	★★★★★
Ameritrade ameritrade.com	454-9272	★★★★	★★★★★	★★★★	★★★½	★★★★½	★★★★★
Merrill Lynch mldirect.com	653-4732[1]	★★★	★★★★½	★★★★★	★★★★★	★★	★★★★½
Datek Online datek.com	823-2835	★★★	★★★★½	★★★★	★★	★★★★★	★★★★½
Charles Schwab schwab.com	225-8570	★★★★	★★★★	★★★★	★★★★½	★★	★★★★
JB Oxford & Co. jboxford.com	782-1876	★★★★	★★★★	★★★	★★★	★★★	★★★★
Quick & Reilly quickandreilly.com	837-7220	★★	★★★★½	★★★½	★★★½	★★★	★★★★
DLJdirect dljdirect.com	825-5723	★★★½	★★	★★★★½	★★★★½	★★★	★★★½
Morgan Stanley Dean Witter msdwonline.com	688-6896	★★★	★★	★★★★★	★★★★★	★★	★★★
Web Street Securities webstreet.com	932-8723	★½	★★★★★	★½	★★★★	★★★★½	★★★
E*Trade etrade.com	387-2331	★★★	★★½	★★½	★★★★★	★★★	★★½
TD Waterhouse waterhouse.com	934-4448	★★★½	★★	★★½	★★★★★	★★★★½	★★½
Suretrade suretrade.com	909-6827	★★	★★★	★★★	★★★★	★★★★★	★★★
A.B. Watley abwatley.com	229-2853[2]	★★★	★★	★★★½	★★★	★★★★½	★★
National Discount Brokers ndb.com	888-3999	★★★½	★	★★★	★★★★½	★★★	★★
American Express americanexpress.com/trade	297-7378	★	★★★★	★★	★★★★	★★★★★	★★
Muriel Siebert & Co. siebertnet.com	872-0711	★★	★	★★★	★★★★	★★★★	★
Mydiscountbroker.com mydiscountbroker.com	882-5600[2]	★	★★★	★★	★★★½	★★★★	★
Dreyfus edreyfus.com	421-8395	★½	★	★★★★½	★★	★★★★	½
Scottrade scottrade.com	619-7283	★★½	★	★½	★★★	★★★★½	½

Notes: [1]Area code 877. [2]Area code 888.

FIGURE 14.1 Online Brokers Scorecard

What to Watch Out For

Unfortunately, the same things that make online trading a blessing can make it a curse as well. Broker-free access to instantaneous trading provides incredible power and freedom for investors. But power and freedom are double-edged swords. It's easy to fall into a trading mentality of buying and selling stocks or mutual funds at every blip in the market.

Studies show that this is exactly the wrong way to build wealth in the stock market. Even purveyors of online trading concede that easy access to the markets may not ultimately be in the best interest of certain investors. "Trading often and heavy is not something that makes you a lot of money," says J. Joe Ricketts, chairman of online broker Overtrade.

A short-term trading mentality is not the only potential problem with online trading. Remember that online trading is only as good as the technology behind the trading system. Some online traders have already tasted the downside of this technology. In October 1997, the Dow Jones Industrial Average fell 554 points and then rose 337 points in record trading of 1.2 billion shares. Many online investors experienced system crashes and were unable to execute trades in time to avoid the bear.

The problems may not always be related to system crashes at your broker. If your Internet service provider is having problems, you may not be able to get on to the Internet, let alone connect to your broker. And if you believe your online trades will always be conducted in nanoseconds, think again. Trades can be delayed for several minutes, depending on the online brokerage firm you're using. A prudent approach is to open at least a couple of online accounts with brokers who also take telephone orders. That way, you give yourself more options should system problems develop.

Online trading systems are also vulnerable to security problems. Although Internet security has improved significantly in recent years, security breaches are still possible. For that reason, security provisions should be as important as commission schedules when selecting an online broker.

Finally, if you're not careful when you execute an online trade, it can cost you dearly. Make sure you review the confirmation screens before you execute an order to avoid any surprises due to a key entry error. For example, suppose you want to sell one hundred shares of IBM at $100 a share. For whatever reason, you make a mistake and enter a sell price of $10 a share. You're in a hurry, ignore the confirmation screen, and push the enter key to confirm your order. Guess what happens? You just sold 100 shares of IBM at $90 below market price for a whopping $9,000 loss. And you have no recourse against anybody—including your online broker—because *you* made the mistake. Pay close attention to every trade you make online.

THE LEAST YOU NEED TO KNOW

"Stock brokerage is not a profession you want your children to go into." This statement was reportedly made by the president of the online trading firm E*Trade Group. Certainly, the advent of online trading and its low commissions is affecting the brokerage community, especially full-service brokers. But online trading is not the only factor making the brokerage business a tougher place to make a buck these days. There are several other ways for investors to access the market without a broker or financial intermediary. No-load mutual funds, which investors can buy directly from the fund family, have been stealing brokerage customers for years. Even if you are utilizing the services of a full-service broker, you owe it to yourself to have at least one online account so that you can enjoy the benefits that both options afford.

15

Asset Allocation Is for Wimps

Once you've amassed two nickels to invest,
it's a good idea to keep them in separate pockets
and not in the same pants.

BEN FRANKLIN

THE IDEA OF ALLOCATING, OR DIVERSIFYING, INVESTMENTS HAS BEEN around for centuries. In Shakespeare's sixteenth century version of *The Merchant of Venice,* merchant Antonio explains that his "ventures are not in one bottom trusted, nor in one place." That translates to "I don't put all of my eggs in one basket or rather, one boat." Asset allocation is all about selecting which eggs to put in which baskets. It's the ultimate protection should things go wrong in one investment sector, as happens from time to time.

Unfortunately, many investors have come to believe that asset allocation is as outdated as Shakespeare's prose. They're quick to remind you that anyone who threw money into a Standard & Poor's (S&P) 500 index fund ten years ago did better than the prudent investor who was intent on allocating investments among large- and small-cap stocks, foreign stocks, and bonds. In this chapter, I'll show you why investment allocation is critical to the success of your long-term investment strategy. You'll learn how to allocate your assets and adjust your allocation plan to keep up with changing times.

163

WHAT IS ASSET ALLOCATION?

Many investors spend sleepless nights worrying about which stocks to buy and sell, which mutual funds to own or dump, or whether to get into bonds and money market funds. All of these different investments are called asset classes. And what classes to be in is a legitimate concern. Investors whose overall investment allocation plan is weak can sustain substantial losses.

Studies show asset allocation—dividing one's investment funds among different asset classes—is the single greatest determinant of investment performance. Unfortunately, many investors blithely sink money into the market without ever formulating an investment allocation plan. If they were to consult a qualified financial adviser, they might act differently. Drawing up an asset-allocation model is the first thing most financial advisers recommend to new clients.

Assets are the total of your short- and long-term investments, ranging from a savings account for your children's education to your own retirement savings. Chances are, you've already got money invested in a retirement plan like a 401(k) plan. I hope you have also set aside some funds for emergencies. As you increase

Allocation Resources on the Web

- Fidelity's Asset Allocation Planner (www.fidelity.com) provides diversification advice, a risk questionnaire, and five model portfolios.

- The Intelligent Asset Allocator (www.efficientfrontier.com) offers comprehensive information on how to build a diversified portfolio.

- Schwab Investor Profile (www.schwab.com) provides a questionnaire to match investors with one of six portfolios that fits their profile.

your investment knowledge, you'll be in a better position to fine-tune your investments to fit your needs.

WHAT HAPPENS IF YOU DON'T ALLOCATE?

Suppose you have all your assets invested in high-tech stocks. Then imagine that something happens to the very foundations of the market, as it did in 2000, when millions of investors suddenly decided tech stocks were overpriced. The resulting sell-off caused the tech-heavy NASDAQ to fall more than 50 percent. If you were heavily invested in the tech sector, you probably got hurt.

So you put your money into bonds and quickly discovered that the bond market was also having its ups and downs. If you got disgusted with bonds and moved your money into a money market account, you didn't make much interest. Although money market accounts are virtually bombproof, they provide far lower returns than stocks.

The bad year in the stock market that started off the new millennium may register as nothing more than an insignificant blip in the future. That's because the stock market has historically been the best long-term investment vehicle, with average annual returns of more than 10 percent over the past ten years.

In the short term, though, the stock market is more volatile than other investments. Consequently, investors with less risk tolerance, like those who are close to retirement, should have a smaller percentage of their investment in the stock market than should younger investors, and they should invest a significantly greater percentage of their assets in bonds.

An individual's risk tolerance and return-on-investment goals are the dominant factors influencing what percentage of total investment funds should be put into each of the three investment categories (stocks, bonds, and cash). These factors also influence the specific types of issues that should be bought in each category. Wise choices deliver the maximum return within your comfort zone for risk, enabling you to reach realistic financial goals without losing sleep.

These are the most important points you should know about asset allocation:

Time is on your side The younger you are (the more years you have until retirement), the greater the percentage of your assets you can afford to put into the stock market.

Stocks mean risk, but they also mean higher returns Those with a higher tolerance for volatility should put more money into the stock market than those in the same age group who have a lower risk tolerance.

Education funds need stocks If you're investing for your kids' education and they are still young, consider putting a greater percentage of their education funds into stocks than in more conservative investments like CDs. Given time, stocks will outperform most conservative investments.

Get professional advice If you've done your research but are still confused about what's best for your situation, consult a qualified financial planner or a good broker for help. Invest in identifying the allocation that's right for you. It's the key to achieving your goals. Studies have shown that asset allocation is the single most important factor in determining returns from investing.

Know your stock funds Before you begin to implement your asset allocation plan, check out mutual funds that invest in specialized sectors, such as foreign stocks and municipal bonds. (See the discussion of these specialized fund types in Mistake #12.)

Always remember that things change. It's never too late to revamp or revise an asset-allocation plan. In fact, if you don't review and revise your plan and your actual allocations at least once a year, you are probably not monitoring your investments as closely as you should.

WHAT'S THE RIGHT MIX FOR YOU?

Your goals, risk tolerance, and time horizon are the keys to determining the right mix for your investment portfolio. For example, your ultimate financial goal may be to retire in style. The decisions you make about allocating your assets earlier in life will greatly affect how soon you can retire and in what style. When considering risk in planning asset allocation, it is most productive to think in terms of your tolerance for volatility. This is because one of the greatest investment risks is the risk of doing nothing—and subsequently missing out on superior returns.

Investors planning to retire in fifteen years who have a high tolerance for volatility may want to have 70 percent of their holdings in the stock market, 28 percent in bonds, and only 2 percent in money market funds. Investors planning to retire in twenty-five years might increase their securities holdings to 80 percent. Those retiring in fifteen years but with less stomach for volatility may want to keep 50 percent in stocks and 38 percent in bonds. For equally volatility-shy people ten years younger, the percentage in stocks could be around 65 percent.

Those retiring in five years are faced with the daunting task of allocating their assets for maximum return without betting the farm. A nasty market dip occurring immediately before retirement could eliminate a substantial portion of their savings. Individuals close to retirement who can live with higher volatility may want to put all their holdings in stocks, weighted toward large-cap stocks, which are more dependable than mid-cap and small-cap stocks. Those who can't take the heat may want to put as much as 48 percent in bonds, 2 percent in money market accounts, and 50 percent in stocks.

If one of your investment goals is putting your kids through college, we noted earlier that you should consider investing their education funds heavily in the stock market while they are young. For example, education investors with a high tolerance for volatility might put 80 percent in stocks, while those who sleep more fitfully might limit their securities investments to 65 percent or even less. Achieving the right mix of investments like small-, mid-, and large-cap stocks and short-, medium-, or long-term bonds to achieve maximum return for your volatility tolerance while maintaining adequate diversification is a tricky business. You may want to consider consulting a qualified financial planner for advice.

EXECUTING YOUR ALLOCATION PLAN

Before you actually invest in accordance with your new allocation plan, be sure you know what you already own. Many people don't know precisely what they own because their portfolios are dominated by mutual funds. If you do some investigating, though, you can find out exactly what your funds invest in. For example, some funds call themselves small-cap. However, given the less-than-stellar performance of small-cap stocks over the past few years, these funds may have veered into mid- or even large-cap territory to boost their returns. Call them to find out or read their latest prospectus. Without this knowledge, you could be under the false assumption that your stocks are diversified across companies by size.

You should also know what types of stocks your funds are buying by sector. If one of your funds is tech-heavy, that's okay, as long as you don't have too much in that fund and are sufficiently diversified with stocks from more traditional sectors, such as manufacturing, which tend to rise when techs fall. Similarly, don't take your short-term bond fund's word that its holdings are all short-term. Find out what the fund defines as short-, mid-, and long-term, and then assess what it actually owns by checking the smartmoney.com. mutual fund Web site.

Finding Help on the Web

SmartMoney magazine offers a free asset allocation worksheet on its Web site (www.smartmoney.com) that helps you build a customized allocation portfolio. You enter key variables, such as your age, income, net worth, spending needs, risk tolerance, and expectations about the future, to determine an asset allocation that's best for you (figure 15.1). Generally speaking, the younger you are, the more you can afford investment options with short-term volatility. As your age or your spending needs increase, you'll want to protect your principal by shifting money toward less volatile investment options, such as bonds. *SmartMoney*'s asset allocation system helps balance your risk tolerance with economic realities so

Asset Allocator

SmartMoney One Asset Allocation System

OUR ASSET ALLOCATION system is designed to help you tailor your asset mix to your own needs. If you become bearish about the stock market, it will reset your allocation towards bonds and cash. As you age, it will adjust your mix. If you use this worksheet to allocate only your retirement accounts, and you have more than ten years to retirement, remember to set both spending scales to zero.

More Asset Allocation

· SmartMoney One for Pare
· SmartMoney One for Retirees

One Asset Allocation Worksheet

Value of all assets invested in:		2-yr. spending	$0	0 — 100%
Cash		10-yr. spending	$0	0 — 100%
Bonds		Leaving to heirs	$0	0 — 100%
Small caps		Yrs. to retirement	0	0 10 20 30+
Large caps		In tax-deferred accts	0%	0% 50% 100%
Intl stocks		Equity in home	0%	0% 50% 100%
Total assets		No. of dependents		0 1 2 3+
Tax bracket	15%	Volatility tolerance		low — high
		Economic outlook		weak — strong
		Inflation forecast		<1% 3% 5%+

HELP
Click on the questions above for key information and help.

FIGURE 15.1 Asset Allocation

that you can create a well-diversified investment program that takes into account the historical relationships between stocks, bonds, and cash.

The biggest factor in choosing specific stocks and bonds to meet your asset allocation objectives is the amount of time and interest you plan to devote to your portfolio. The more work you're willing to put in, the greater your potential returns. Portfolios that rely more heavily on individual stocks generally require a lot more attention than fund-laden portfolios.

IS ASSET ALLOCATION AN ART OR A SCIENCE?

The debate over the nature of asset allocation has increased in intensity over recent years as some planners have sought to objectify the process to de-emphasize conceptual thinking and judgment. The latest manifestation of this movement is the myriad of software programs that are sold to do the job that financial advisers have been accomplishing for decades with pencils and calculators. Today, most financial planners have replaced these outdated tools with software programs called optimizers to help determine how best to allocate their clients' assets.

There's nothing wrong with using software to take the numerical drudgery out of the asset allocation task, but these optimizers do pose a problem. They lend an air of scientific certainty to a task that rightfully demands subjective judgment as well. If asset allocation were indeed a pure science, then most or all optimizers would render the same configuration when fed data about the same investor. But they don't. The slightest change in input data can yield disproportionate changes in results.

Regardless of whether you call on a financial planner's experience or depend on allocation software to develop your allocation plan, the process demands judgment calls. Some of the software programs incorporate points at which human judgments can be factored into the process. The myriad differences between one investor's situation and another's require just such human judgment.

Just as financial management style varies from one adviser to the next, so too do the approaches of the professionals who develop allocation plans. Unfortunately, some try to apply standardized solutions to a problem that is anything but standard. The matrix of possible asset allocations is virtually infinite. If you choose to hire an expert for help, look for one with allocation experience. If you're thinking of developing a plan without professional assistance, be prepared to do a lot of reading—even if you're a knowledgeable investor.

GETTING STARTED

Asset allocation is a crucial first step in creating a well-diversified portfolio. Let's suppose you're a conservative investor saving $200 a month, with 75 percent of that money going into high-volatility equities and 25 percent going into medium-volatility equities. As far as you're concerned, your investments are allocated. Then you read an article in *Money* magazine and fill out the diversification worksheet that accompanies the article. It shows that 50 percent of your assets should be in large-company stocks, 30 percent should be in small-company stocks, 10 percent should be in bonds, and 10 percent should be in cash.

Now what? First you identify into which categories in the asset allocation model the funds and/or stocks you already own fit. Say you own a medium-volatility large-cap fund. Count that fund as part of your 50 percent allocation to large-company stocks. Count your high-volatility small-cap fund as part of your 30 percent small-company allocation. Figure out where your retirement investments fit as well. Then see what your actual current allocation percentages are. Work from that point to buy, sell, or add to categories to match the allocation you have decided is right for you.

Make sure that whichever allocation approach you choose addresses both your short- and long-term investment goals. Money already earmarked for short-term goals might include savings for a down payment on a new house or for a child's college tuition that's just a few years away. Because you have no time to make up a short-term downturn in the stock market, those kinds of savings demand a more conservative approach.

Once you've allocated your investments, be sure to monitor those allocations at least once a year. Say, for example, that your ideal allocation is 10 percent cash, 15 percent bonds, and 75 percent stocks with the stock portion split equally between large-company, small-company, and international equities. Let's assume that as the year progresses, your large-cap stocks soar for a 20 percent gain, but your small caps decline 10 percent; everything else stays about the same. At the end of the year, you'd have several ways to restore the balance. You could use new money to buy more small-cap stocks or to increase your position in bonds.

Yogi Berra once said, "When you come to a fork in the road, take it." Here's one more way to diversify: When you come to a fork in the investing road and must decide between two promising stocks in different industries, consider going both ways. Buy some shares of each to fill your portfolio with as broad a selection of stocks as possible. Just be sure the two stocks are dissimilar to each other. Some investors think owning five or six stocks makes them diversified, but that's not the case if some of those stocks are in the same industry group.

THE LEAST YOU NEED TO KNOW

Apportioning your long-term investments among various types of stocks or mutual funds and fixed-income investments—like a money market account—makes sense for most investors. Study after study has shown that portfolios invested in different kinds of assets perform better and are less risky than portfolios that are heavily weighted toward one type of investment.

Asset allocation isn't the hurdle some investors think it is if you follow the advice offered in this chapter. But since uneven price movements can upset category balances over time, review your allocations and adjust them as needed at least once a year. This has the added benefit of lending a vital measure of discipline to your investing. It prods you to take the appropriate amount of risk when you're feeling overly cautious. It reins you in during those times when the sky seems to be the limit.

MISTAKE 16

I Don't Follow Industry Trends

When the bull is running down the street, grab it by the tail and hang on for the ride.

BUFFALO BILL

ROUGHLY HALF OF A STOCK'S MOVE UP OR DOWN IS DUE TO THE strength of its industry. If you don't check out the health of a stock's industry before you buy it, you could find yourself owning a loser. Look what happened to Sun Microsystems in the fourth quarter of 2000. The company had met all of its earnings and sales projections. But because the personal computer market had gone soft when companies such as Compaq and Dell announced disappointing earnings, Sun Microsystems suffered as well, even though its earnings were up (figure 16.1).

Now take a look at the computer systems industry graph in figure 16.2. This graph represents a composite of the average price of stocks in Sun's industry. As you can see, the industry started downtrending in November 2000; Sun's downtrend began at the same time. In fact, the industry graph and Sun's graph follow almost identical downtrend patterns. The lesson this teaches us is that even great industry leaders such as Sun Microsystems can't overcome a precipitous drop in their industry's fortunes.

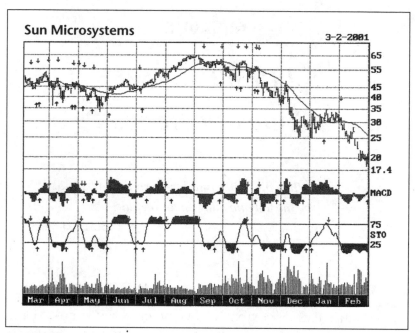

FIGURE 16.1 Sun Microsystems

MONITOR INDUSTRY PERFORMANCE

It's important to track the performance of an industry before you invest in any of the stocks in it. As a rule of thumb, it pays to look for the best stocks among the top forty of the 197 industry groups. Here's a case where herd mentality works to your advantage. Studies show that 37 percent of a stock's price movement is tied directly to the performance of its industry. Another 12 percent is due to strength in its overall sector.

A sector is a broader grouping than an industry group. For example, the Leisure and Entertainment sector contains the Media

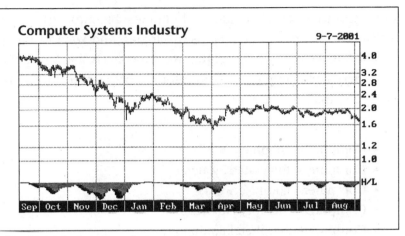

FIGURE 16.2 Computer Systems Industry Graph

industry group. Industry groups can also be subdivided into sub-groups. Within media, for example, there is:

- Media—Books
- Media—Cable TV
- Media—Newspapers
- Media—Periodicals

You don't have to scan every single stock to find out which industries are leading the market. *Investor's Business Daily* ranks 197 different industry groups by the price performance of all stocks in each group over the latest twelve months. This is a realistic period over which to observe market trends.

Why are there so many groups? Because the U.S. economy is fragmented, and industries tend to spawn related businesses that become industries in their own right. Not only do many segments or subgroups make up an industry, but new subgroups are forming all the time as new products, technologies, and ways of doing business make possible things that were inconceivable only a few years ago. For example, the computer sector is not just personal computer makers. It is also:

- Computer—Graphics
- Computer—Integrated Systems
- Computer—Local Networks
- Computer—Memory Devices
- Computer—Peripheral Equipment
- Computer—Services
- Computer—Optical Recognition
- Computer—Software

The more specific the industry classifications, the easier it is to pinpoint specific segments that are leading or falling behind.

Stocks, like people, move in groups, and each market cycle is led by specific industries. The phenomenon is quite natural and is usually due to positive events that are taking place within an industry. For example, among the best-performing groups in the consumer-led boom of the 1980s were apparel manufacturers and retailers. The subgroups that did best were those involved with women's apparel. They were benefiting from an influx of women into the workforce. Manufacturers, such as Liz Claiborne, and retail chains, such as The Limited, enjoyed years of booming sales and earnings as women shopped for career clothes and had money to pay for them. In the 1991 bull market, medical and health care companies led, and computer and electronics issues set the pace in the late nineties.

Although there are exceptions, industries that lead through one bull market don't usually lead in the next cycle. In the 1995 bull market, technology stocks were the rage as corporations poured money into new computers to boost productivity and profits. But more tech subgroups participated than did computer manufacturers. In fact, manufacturers of personal computers lagged behind other computer subgroups even though they outperformed the broad market.

Using Industry Ratings

As I said before, most of the best-performing stocks are in the leading industry groups. So, scanning an industry-rankings list will tell you if a stock you're considering is in a leading industry. Pay close attention to the top 20 percent of industry groups because studies show the greatest market winners are stocks in industries in the top 20 percent of the rankings. Avoid the bottom 20 percent of groups—that's where you'll find the losers. Historical analysis also shows that the stocks within the top half of the industry groups significantly outperform those in the bottom half. Once you've zeroed-in on a stock, check to make sure at least one other stock in the same industry group is showing leadership as a way of confirming your selection.

Knowing how to read sector movements helps you judge the strength of the overall market. Different sectors perk up at different stages of the business cycle. For example, the defensive sectors, which include supermarket chains and utilities, are sometimes viewed as havens during market slumps. People don't significantly change their spending in these industries even when times are tough. These industries typically rise during times of economic weakness or when investors think the economy is headed down. The high-technology sector tends to be strong during expansion phases.

There are other ways to get a picture of market behavior. *Investor's Business Daily* (*IBD*) also tracks a number of market sector indexes by performance over the past three months. The list includes *IBD*'s proprietary sector indexes plus others that are widely followed, such as the Dow Jones Transportation Index. Another excellent way to spot market leadership is the table of new fifty-two-week price highs located on *IBD*'s Industry Groups page. Watch daily for the top six sectors showing the most stocks making new price highs.

Watch for Follow-On Effects

Sometimes, a major development happens in one industry and related industries later reap follow-on benefits. For example, in the late 1950s the airline industry underwent a renaissance with the introduction of jet passenger planes. The increase in air travel a few years later spilled over to the hotel industry, which was more than happy to expand to meet the rising number of travelers. More recently, we've witnessed the ascent of the Internet industry. The Web has helped the securities industry, in turn, attract thousands of online investors. Retailing, media, and other industries are enjoying the coattail effects of the Internet as well.

However, some industries and individual stocks don't ride the leaders' coattails. Don't assume that just because it's the rainy season, umbrella manufacturers will suddenly surge. Look for quality companies capable of producing healthy sales and earnings from exceptional products and services. Table 16.1 provides a historical perspective of how various industries have fared since 1958.

TABLE 16.1 Leading Industry Groups Through the Years

Dates	Top Group	Top Company	Reason for Position
4/58–6/60	Electronics	Fairchild Camera	Transistor developed
5/58–4/61	Vending Machines	Vendo	Provided convenient service
8/58–4/61	Bowling	Brunswick	Automatic pin spotter developed
8/58–4/61	Publishing	McGraw-Hill	Advertising revenue
5/60–12/61	Tobacco	Phillip Morris	New filter cigarettes
12/60–11/61	Savings & Loans	Great Western	Increased demand for loans
11/62–7/66	Airlines	Northwest	Improvements in jet aircraft
1/65–4/66	Color Televisions	Motorola	Color TV becomes popular
7/65–4/66	Semiconductors	Solitron Devices	Increased military spending
12/66–12/67	Computers	Digital Equipment	Improved office procedures
1/67–5/69	Hotels	Hilton Hotels	Increase in air travel
5/67–7/69	Conglomerates	U.S. Industries	Acquisition craze
9/67–6/69	Mobile Homes	Redman	Demand for low-priced homes
8/70–1/73	Retailing	Levitz Furniture	Growth in disposable income
9/70–7/71	Coal	Eastern Gas	Need for more power
10/70–5/72	Building	Kaufman	Increased housing demand
11/70–1/73	Restaurants	McDonald's	Demand for convenience food
12/70–1/74	Oil Service	Halliburton	Increase in oil consumption
4/71–5/72	Mobile Homes	Winnebago	Increase in mobile home parks
2/73–8/74	Gold and Silver	Homestake Mining	High inflation
10/74–12/77	Coal	Falcon Seaboard	Energy shortage

Continued overleaf

Dates	Top Group	Top Company	Reason for Position
9/75–9/78	Catalog Showroom	Best Products	Space-saving shopping
8/76–9/78	Hospitals	National Medical	Medicare pays for services
9/76–12/80	Pollution Control	Waste Management	Increased environmental regulation
1/78–11/80	Electronics	AVX Corp.	Demand for computers
2/78–5/81	Small Computers	Wang	Reduced cost of small computers
1/79–5/81	Oil	Tosco	Shortages due to war in Middle East
12/81–11/83	Apparel Retailing	Gap Stores	More women in workforce
4/82–9/83	Discount Stores	Wal-Mart	Demand for lower prices
6/82–6/84	Military Electronics	EDO Corporation	Reagan increases defense budget
7/82–1/85	Building	Pulte Homes	Home buying by baby boomers
6/84–6/87	Cable Television	Viacom	New programs drive demand
2/85–10/87	Computer Software	Microsoft	Need for software to support PCs
3/88–7/90	Sports Shoes	Nike	Fitness now in fashion
10/88–1/92	Outpatient Health	Surgical Care	Cost advantage over hospitals
10/90–3/95	HMOs	United Healthcare	Reduced health care costs
4/95–5/98	Communications	Nokia	Huge demand for cell phones
3/96–6/99	Computers	Cisco	Web-driven computer sales
7/96–3/00	Automobiles	Chrysler	Aggressive demand for SUVs
4/00–12/00	Oil	Tosco	OPEC cuts supply to raise prices
11/00–6/01	Finance	Washington Mutual	Cheap interest rates

THE LEAST YOU NEED TO KNOW

Much of a stock's move is due to the strength of its industry. You want to own stocks in industries that are displaying strength and market leadership. Different industries move into market leadership positions as economic conditions and consumer trends change. You can identify new leaders by watching the *Investor's Business Daily* Industry Prices table and the top five industry sectors with stocks making the most new price highs. The stocks you buy should be in the top 20 percent of industry groups. It's even more significant when the industry group has been moving up the Industry Prices table.

17

I Buy Low-Priced Stocks Because They're Cheap

One of the great mistakes made by investors is paying too much attention to prices instead of values.

CHARLES H. DOW

MANY INVESTORS LIKE TO BUY LOW-PRICED STOCKS—STOCKS WHOSE share price is in the single- or low-double-digit range. There's nothing wrong with that as long as those stocks have value. Unfortunately, some buy these low-priced stocks simply because they can buy more shares. However, the number of shares you have in your portfolio has nothing to do with your portfolio's cash value. The growth of each stock's share price is where the real value lies.

Astute investors have an entirely different view of what constitutes a "cheap" stock. They look at value rather than stock price alone. In terms of value, a $100 stock may actually be "cheaper" than a $10 stock. Investors looking for value seek out low price–earnings ratios or exceptional annual earnings growth, and carefully consider other critical financial information.

PRICE DOESN'T EQUAL VALUE

One thing you should never do is judge a stock by its price alone. Even if you have only a few dollars to invest, base your buying decision on a stock's value, not its price. There is no rule that says you have to buy an even lot of shares—that is, a block of one hundred shares or its multiples. Odd lots are just as easy to buy and sell as even lots. Look for the best stock at any price. If your choice is between buying ten shares of a $100 stock with a growth rate of 20 percent and a price–earning (PE) ratio of 20, or buying two hundred shares of a $5 stock with a growth rate of 20 percent but with a PE of 30, buy the $100 stock with the lower PE ratio.

What may look like a bargain in the stock market may turn out to be no bargain at all, but big trouble in the making. Say you have been following a stock for a period of time to get a feeling for its normal trading range. Then one day you notice its price begin to drop. You continue to watch and the price continues to fall. You check the company's financials and see that its most recent earnings report was positive. Yet the price of the stock continues to drop to the point at which you can no longer resist it. You buy some shares at what you think is a bargain price. Unfortunately, after you buy it, the stock falls even further. Only when its next earnings report comes out do you realize why the stock dropped so dramatically. The new report reveals that the company has hit some serious financial turbulence.

Be wary of stocks that unexpectedly begin to fall, particularly during a period when the overall market is moving up. The company's most recent earnings report may be of no value in assessing the strength of the stock because the problems are probably more recent. You need to dig deeper. Call the company and talk to its investment relations manager. Don't be shy. The manager's job is to talk with investors like you. Search for recent news on the company to see if it is encountering financial trouble. Chances are, there's a good reason for the drop in price and a good reason to stay clear of the stock. On the other hand, you might find that the company is still doing well despite the drop in its stock price. If the price drop is just part of the normal market flow, it could signal a good time to buy at a bargain price.

WHY TO NOT BUY CHEAP STOCKS

Perhaps you think you'll hit the jackpot by buying a low-priced stock that might make huge gains. Some investors equate a "cheap" stock price with "value." If a stock costs just $5 a share, they argue, then they can't lose a whole lot, right? Wrong. The truth is that consistently making money with low-priced stocks is about as likely as winning the lottery.

Think of a stock's price as a measure of its quality and its potential. Stocks selling at less than $10 a share have a much smaller chance of making major advances because they're usually companies lacking good performance records. Professional investors tend to shun low-priced stocks because they're lightly traded, which makes it more difficult for these investors to move in and out of the stock.

A study of the best stocks of 1996–97 found that, on average, they made their big jumps when trading at about $25 a share. Only three of the 120 stocks studied were trading at less than $10 a share. So, instead of looking for "cheap" stocks, look for new highs in quality stocks. Stocks that are coming out of a price consolidation period and that are making solid advances on surges in buying volume are the ones you should consider. As soon as you spot a buy point, and if all other factors (like good earnings growth) are in place, snatch up that stock.

PE RATIO KEY TO VALUE

The price–earnings ratio—stock price divided by earnings per share—is the most commonly used measure of a stock's value. Many investors decide which stocks to buy and sell based largely on the PE. Value investors look for stocks with inordinately low PEs, not for "cheap" stocks that sell for a few dollars a share. Stock PEs are listed every day in the stock tables of most major newspapers. Investors often watch the PE as closely as they do the stock price itself. It's a measure that every serious investor should understand.

In terms of value, a $100 stock may be cheaper than a $20 stock. A $20 stock with earnings of $1 per share has a PE of 20 (20 divided by 1). A $100 stock with earnings of $10 a share has a PE of 10 (100 divided by 10). PEs are a lot like golf scores—lower is better, other factors being equal. Most established blue-chip stocks have PEs in the range of 10 to 50. Value investors tend to focus on stocks with PEs of 30 or under. Consider this analogy: If you could buy a business earning $1 a year for $10 (PE of 10), that would be a much better value than paying $30 for a business with that same $1 of earnings (a PE of 30).

So why doesn't everyone buy stocks with the lowest possible PEs? Because some companies really are worth more than others. Great companies with fast earnings growth command a premium over slower-growing companies, as well they should. Investors are generally willing to pay a price premium for higher-PE stocks that

---

Fairly priced stocks have PEs that roughly reflect their earnings growth rates. The Wall Street rule of thumb is that if a company's earnings are growing at 30 to 40 percent, you can apply a 30 to 40 PE multiplier. If they are growing at 15 percent per year, you can apply a 15 PE multiplier.

are growing at 30 to 40 percent per year compared with stocks that are growing at 10 to 15 percent.

When evaluating a stock's PE ratio, be aware that the average PE ratio differs from industry to industry. For example, stocks in the biotech industry may sell at an infinite PE ratio because of the low earnings that are being made in the industry. A more mature industry might sell at an average PE ratio of 7. So compare the PE of a stock you are investigating with the average for its industry to better gauge its relative value. Another point of comparison is a stock's historical PE ratios. A stock that has maintained a 20 PE through most of its history would probably be a safe buy at around a 20 or lower PE, assuming its earnings are still about the same. If its PE has climbed closer to 30, you might be better served to look for other opportunities and wait for the PE of that stock to drop back down to its normal range.

SHUN THE LITTLE GUYS

Assume you have two stocks on your potential "buy" list: one at $2 and the other at $20 a share. Which one should you pursue? Do what the institutions do and check out the $20 stock.

Some investors focus on low-priced stocks hoping to reap big percentage gains if the stock moves from $2 to $4 in a short time. Great stocks don't start from such modest price levels. As stated earlier, most of the market's biggest winners began their huge runs after their stocks were trading for $25 a share.

Mutual funds, insurance companies, and other large investors move most of the money in the market. A stock needs to trade at a price high enough to spur a steady flow of trading. Its floating supply, or float—the number of shares held by willing sellers—also must be large enough for these big institutional investors, who buy and sell thousands of shares daily, to enter and exit the stock smoothly. For a stock to have a healthy, sustained run, it usually must attract the attention of these institutional investors, the market's most important players. If they determine a company isn't worth their investment, there's probably a good reason.

Institutions also avoid low-priced shares because of the sheer volume of money they have to put to work. With billions of dollars to invest, they often can't take a meaningful enough position in a cheap stock to make a difference in their returns. One percent of a $10 billion fund is $100 million. Investing a sum like that in most small companies would be the equivalent of buying them out. And many small companies aren't even worth $100 million.

YOU GET WHAT YOU PAY FOR

Shirts and sweaters find their way into outlet malls when they're out of style. Retailers slash prices to entice shoppers. Though bargain hunting may be fine for clothes, it doesn't work well with stocks. All too often with low-priced shares, you get what you pay for. Why? Because the market is painfully efficient at putting a price tag on a company's future value.

If the market says a firm is worth only $2 a share, investors have probably spotted a deficiency. Low-priced stocks tend to be young and untested, or perhaps they have fallen from some bad financial news, or they are old leaders long past their prime. They may also have low earnings, or worst yet, be losing money. Stocks with market caps of less than $30 million don't generally have long-term records. Whatever the reason for the low price, it's not wise to argue with the market's verdict.

As a company matures or turns around, its price will reflect those changes. Wait until you see evidence of a transformation in the form of a rising stock price before risking your money. It's also smart to wait for a stock to rise to the level at which institutions will buy it.

THE LEAST YOU NEED TO KNOW

Stocks tend to run in packs. Make it your goal to latch on to the leaders of the pack, not the laggards. The leaders are the first out of the gate when the market improves. They may not be the biggest companies in their industry, but they're the fastest growing, most innovative, and most efficient firms in their fields. They report top-notch sales and earnings growth. Because of it, their stock demands a good price.

Yet many investors think these stocks are "pricey" and look elsewhere for "cheaper" stocks. Or their brokers may recommend a plodding rival that's a "real bargain." Such thinking shows its folly a short time later when the leaders take off and the cheap stocks don't show any true strength. If they rally at all, it's because they're being swept up with the rest of the group and the general market.

Always remember: You get what you pay for. Cheap stocks tend to be mediocre companies that are just getting by rather than forging ahead. As a result, they lack critical institutional support.

MISTAKE 18

I Like to Play
Margin Games

The margin-debt hole is deeper than you think.
How long can you hold your breath?

GERRI DETWELLER

TIM NELSON KNEW ALL ABOUT TAKING RISKS. HE HAD SURVIVED SOME rough times in Vietnam and had gone on over twenty covert missions before he finally retired from the Marines. He had an iron stomach for anything and decided he would make a fortune investing in the stock market with a $50,000 nest egg that he'd saved for that purpose. He opened an online account with a margin option.

Given the $50,000 in Tim's online account, his broker was eager to lend Tim another $40,000 on margin, secured by the value of his portfolio. That almost doubled Tim's gambling chips. At first, he made small buys in blue chips such as Cisco and Dell. As his profits grew, so did his confidence.

When the market is rocketing upward, all investors think they are geniuses. This can be especially true of those who use margin to propel the rocket, as Tim did. But when the market turns south and the rocket comes back to earth, it can be a different story. Tim had loaded up on tech stocks using his margin account, only to lose it all in the great tech sell-off that occurred in 2000 and 2001.

WHAT IS A MARGIN ACCOUNT?

When you open a brokerage account, you have a choice of two types. You can open a cash account or a margin account. A cash account is a simple account you use to buy and sell securities. You pay for your transactions with the money in the account. A margin account is a credit account. You buy securities by paying a certain percentage of their purchase price and borrowing the remainder from the brokerage firm. With a margin account, you are in effect taking out a secured loan against your own portfolio.

The advantage of a margin account is that you do not have to sell any of the equities in your portfolio to obtain cash to buy more securities. Furthermore, you have no repayment schedule. You're free to repay the loan at any time, unless your collateral falls below the required amount. That collateral is the value of the wholly owned securities in your portfolio. While most investors use the cash borrowed in this way to buy additional securities, you can use it for any purpose. Investors who engage in short sales, which I'll cover later in this chapter, also need a margin account.

SETTING UP A MARGIN ACCOUNT

To buy on margin, you must have a margin account. When you open a margin account, you sign a margin agreement form, which outlines the rules for using the account. You can put up your collateral in cash and/or securities. Once the cash and/or securities are in your margin account, you can borrow on margin anytime without having to complete any other forms. You can also add money or securities to your account at any time.

The *initial margin* is the minimum amount of collateral a margin investor must pledge at purchase. The minimum collateral that must stay in the account is called the *maintenance margin*. If the value of the margined securities drops and the account value falls below the broker's maintenance margin (usually about 30 percent of the loan), you'll get a margin call by letter, telephone, telegram, or other means. This is a demand from the broker that the account be brought back up to its maintenance margin. You do this by depositing cash or fully marginable securities into the account. However, only a percentage of a security's market value can be used to meet a margin call.

If you fail to meet the margin call, your broker is authorized by the margin agreement form you sign to sell the margined securities and any other collateral needed to repay the loan, interest, and commissions. You are responsible for any deficit that may remain after your assets are sold. NASDAQ requires a maintenance margin on equities of 25 percent. However, your broker may impose higher margin maintenance requirements.

MARGIN ACCOUNT LIMITATIONS

The Board of Governors of the Federal Reserve Board (FRB) applies restrictions on margin lending practices. You may not borrow up to the full amount of your portfolio. The FRB regulates the amount of credit brokers can extend to its customers. Currently, you can borrow up to 50 percent of the value of your marginable stocks to make a new purchase. In the past, the percentage has varied between 40 and 100 percent.

The New York Stock Exchange (NYSE) Minimum Initial Equity Requirement states that your equity must be at least $2,000 whenever you enter into a new margin account transaction. The NYSE Minimum Maintenance Rule requires that the equities in your account be at least 25 percent of the current market value of your margined securities.

All of these requirements are minimums and can be increased at any time by your brokerage firm or by the regulatory agencies of the securities industry. Not all securities are fully marginable. Your brokerage firm may have its own requirements; your broker can tell you which rules do not apply. Brokers charge interest on margin loans at varying rates, depending on the amount you borrow.

You cannot register shares purchased on margin in your name and have certificates sent to you for those shares. The shares must remain in your margin account in "street name." Any dividends such shares pay will be credited to your account. You may remove shares from a margin account only after you have repaid the amount you borrowed on margin to purchase those shares. If the value of the collateral in your margin account rises, you can withdraw the amount over the minimum requirement or use it for additional investments.

HOW BUYING ON MARGIN WORKS

Margin accounts let you magnify your gains if you choose your purchases wisely. But if you choose unwisely, a margin account will also magnify your losses. You benefit from buying on margin only if the stocks you purchase rise in price. If they stay the same or, worse, drop in price, you lose. Plus, you must pay interest on the margin whether or not the stock price rises.

Let's take an example. Suppose you purchase a stock that's trading for $11 a share. You have only $5,500 to invest, so you buy 500 shares. A year later, you sell the stock for $33 a share. You receive $16,500 before commissions on a $5,500 investment, or the equivalent of a 200 percent return on your investment. Not bad. However, what if instead you had used your margin account.

Suppose you bought on margin 1,000 shares of an Internet stock for $11 a share. You put up 50 percent of the stock's purchase price ($5,500) and borrowed the other 50 percent from the brokerage firm. The next year, the stock is valued at $33 per share. If you sell the stock and repay the broker, you are left with $27,500 ($33,000 from the stock sale less $5,500 plus interest owed to the broker after commissions and interest charges; interest charges and brokerage fees were not included to simplify the example.) That's a much spiffier return on your $5,500 investment.

However, what if that same stock had dropped in price to $8? In the cash transaction, you would receive $4,000 back (excluding commissions) from your original $5,500 investment. In the margin transaction, you would receive $8,000, repay the $5,500 you borrowed from your broker, and be left with $2,500 of your original $5,500 investment (excluding commissions and interest).

WHEN TO BUY ON MARGIN

Here's an example of when you might want to buy stock on margin. Suppose you believe that a particular stock will rise in price. It

Margin Accounts Simplified

A margin account is essentially a collateralized line of credit. You may use proceeds from a margin account for investments or for other purposes. You pay interest on money you borrow from a margin account. If you use the margin to buy securities, you must meet certain minimum margin requirements and maintain the appropriate amount of collateral. If the collateral level falls, you can expect a margin call.

is currently trading at $15 per share and you believe it will soon hit $20. You only have $3,000 in cash—enough to buy two hundred shares. You borrow $3,000 on margin and invest the total $6,000 for four hundred shares. The stock hits $20, and you sell, adding $8,000 to your cash account. You pay back the $3,000 you borrowed plus $100 interest, leaving you with a tidy gain of $1,900 on your original $3,000 investment ($8,000 − $3,100 − $3,000 = $1,900). If you had not used your margin account and had bought only two hundred shares, your gain would have been only $1,000 ($4,000 − $3,000). The chance to magnify your gains is what buying on margin is all about. However, if the margined stock had declined to $10 a share and you had sold, your losses would have been $2,100 ($4,000 − $6,100).

Buying on margin is a strategy for the short term, since holding onto borrowed money too long can result in a loss. When you buy on margin, you are responsible for meeting all margin calls promptly, and you are responsible for repaying all funds borrowed, even if the amount exceeds the value of your account.

As with all investing, there is risk in buying on margin. One of the biggest reasons people lost fortunes in the stock market crash of 1929 was that they borrowed too much and couldn't pay back their loans. The government stepped in soon after to set margin limits.

WHICH SECURITIES CAN BE MARGINED?

The Board of Governors of the Federal Reserve System publishes a list of marginable securities. Most brokerages will extend margin on the following types of securities:

- Listed common and preferred stocks
- Municipal bonds
- Federal government bonds, notes, and bills

- NASDAQ securities
- Convertible bonds (if convertible into a marginable security)
- Corporate bonds (if rated Baa or higher by Moody's)

Check with your brokerage firm to determine if a security is marginable. A higher maintenance requirement is imposed on some securities. Some securities are marginable only up to a certain value. For most initial public offerings (IPOs), there is a waiting period of at least thirty days after they begin trading before they become marginable. Certain mutual funds and all options may not be bought on margin or used as collateral in a margin account.

SELLING SHORT

Margin accounts are not used just for buying. You can also use them to sell securities. This is called selling short, or shorting.

You may have a "long" or a "short" position in a security. When you have a "long" position in a stock or bond, you actually own the security. On the other hand, sometimes you may want to take advantage of a price movement in a security you don't own. When you do this, you take a "short" position by borrowing the security.

A short sale involves "borrowing" a security from your broker and selling it with the intent of repurchasing it later to repay the loan. You might sell short if you believed the price of a security was going to drop and you could repurchase it much more cheaply than the price at which you sold it. Looked at another way, short selling is about selling high and then buying low.

Buying on margin is a simple process but it's also risky. Remember that if you buy a security on margin and it nose-dives in value, you cannot rescue it with more margin buying.

When you short, you sell securities you do not own. You have to buy the shares back at some point because you must return them to the brokerage firm. Once you sell the borrowed securities, you hope that the price falls, so that you can buy back the shares at a lower price. If the price rises, though, you may be forced to buy shares back at a higher price, losing money on the transaction.

For example, let's say you believe that XYZ Inc., which is trading at $10 a share, is going to fall very fast. You borrow one hundred shares of XYZ from your broker and sell them for $1,000 ($10 × 100). Soon afterward, the stock drops to $4 a share and you pay $400 to buy back the one hundred shares, which you return to your broker. You come out $600 ($1,000 – $400) ahead before commission and interest.

However, if XYZ Inc. becomes a hit and its price rises, you'll take a loss. Say the price rises to $15 a share by the time you must repay the shares. It will cost you $1,500 to replace the one hundred shares you sold for $1,000 (plus commission and interest costs as well).

Also keep in mind that, while you have a "short" position in a security, any dividends the security pays or interest it earns must be distributed to the party from whom you borrowed the security, even if you did not actually receive the dividends or interest. The broker can also call the security—demand that you return the shares—at any time regardless of whether the price is up or down.

Rewards and Risks of Selling Short

Investors use short sales to make gains in a declining market or to hedge against losses in an investment. If you sell short and buy back at a lower price, you stand to make larger gains than if you had a long position in a security that declined in value below your

Short Selling Simplified

Here's a summary of how selling short works:

1. You borrow a security from your broker.
2. You sell the security at its current price.
3. You buy the security back when you believe the price has fallen sufficiently or when the broker calls for it (whichever comes first).
4. You return the security to the broker.

purchase price. For example: You borrow one hundred shares that have a market price of $35 a share. You sell those shares for $3,500. The share price later falls to $25 and you buy back the shares for $2,500. You have made a profit of $1,000 ($3,500 – $2,500).

As with any investment strategy, there's a downside. If you are incorrect, you may have to repurchase the borrowed security at a price higher than what you sold it for. Using the previous example again, if the price of the stock increases from $35 to $40 and then you have to buy back the shares, you have to pay $4,000 for them, a loss of $500.

An important thing to remember when selling short is that there is a limit to the amount of money you can earn if you are correct. However, your potential for losing money is unlimited. This is the case because what you can make is limited to the difference between the stock's current market price and the floor price for all securities, which is $0.00. On the opposite end, a security can hypothetically appreciate indefinitely. This means that when you sell short, your losses could build indefinitely if you do not close out the position.

You need a special brokerage account to participate in short selling. All orders to sell a security short must be placed in a short account. You must have margin privileges with your brokerage firm to have a short account. Since selling short requires that you borrow from your broker, you will need to establish credit with your broker and abide by the rules for borrowing against your account.

THE LEAST YOU NEED TO KNOW

You can make money using margin accounts to leverage your investment returns if you're careful and know what you're doing. Conversely, you can lose a lot of money if you buy on margin and the market crashes. For this reason, it is vitally important that you put stop-loss transactions in place on any stock that you buy on margin.

MISTAKE

I Drop My Guard After a Big Gain and Lose It All

Always try to rub up against money, for if you rub up against money long enough, some of it will rub off on you.

DAMON RUNYON

*A*S FAST AS STOCKS ADVANCE DURING RALLIES, THE RETREATS COME EVEN faster. If you don't spot market tops (peaks) quickly, your hard-earned profits can vanish in a few days. So keep a close eye on the major market averages and the prices of leading stocks. You can also get a confirmation that a market is about to top out from the market's leading stocks. The leaders will be rolling over during the first couple of distribution days, where their tops may take the form of a *climax run*, moving into record territory during the day, only to close near the low of the day.

Yahoo! Inc. offers a classic example of how complacency with this great stock could have cost you plenty in the long run. Figure 19.1 shows how well Yahoo! was trading as we entered 2000, filled with the promise of more good investment times as we had enjoyed in the late 1990s. The stock had consistently traded at well over $150 a share and even hit a high of $250 in January 2000. In late March, though, many of the tech stocks started to run into trouble as massive sell-offs began to dilute their share value.

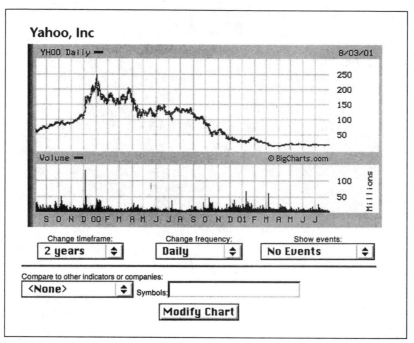

FIGURE 19.1 Yahoo 2-year Chart

On the surface, the sell-off didn't appear to bother Yahoo!, which surged to over $200 in April. But even great stocks can't overcome a weak industry forever. Yahoo! plunged to $125 in May and then fell below $50 a share in October and November. If you owned Yahoo! and weren't watching what was happening, you could have lost 75 percent of your investment.

WHAT DRIVES BIG GAINS IN STOCKS?

Research shows that earnings growth is the single most important indicator of a stock's potential to make a big price move. The companies with the best earnings growth are the ones that will in fact continue to grow. Stocks with poor current earnings won't go anywhere. How many times have you kicked yourself for passing up a great stock such as Microsoft or Home Depot? There were signs that these winners were about to make major moves before they became household names. There were also lots of signs when they fell out of favor in 2001.

Earnings, also called profits or net income, are what a company makes after paying all its obligations. Companies often conclude their quarters at the end of March, June, September, and December, though some companies end their quarters in different months. There are two ways of reporting earnings: a bottom-line total and a per-share amount. The per-share figure is calculated by dividing the company's total earnings by the number of shares it has outstanding. For example, if XYZ Corporation has 45 million shares of stock outstanding and reports earnings of $35.8 million, its earnings per share would be eighty cents ($35.8 million divided by 45 million shares). The per-share amount is the relevant number for investors.

Yahoo!'s stock price surged 458 percent in seven months starting in September 1998. Right before this phenomenal move, Yahoo! reported three quarters of earnings growth of 400 percent, 500 percent, and 800 percent respectively, which were clear indications Yahoo! was building a strong track record and was poised for further growth.

A comprehensive study of the greatest stock market winners dating back to 1953 by *Investors Business Daily* looked at all the stocks that doubled, tripled, or went up even more in value. It analyzed every fundamental and technical variable in all these stocks. What emerged were common earnings characteristics among the big winners:

- Three out of four companies averaged earnings increases of 70 percent or more in the quarter right before their stocks started to take off.

- Three quarters of the top stocks averaged annual earnings advances of at least 30 percent in the three years before their major price move.

Earnings research continues today, and it consistently confirms the significance of strong earnings growth. These studies also reinforce that under a variety of market conditions, selecting stocks based on outstanding earnings performance works. When it comes to investing, look at a company's quarterly and annual earnings record. If you find a winning stock with great earnings potential, buy it. But don't get complacent after you buy it. Watch it closely and be prepared to sell if the situation changes, as it did with Yahoo!.

THE PAIN OF SELLING

Why do investors tend to hold on to their winning stocks long after they become losers? There's a general agreement among psychologists that humans are primarily engaged in finding ways to decrease their amount of pain and raise their amount of pleasure. Pain avoidance and pleasure seeking are familiar concepts that certainly dominate marketing, advertising, and investing. Many other forces are undeniably at work as investors face decisions about selling, but comfort seeking and pain avoidance are extremely powerful.

In a world that keeps moving faster and faster, where technology both amazes and scares us, we are all looking for any anchor against pending storms. Great companies whose stocks have treated us well frequently act as psychological bedrock. We strongly resist any suggestion to sell.

At a most obvious level, making a profit represents pleasure for all of us, while suffering a loss is painful. Let's look at how our subconscious pain-avoidance and comfort-seeking tendencies cause us to drop our guard after we buy a winning stock.

Why Holding Feels Good

When we own a good stock, holding it maintains our zone of comfort. Taking action to change things—for example, selling it—makes us uneasy. Holding keeps us close to our past, to memories and feelings we cherish. Many investors hold stock in companies whose fortunes peaked years or even decades ago. They have a hard time explaining why they resist selling these stocks despite obviously dim prospects for these companies' recovery.

Some people become emotionally attached to a stock. They may love it because it's made them a lot of money, or at least a large paper profit. That's reason enough, as long as the situation doesn't change. Some people bond with a stock and are reluctant to sell it because they inherited it from a relative. Or maybe their grandfather worked for the company or the firm was the major employer in the town in which they grew up. Or they may simply have owned the stock for many years and have grown attached to it. Unfortunately, such investors often hold on to stocks such as these for sentimental reasons even though those stocks have turned into poor performers. Their nostalgic feelings about the stocks make it difficult for them to sell out their positions.

Our primary inclination is not to sever ties and terminate a comfortable relationship. Holding on to a stock represents staying in our comfort zone. Selling means deliberately walking outside that zone, which represents taking a risk. It doesn't matter that a stock may have become grossly overvalued, or may have lost its fundamental greatness, or is having trouble making its profit projections. We tend to cling to our old favorites no matter their current merit.

From the late 1980s into the early 1990s, computer stocks, such as IBM, held a mystical power over their shareowners despite the rapid sea of changes that were occurring in the computer industry. Investors held IBM as a matter of nearly religious conviction due to its past merits—even when IBM's earnings started declining in 1986. In late 1993, the stock bottomed below $40, down some 75 percent. To develop a mind-set that will enable you to sell stocks when the time is right, you must battle nostalgia and the tendency to cling to old moorings.

Why Selling Feels Uncomfortable

Selling requires a significant change in thinking. When we bought that great stock, its prospects were outstanding. It represented value and opportunity. Now, whether the stock has done well or faltered, choosing to sell means pivoting 180 degrees. Liquidating means that a position we once believed to be correct is no longer so. The company is no longer underpriced, or its prospects are not what we expected.

Maybe we've already been on the wrong side of the market for some time and are now admitting a change is warranted. Either way, selling is like saying we now believe that what we thought

---

Holding postpones coming to closure. We hold losing stocks with the hope they will rally. But we pay dearly to avoid the emotional pain of selling, as potential losses grow worse. Selling could stop the losses, but it takes courage to implement this action.

earlier was mistaken. Many of us have great difficulty admitting we were wrong. If you place a strong value on self-esteem, the reversal of position inherent in selling is likely to be an especially difficult battle zone for your ego.

We live in a time of high expectations driven in part by computers and high-speed communications. Precision is possible and increasingly expected. Time is telescoped. We've become impatient with delays. We expect perfection. At work, we function in an environment that demands zero defects and immediate paybacks. Our favorite professional sports team is labeled a failure if it doesn't take the championship two years in a row.

This perfectionism makes us recoil from the sell decision. Avoiding that choice is the least uncomfortable course of action. When we sell, we know we won't receive the top price unless we're extremely lucky. Selling puts us in yet another situation in which we can be proved less than perfect. So we avoid the idea—and hold on by default.

Surprisingly, holding makes us feel better than selling. To sell a loser is to admit our human fallibility and to wipe out any possibility of vindication. If we sell a loser, it's gone. Should the stock's price increase after we sell it, we would have compounded our error. So we preserve the hope of ultimately being a winner by holding. Even though an objective assessment of a stock's prospects may provide little optimism, we can continue to hope for a miracle as long as we hold the stock.

If there's a poor-performing stock in your portfolio that you won't sell for sentimental reasons, here are the facts of life: The stock doesn't know you own it. It doesn't care about you, and it has no emotional attachment to you. It doesn't have any opinion one way or another about whether you hold it or sell it. So if it's not performing, get a divorce. Kiss it good-bye, and put your money into a stock with more potential.

When you're thinking of selling, tear down any protective shields around your ego and accept the consequences of your decision. One of the worst aspects of losing money in the stock market is its effect on our thinking. A loss not only leaves us poorer but also makes us feel foolish, stupid, or perhaps inadequate. But postponing the pain only increases the loss—and extends the emotional effects.

Commission Phobia

Some investors balk at accepting a broker's advice to sell a stock because they suspect that advice is driven by a desire to make more commissions. This is called *commission phobia*. It's a smokescreen that is dangerous to realizing potential profits from stocks. Investors often display commission phobia when their investment has gone down or has appreciated so little that the commission will wipe out the gain. If the stock has enjoyed a substantial gain, they seldom complain about commissions.

Commissions are more visible in stocks, commodities, and options than in most other products or services because securities prices are publicly quoted in the media. Investors pay commissions to trade stocks as a way of rewarding the people who do the trading for them for their time and expertise. Commissions are built into the purchase price of other types of products. In fact, built-in commissions for goods such as cars, shoes, and washing machines are immensely higher than stock commissions.

Like taxes, commissions are neither a surprise nor a rules change in the stock market game. Having to pay a commission is not a valid reason not to sell a stock. Except in a small handful of circumstances, there is no way to sell a stock without paying a commission.

Tax Phobia

The Tax Reform Act of 1986 had at least one positive result: It removed an artificial excuse for not selling stocks. The Act legally erased the distinction between long- and short-term capital gains. Until then, many investors had used the tax incentive to hold stocks for the long term as a justification for not selling. Unless an extremely large gain was involved and the time remaining to qualify for long-term status was very short, tax reasons for not selling were considered foolhardy. But sensitivity to tax treatment was nearly a religion for many investors.

Unfortunately, the existence of federal and state taxation on securities gains remains a stumbling block for some investors despite the elimination of the distinction between long- and short-term gains. Using taxes as a reason for not selling is illogical, but tax phobia still grips many investors. No one likes to pay taxes, of course, but paying taxes on capital gains is a reality of investment life. Not wanting to pay tax on a gain is just another rationalization for not making a sale decision. Ignore taxes. Sell when the time is right. Not cashing in on a profitable stock because of an unwillingness to pay taxes is self-defeating.

THE LEAST YOU NEED TO KNOW

Successful investors recognize, understand, and avoid the conscious and subconscious psychological reasons that keep others from selling their stocks when the time is right to do so. If you recognized some aspects of your own behavior in the attitudes discussed in this chapter, you'll now be better equipped to deal with them. These negative attitudes keep you from cashing in on winners or from selling stocks that are past their prime.

For many investors, selling is a more challenging arena than buying. Keep in mind that the capital losses that result from holding too long include opportunity costs. Selling a stock that's going nowhere and replacing it with a stock that has a better chance of increasing in value is smart investing.

MISTAKE

I Do Not Need a Bear Market Survival Plan

Bears have a way of sneaking up behind you and grabbing you where you least expected it.

DANIEL BOONE

THERE'S NOTHING LIKE A LITTLE MARKET CARNAGE TO UNLEASH A FLOOD of what's called "bogus bear-market advice" stories. You know what I'm talking about. These stories begin with a recitation of some scary facts about past bear markets such as, "It took 302 months for investors to break even after the crash of 1929." But the notion that you ought to be doing something radically different after a crash has always struck me as absurd—unless you were doing something radically wrong to begin with.

Surviving in the stock market game does demand a bear market survival plan, though. If you don't have one already, it's time to develop one. The key is not to panic. With some financial housecleaning and a bit of reallocation, you'll be ready when the bull thunders back in. This chapter provides some commonsense guidelines for making it through tough times in the investment arena.

DON'T PANIC

In the midst of a market decline, tuning in to CNBC or CNN can easily give you the impression that Armageddon has arrived and it's just a matter of time before marauding bands of disgruntled investors start sacking and pillaging the stock exchanges. But bear markets, typically defined as a decline of 20 percent or more in one of the indexes (e.g., the Dow Jones Industrial Average [DJIA] or NASDAQ), are facts of investing life. The Standard & Poor's (S&P) 500 has experienced fourteen of these 20 percent-or-greater declines since 1929.

Bears can be severe. They can maul one exchange and leave the others alone. We saw this occur in 2000, when the tech-heavy NASDAQ was thrown into a bear market while the DJIA remained relatively stable.

The S&P declined 43 percent during the 1973–74 bear market and didn't recoup that loss for three years. The NASDAQ sank more than 50 percent in 2000 and hit a two-year low in 2001. But don't panic. Remember that each bear market always gives way to another bull market.

REASSESS YOUR PORTFOLIO

Over the years, you've heard all the advice about allocating your holdings among stocks and bonds. If you're like many investors, you've also ignored that advice because putting even more money into high-flying stocks such as Qualcomm and Oracle worked much better. If you've gotten a taste of what it's like to lose money in a bear market, it's a good time to rethink how to divvy up your portfolio. (Review the advice about asset allocation in Mistake #15.) If you're completely unfazed by a bear market, and can stomach even more, then go ahead and keep all your money (or what's left of it) in stocks. But if your tolerance for risk seems to have waned, you might want to consider adding some bonds to your investment mix.

As you reallocate your portfolio, don't sell your high-quality stocks that have momentarily fallen. Instead, sell off all your losers, stocks that seemed like a good buy at the time. You know, mistakes such as the initial purchase offering you bought for $200 on its first trading day that's now selling for $20. While you're at it, re-examine your sector weightings. A 60 percent tech stake seemed to have all upside and no downside in the 1990s. Now that you've seen how far and how fast tech shares can dive, scale back your tech weighting to a merely aggressive 40 percent or even a more conservative 10 to 20 percent of assets, assuming the market has not done it for you already.

KEEP ON INVESTING IN STOCKS

The hardest part of a bear market plan is to continue to follow the market. When stock prices melt, all our instincts tell us to unload the stocks we have, avoid buying new ones, and turn a deaf ear to the financial media. We're afraid stocks will go even lower. But this attitude makes little sense for long-term investors.

Researchers at T. Rowe Price recently looked at the six bear markets in the S&P 500 over the past thirty years to see how three different types of investors would have fared if each had invested $10,000 on the eve of a bear market.

The "stock investor" kept all his money in S&P 500 stocks and added an additional $100 every month. The "cash investor" bailed out once the index declined 10 percent, and put all his money and subsequent additions of $100 a month into T-bills. The "switch investor" did exactly what the cash investor did, except he put all his money plus $100 a month back into stocks once the S&P 500 regained its prebear peak.

So how did these three investors do? In the relatively brief bear markets of the 1980s and 1990s, the stock investor quickly caught up with the cash and switch investors. For example, within two years of the 1987 crash, the stock investor had the most money. In the generally longer and tougher bears of the 1960s and 1970s, it took more time for the stock investor to come out ahead, but he always did.

Of course, you could come up with thousands of different scenarios with different outcomes, depending on how much money you start with, how much you add, and what kind of stocks you buy. But the strategy of putting most of your money in stocks makes as much sense today as it ever did. Assuming that you are a long-term investor who makes rational, informed decisions and knows that volatility is a natural part of stock investing, you'll do just fine. If you're not that kind of investor, consider the market's plunge as a wake-up call to put your money into a money market account.

Tom Peters put the right spin on the word *mistake* when he said, "The essence of innovation is the pursuit of failure, one's ability to try different things and not be concerned about making mistakes, as long as you don't repeat the same mistake." All great investors share the belief that they need to experiment, innovate, and be daring in their thinking. You can't be innovative with your investments without making mistakes.

Stocks Fall Faster Than They Rise

While it's often good to buy stocks when they're down, it can be a mistake to jump on board too soon. When a stock takes a hit after a disappointing earnings report or in a downtrending bear market, bargain hunters are often quick to buy in to the stock before the market pushes the price back up. However, in most cases there is no need to hurry. Stocks tend to fall much faster than they rise. If the market has had a major correction, or a stock you follow has had a sudden free fall, be patient. Wait for the stock or the market to begin showing some upward momentum. You may not get in right at the bottom, but you can avoid buying a falling star midway through its plunge.

In 1987, when the market dropped 25 percent, it ultimately began to move back up. But it took more than a year to regain all the ground it had lost. There was plenty of time to analyze the situation, look for an upward trend, and buy in to the market while prices were still depressed.

As an investor, my biggest weakness probably has been my impulse to buy a stock shortly after a steep drop. I owned a couple hundred shares of telecom equipment maker Viasat when it was trading in the $50s. When the company issued a disappointing earnings report, its stock suddenly plunged to $15 a share. I watched it for a couple of days, saw that it was hovering around $25, and decided to double up my holdings before it moved back up. It never did. At last check, the stock had dropped 40 percent to about $15 a share. Figure 20.1 graphically displays the wild ride I was on over a twelve-month period of time with Viasat.

PROTECTIVE STRATEGIES FOR BUYING THE BEAR

Certainly, there are times when a fallen stock can rebound quickly. But just in case things go the other way, there's one precaution you can take to ensure that you won't get mauled too badly by the bear. Put in a stop-loss order to sell the stock at a specified price if it keeps dropping. Stop-loss orders are explained fully in the glossary.

Figure 20.1 Viasat Graph

For instance, let's say you buy XYZ Inc. at $15 a share after a steep drop. You could put in a stop-loss order at $13.50 so that if it drops another $1.50, or 10 percent, you automatically sell out at a small loss rather than ride it down 50 or 60 percent like I did with Viasat. If the company turns around, you can always buy back in to the stock later. Just don't rush it. Remember, stocks fall faster than they rise.

Watch Out for Sucker Rallies

The way everybody hopes for capitulation in a bear market, you'd think it was something really delicious. Far from it. To market experts, capitulation refers to the explosive selling climax that comes when investors, battered by losses, finally give up and rush for the exits. So why do people hope for such a rout? In a bear market, a capitulation signifies that the market has finally hit bottom, meaning stocks are ready to go back up.

Technical analysts have a precise definition of capitulation, based on the appearance of several market indicators. One sign analysts point to is heavy downside volume, when the overwhelming majority of trading comes on downticks in stock prices. That's a signal that most investors are ready to bail once prices reach certain low levels. On the Monday before Thanksgiving 1998, the NASDAQ plunged 5 percent and downside volume exceeded upside volume by a ratio of 8 to 1. That's nothing compared with the 25 to 1 ratio that many technical analysts consider the telltale sign of a true bottom.

Another technical indicator of capitulation is the number of new fifty-two-week lows set in a single day. When the NASDAQ hit a new low of 737 and the Big Board dropped 231 points in 1998, many analysts were saying, "That's not good or bad enough." They were right. On October 8, 1998, the market bottomed out as a result of the financial crisis in Asia. The NASDAQ posted 1,639 new lows, marking the beginning of a significant rally out of bear territory.

Michael Burke, editor of the *Investors' Intelligence* newsletter, looks beyond the number of fifty-two-week lows. He checks to see whether new-low stocks end the week with a gain. When everyone has thrown in the towel and then a lot of stocks bounce back by the end of the week, he figures an inflection point may have been reached. If the gains don't appear by Friday, however, "there's not enough capitulation," he says.

Burke's much-looked-for indicator didn't arrive on Friday, October 28, 1988, as the huge rally, rebounding from Thursday's plunge, fizzled out in the last two hours of trading. The NASDAQ Composite Index, which had surged 152 points early in the day, ended up just gaining 47 points, to 2,645. The Dow Jones Industrial Average also gave up a triple-digit gain, to post a 41-point loss to 10,373.

When Negative Sentiment Is Positive

Many analysts also look at certain "sentiment" indicators, such as the *Investors' Intelligence* Sentiment Index and *Market Vane's* survey in its *Bullish Consensus* newsletter. The *Investors' Intelligence* Sentiment Index is a weekly survey of 130 investment newsletter writers that ascertains whether they're bullish, bearish, or looking for a correction. If they're more optimistic than we would expect them to be, that is a good sign. If the results reveal that 55 percent of newsletters were bullish, much more than might be expected with what's going on politically in the country today, then that is a strong indication that we are about to enter a bull market.

THE LEAST YOU NEED TO KNOW

Make sure you know what constitutes a bear market and how to recognize the beginning symptoms before the bear takes over. That will give you a chance to get out of the market before it turns really ugly. As a general rule, even if you are invested in great stocks, the bear will drag them down. Your best move is to get out of the market and sit on the sidelines and wait until the market bottoms out. Then, be patient when you buy back in to the market as it begins to move up into bull market territory. You'll find plenty of bargains along the way.

MISTAKE 21

I Never Learn from My Mistakes

If I had to live my life again, I would make the same mistakes, only sooner.

TALLULAH BANKHEAD

*I*F YOU DON'T PAY ATTENTION TO WHERE YOU'VE BEEN WHEN YOU INVEST in stocks, you'll make countless errors in judgment and timing that will cost you thousands of dollars. You'll buy stocks that suddenly go down and continue to drop after you buy them. You'll sell stocks that suddenly go up after you sell them—and that drop back down again if you buy them back.

The sooner you start learning from your mistakes and relying on some tried-and-true investment strategies, the sooner you'll start making money. To get where you're going with the least amount of pain, you need to know where you've been—and to learn from the mistakes you made there.

In this chapter you'll look at some ways to avoid stock market investment pitfalls. You'll see that mistakes aren't the end of the road, as long as you don't repeat the same ones over and over again. If you learn from your mistakes, the law of averages will bail you out. Persistence, coupled with the market's rocky but inevitable ascent, should ultimately increase your portfolio.

GET YOUR FEET WET

It's not just the money that keeps some people out of the stock market. It's the emotions, the fear of the unknown, and apprehension over the drudgery of dealing with stock tables, earnings reports, account statements, and all the other aspects of financial responsibility in general. Instead of viewing investing as drudgery, approach it as a hobby or a game, like Monopoly with real money. As your portfolio grows, so will your interest in the game. Soon you'll find yourself trading stocks, hunting for bargains, scouting for hot tips, joining investment clubs, comparing your performance with those of your friends, and crafting your own strategies to land that next big winner.

Don't worry about your inexperience. Even America's most successful investment managers were inexperienced novices at one point in their lives. But they took the first step, bought their first stock, and began to learn how the game was played. Investing is no different than any other pursuit. You can follow a sport for years, watch it on TV, and read about it in the newspaper, but until you lace up the Nikes and get in the game, you can't really understand how it's played. Similarly, you can follow investing from the sidelines, read some books, attend some seminars, and watch the financial news, but the only way to learn the real lessons of the market—the emotions, the discipline, the execution—is by putting your own money on the line. As the adage has it, you can't win at gambling with your hands in your pockets.

Don't fear mistakes. Every successful investor has made them—and continues to do so. The only certainty about the stock market is that there is none. If you have enough time, the stocks of most companies that remain in business will go up. Remember, Babe Ruth had 714 homers, but he also had 1,330 strikeouts that no one ever talks about.

FORGET THE EXCUSES—
GET IN THE GAME

The worst excuse for refusing to invest in stocks is the attitude, "Well, the market's kind of down right now. I'd rather wait until things turn around." That's like saying, "I'd really like to buy a new suit, but Macy's has that ridiculous 30-percent-off sale going on right now, so I think I'll wait. When prices get back to normal, then I'll buy the suit." The stock market is one of the only venues of commerce in which consumers shrink from bargains. When stocks are on sale, that's the time to buy.

There is always uncertainty in the market, with every stock and every sector. I was asked on a talk show about one of my top stock picks. It was a bank stock that had done very well over the past ten years. But the interviewer questioned the timeliness of the pick, suggesting that if interest rates should take a sudden upward turn, that could hurt the prospects for the company.

I answered, "Yes, that could happen. The wolf is always at the door. Every day, every week, every month, every year, interest rates could go up and bank stocks could go down. And with every stock and every sector, you could find a similar wolf at the door ready to spoil a stock's peaceful ascent."

But if you worry about every possible negative element that could affect a stock, you will never invest in stocks. At some point, if you're going to make it in the stock market, you have to get over your fears and put your money on the table. You wouldn't get very far in poker if you assumed on every hand that one of your opponents might be holding four aces. You'd never bet, no matter how strong a hand you held.

Professional gamblers know how to play the averages, and so should you. They know they will lose some hands, just as you need to assume some stocks will drop from time to time. But most of the time, the quality stocks in your portfolio will provide solid returns. The greater evil is to let your fears keep you out of the market. To make money in the market, you've got to ante up and play the game. Over time, you should come out a winner.

THE EXPERTS MAY KNOW
LESS THAN YOU

In his investment classic, *A Random Walk Down Wall Street,* Burton Malkiel debunks virtually every popular theory of stock selection employed by the gurus of Wall Street. Malkiel, a Princeton professor, first published *Random Walk* and his dart-throwing chimp theory in 1973 amid much controversy. He contends that a blindfolded chimpanzee throwing darts at the *Wall Street Journal* can select a portfolio that will do as well as one carefully selected by the experts. Malkiel's book has survived to its sixth edition, and he has stuck to his premise, insisting that time has proven him right.

I don't recommend selecting stocks by throwing darts at the *Wall Street Journal,* but a passive investing approach has, over time, outperformed 60 percent of actively managed portfolios. Some investors may read a sense of hopelessness into Malkiel's message, but he's actually bullish on the stock market itself. He just believes that investors could find a better use for their time than poring over annual reports, balance sheets, and other research materials to get an edge on the market.

Stocks are almost always priced fairly relative to the information currently available on those stocks. That's what is known as the "efficient market theory," and it evens the playing field for all investors. The theory posits that stock prices fully reflect all known information. Uninformed investors buying a diversified portfolio at the tableau of prices set by the market will obtain a rate of return as good as those achieved by the experts.

HIGH VOLATILITY
DOESN'T MEAN HIGH RETURNS

Another theory that Malkiel shoots down is the perception that riskier stocks bring higher returns. Malkiel defines risky stocks as those with high volatility. There is a measure of volatility in the stock market known as "beta." The higher a stock's beta, the more volatile the stock. Some investors have assumed that stocks with higher betas, while more volatile in the short term, offer better average long-term returns. However, a 1992 study by Eugene Farna and Kenneth French showed absolutely no correlation between beta and performance. Malkiel also conducted his own study of high-beta stocks, and found that the highest beta portfolios had the lowest returns. What's clear is that if you think you can get a dependably higher rate of return by buying a high-beta portfolio, you will likely be badly disappointed.

Malkiel shoots down several other timeworn theories as well. He admits that there may be some seasonal patterns in the stock market, that stocks with low price–earnings (PE) ratios can sometimes outperform the market, and that there may be some evidence of short-run momentum in the market. But he contends that closer analysis reveals that none of these theories is consistently reliable. He also challenges the theory that you can earn a higher rate of return by buying stocks with relatively high dividend yields. According to

Malkiel: "This phenomenon does not work with individual stocks. We tried simulating strategies. If you simply purchase a portfolio of individual stocks with the highest dividend yields in the market, you will not earn a particularly high rate of return."

What is clear is that no single investment strategy will bring you above-average returns every single year. To play the market successfully, you need a combination of investment strategies, patience, and conviction to see you through the down times. You must also have the courage to buy when stocks are down and everyone else is selling as they flee to the sidelines.

CULTIVATE PATIENCE

If you've followed a stock closely, you have a good idea of its trading range and a lowball price you'd like to pay for it. But stocks don't always cooperate. Sometimes they unexpectedly move up a few dollars before you have a chance to buy in at the price you want. If the price continues to climb, you might be better served forgetting that stock and moving on to another stock. There's a good chance that if you wait, your patience will be rewarded. Nothing goes straight up. All stocks go through periodic lulls. Wait for the stock you want to drop back into your target price range.

All great companies with outstanding long-term financial track records hit an occasional lull due to cyclical Wall Street trends. A study by *Investor's Business Daily* found that ninety of the best one hundred stocks had periods over the past decade when they traded below their two-year low price. When stocks are down simply because their industry sector is out of favor on Wall Street, there are great bargains to be had on great stocks.

SELL THE PAST AND MOVE ON

As I've said before, weed out your losers as quickly as possible. If your earlier judgment turns out to have been incorrect and a company you liked comes out with an unexpectedly low earnings report, get out of the stock. Also, sell a portion of your holdings in a stock if its PE ratio gets too high or if the stock grows so quickly that it accounts for more than 20 percent of your portfolio.

Watch your stocks closely to make sure they stay on track. If there is some fundamental change in the business or the dynamics of an industry, or if a stock can't meet its earning projections, sell it. Quickly unload stocks that don't meet your expectations and move on. Be willing to take lots of little losses, but never ride a stock down for a big loss. Sell signs include changes in management strategy and failure to execute. For example, if profit margins are down, key personnel are leaving, products are coming out late, costs are out of control, and earnings are lower than projected, you have all the signs that management is not executing a viable plan. Your goal should be to accumulate a portfolio of winners. If you mistakenly add a loser to your account, dump it and move on to something more promising.

KEEP YOUR HEAD ON STRAIGHT

It's often been said that if you can keep your head on straight when all others are losing theirs, you'll win every time. Success in the stock market requires a combination of many traits, including intelligence, patience, persistence, and luck. But nothing is more important to successful investing than the ability to maintain your emotions through good and bad times. Buy when stocks are down and investors are fleeing the market. Sell when market euphoria has pushed prices up beyond reason. If you sell your losers and keep your winners, you will enjoy tremendous, sustained success in the market.

Fear, greed, and the other extremes of emotion only get in your way. If you can keep your cool and make your investment decisions based on solid research and long-term market trends rather than on emotion, you'll be way ahead of the game.

You may not be able to put as much time and effort into your portfolio as mutual fund managers put into theirs, but you don't need to maintain a portfolio of one hundred to two hundred stocks, as they do. Before you buy any stock, learn as much as possible about the company to determine if it's likely to perform well over the long term. Take advantage of volatility and build a position in the stock when it's down.

A FOOLPROOF WAY
TO MATCH THE MARKET

Despite devoting long hours every day to researching companies and tracking the ups and downs of the Dow before they buy or sell, most Wall Street investment managers trail the overall market average over the long term. How can the small investor outperform most of these gurus? By using dollar-cost averaging to invest in index funds. (For a review of the dollar-cost averaging strategy, see Mistake #5.)

One of the easiest ways to play the market is to buy a broad cross section of index funds that mirror the overall market. Indexing allows investors to buy securities of all types with no effort. It can also be a good approach for investors who fear making mistakes picking individual stocks or who have trouble learning from the mistakes they have made in the past.

Index funds typically outperform the majority of actively managed mutual funds. While I grant there are active portfolios that outperform index funds, they are not the same from year to year. There's no way you can know for certain how an actively managed fund will perform.

Indexing Versus Hands-On Stock Picking

Here's a challenge to those of you who enjoy playing the market: Set up two portfolios—a passive portfolio using index-fund dollar-cost averaging and an active portfolio using your own buying and selling strategies. Compare the results periodically to see which portfolio does the best. Unless you beat the odds, your passive, worry-free portfolio will earn more than your actively managed portfolio.

THE LEAST YOU NEED TO KNOW

Even the greatest of all stock market investors make mistakes. But these investors know where they have been, and use what they

---

Index funds make it easy to set up a passive portfolio. To ensure greater diversification, invest in two or three different index funds. Many index funds offer automatic investment plans in which a set amount is deducted from your checking account regularly. Here are two funds to consider. Both mirror the S&P 500 index:

- Fidelity Spartan Market Index Fund: 800-544-8888
- T. Rowe Price Equity Index Fund: 800-638-5660

learned to their advantage. Peter Lynch once said, "I never make the same mistake twice."

You *will* make mistakes if you invest in the stock market. The important thing is to take them in stride and move forward. Make prudent decisions and don't let your emotions override your better judgment. Quickly dumping your losers and replacing them with winning stocks will keep losses in check. Index fund investing is another approach. This low-effort strategy can reduce anxiety about making mistakes while producing better returns than those of many professional managers.

MISTAKE 22

Who Cares What the Institutional Investors Are Doing?

Always remember that you are only a small frog in a very big pond when investing in the stock market.

JUDY CRAWFORD

A NY PARTY IS LIKELY TO BE SHORT-LIVED IF ONLY A HANDFUL OF FRIENDS show up. A stock that's trying to break out of a base and move up the price ladder needs some big sponsors to keep the festivities going. Without heavy trading volume to fuel its climb, any high-flying stock will likely stall. Large institutional investors—the mutual funds, insurance companies, and banks—need to be on board. They have the buying power to move stock and market prices.

Keeping an eye on your stock's daily trading volume is just as important as watching its price. Although price movements ultimately determine your profits when you sell, trading volume offers clues about where the price is headed. Volume shows what the big institutional investors are doing. Their participation is essential if a stock is to make any kind of upward move.

A spike in the price of a stock is usually an indication that some of the big players have suddenly taken an interest in the stock and are buying it. Conversely, a significant drop in its price is an indication that it has either fallen out of favor with institutions or that they're taking profits by selling shares.

WHY SPONSORSHIP IS CRITICAL

Institutions such as mutual funds pack a lot of buying power. But it's not just their girth that individual investors can take advantage of. Top-notch mutual funds are filled with Wall Street's best and brightest portfolio managers, who depend on quality research to select winning stocks and build track records for themselves. Large institutional holdings are a positive factor you should consider when evaluating a stock. If the big players like a stock, its fundamentals must have longer-term merit. When you see high-quality funds buying into a stock, it's a strong endorsement that the company's fundamentals and business operations are in order.

IT'S A JUNGLE OUT THERE!

The worth of stocks has grown almost thirty-five-fold, from $200 billion in December 1980 to $1.95 trillion at the start of the new millennium. In that same twenty-year span, the value of the stocks listed on the New York Stock Exchange grew sevenfold. With more baby boomers coming into their primary asset-accumulation years and realizing that they must invest for retirement, market participation has risen significantly.

The New York Stock Exchange estimates that institutional activity accounts for about 70 percent of all daily trades. Such dominance on the trading floor presents both a problem and an

You want to own stocks that are owned by the institutions that hire successful money managers with the skills for picking winning stocks. A stock that is
enjoying strong buying by top-performing institutions has a greater probability of making you money. However, don't pick a stock on volume, accumulation, or sponsorship numbers alone. Make sure the company's earnings,
sales, and other fundamentals are strong.

opportunity for individual investors. In a nutshell, the problem is
that institutional buying and selling destabilizes the market, especially since many large investors are increasingly short term in
how long they hold a stock. They chase price or earnings momentum rather than focus on long-term value. The slightest deviation
from analysts' consensus estimates triggers major and rapid institutional activity: buying and selling that can dramatically affect
the price of a stock overnight. Usually such price adjustments are
more extreme on the downside than on the upside because institutions are averse to losing money. For example, institutional sell-
offs were the alleged cause of the sudden one-day stock market
meltdown that occurred in October 1987.

AVOIDING THE INSTITUTIONAL STAMPEDE

Some investors have decided that the best way to beat the institutions is to join them: to invest in stocks only through mutual
funds. Unfortunately, that choice simply increases the institutional dominance of the market. If you want to do your own stock
picking, how can you keep track of what the institutions are doing
so you won't get trampled? Watch the average trading volume in
the mutual fund tables published daily by the *Wall Street Journal*
and *Investor's Business Daily*.

To understand how institutional investors can affect the price of a stock you own, let's look at an example. Suppose a company in which you own stock misses its earnings estimate. Suppose that in response to that bad news, one of the institutions that also owns stock in the company takes evasive action, dumping its shares. Say the company in question is small, with just a million shares of stock outstanding. If the institution owns 5 percent of the company's shares, that means there are 50,000 shares of the stock up for sale, a number that will certainly drive the price of the stock down. The higher the number of shares, the more severe will be the tornado. The institutional investor will have the bad news well before you and will execute a sell order before you even know what's going on. If you're in the path, you'll get trampled.

Any investment consultant will tell you that all investment information is worthless unless you're willing to analyze it and act upon your convictions. Knowing how heavily exposed a stock is to the possible ravages of institutional herd selling will generate only bad headaches unless you take remedial action. The worst action to take when an earnings disappointment makes the big players run for cover is to not join them. Their selling creates maximum downward pressure on the price and peak emotional strain on other holders. If you don't constantly monitor your stocks, you will be late seeing the bad news. Never buy after bad news, no matter how much of a bargain the stock seems to be, or you'll get clobbered again. Get out of the stock as quickly as you can and wait for the institutions to start buying again before you jump in.

Profiting from the Stampede

In a bull market, where earnings expectations are high, stocks with high institutional holdings tend to generate upside price action because everyone is eager to buy. The most prudent course is to sell at market on any rally shortly before the stock's quarterly earnings due dates and step aside to see what happens. Clear out of the jungle before the selling stampede season starts. You can always buy back in when things settle down.

An alternate course of action is to place a stop-loss order fairly close to the current price a week before a company is scheduled to report earnings. The stop-loss order will guard against any potential damage to your portfolio in case a company misses its projections. You should be less concerned about staying in a good long-term position than about preventing a loss.

LEADING STOCKS HAVE SUPPORT

Many market analysts consider large holdings by institutional investors as a positive factor when evaluating a stock. Their logic says that if the big players like a stock, it must be good, which is positive in terms of longer-term fundamental merit. Even a superior stock will fall on occasion, though. When that happens, institutional investors who are heavily invested in it will take steps to make sure the stock's decline from its peak doesn't snowball into a severe drop. They'll step in and buy on days when the stock spikes down.

Their support reveals itself vividly in a stock's daily and weekly price and volume charts. As a stock sells off, shaking out "weak" holders, a long vertical line stretching from the session high to the low appears on the stock's daily chart. This new line will be longer than comparable lines in previous trading days.

Later in the session, large investors buy the stock, while trading volume stays heavy. At the end of the trading session, the hash mark, which shows the stock's closing value, often appears in the upper half of the line on the stock's chart.

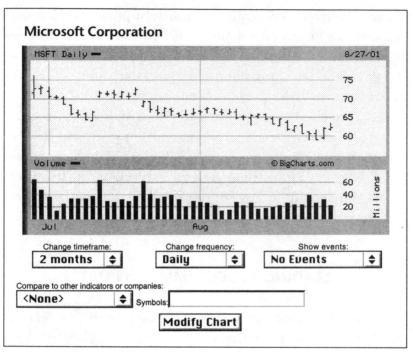

FIGURE 22.1 Microsoft Corporation

Figure 22.1 illustrates what the hash marks looked like on Microsoft's chart in early 2001. For example, look at the hash marks for the last two trading sessions in February. The vertical lines represent the high and low trading prices for Microsoft's stock during each of the two days. The horizontal line to the right of each vertical trading line represents the closing price of the stock. The higher the horizontal line, the closer Microsoft closed to its daily high, which is an indication of strong buying activity. If it goes the other way, it is an indication of strong selling activity.

These reversals show up on weekly charts as well. In either case, they can mark the end of a stock's slide, which generally should not exceed 40 percent from its prior peak. They're telltale signs of institutional support, a key ingredient of a winning stock. Such stocks stand a better chance of forming bullish patterns that break out of an extended advance.

THE POWER OF BIGNESS

All investors wish they could be the very first buyers of the next Microsoft, Wal-Mart, or Cisco. But savvy investors don't go out on a limb alone. Buying the shares of a fast-growing company early and holding on is the path to truly outstanding gains. But it also pays to wait until institutional investors start shoveling money into the stock. Their sponsorship provides constant buying support over the long run as winning stocks rise to new highs, backtrack a bit, and break out yet again to new highs.

Of the ninety-five top-performing small and mid-cap stocks in the late 1990s, all but nine were held by at least one major mutual fund prior to their blastoff to new highs. On average, each stock was owned by twenty-five different funds, according to *Mutual Fund* magazine. After taking an initial position in a stock, a fund manager usually builds on it.

Let's say a $1 billion fund decides to put 1 percent of its assets in a stock trading at $40. It will have to buy 250,000 shares of that stock, usually over a period of days, weeks, or even months. Snapping up too many shares too fast could overheat the stock and leave it vulnerable to steep pullbacks if other shareholders decide to sell their shares and take a profit. Where one top fund treads, others soon follow. The sustained buying power of these institutional investors drives the stock price ever higher. Funds often step in and buy more shares when a stock, after having risen in price, starts to wane. A true winner will periodically fall to its fifty-day moving average price and then bounce off it as institutions increase their positions. A stock trading at its fifty-day moving average is attractive to fund managers when the moving average is on the upswing. This method helps keep the fund's overall cost per share low.

THE LEAST YOU NEED KNOW

Institutional investors represent the bulk of trading activity in the market. As such, their buying and selling power can move a stock's price up or down dramatically. Learn to spot which stocks institutions are buying and selling by watching for a surge in trading volumes—and don't fight the tides. You may have found an outstanding company that meets all of your strict technical and fundamental analysis criteria. But if the institutions aren't buying that stock, it probably isn't going anywhere. Be patient. Wait for the big guys to buy in.

MISTAKE

Bonds Just Don't Interest Me

*I've been poor and I've been rich and have
decided that rich is better.*

SOPHIE TUCKER

HAVE YOU EVER NOTICED HOW PEOPLE'S EYES GLAZE OVER WHEN YOU mention the word *bonds*? These shortsighted individuals are among the legions of the uninformed riding the boat of missed opportunity. The fact that you're reading this indicates you're savvier than the average investor. So, welcome to the world of bond investing.

You can decrease your aggregate investment risk by putting some of your money into bonds of various types. By allocating a specific slice of your investment pie to corporate bonds, which are substantially different from stocks and react to different stimuli, you help guard against your whole portfolio getting hit hard all at once.

Bonds are a stimulating and dynamic investment vehicle with almost limitless possibilities. There are different ways to diversify your bond investments. You can invest in maturities that fall along different places on the yield curve. You can buy bonds with substantially different coupons, or yields. If you are not averse to risk, you can invest in bonds with lower ratings, but higher yields. You can also diversify among different types of issuers.

Bonds may be intimidating, but they can have sex appeal. From the tried-and-true Treasuries to municipal, zero-coupon, and corporate issues, there is a bond type for every investment temperament. And you can diversify among types or within them. If you're heavily invested in tax-exempt bonds of issuers in your state, for example, you can diversify by buying out-of-state municipals that present good value.

Don't be discouraged if you don't know much about bonds to start. Many folks in the finance industry don't understand them either. After you've done some research into these vehicles, you may hear yourself commenting at your next get-together: "Aren't you totally jazzed the Fed lowered rates? I just extended out the curve and went long on a bunch of zero coupons."

One of the reasons bonds have remained shrouded in confusion is the jargon used to talk about them. This chapter focuses on corporate bonds. You'll need to employ the same research diligence you use for stock selection to assess the health of corporate bond issuers.

UNDERSTANDING CORPORATE BONDS

Corporations issue bonds. It therefore follows that much of the research you do when investing in corporate bonds is similar to what you would do for stocks. You evaluate a company's financial strength, its products, management, competitive pressures, and so on. In fact, the value of a corporate bond often tracks the health of the company that issued it even more than it is affected by movements in interest rates.

If the issuing company is financially strong and enjoys an excellent credit rating, corporate bond prices go down less than other types of bonds issued by less-stable companies. Investors often look for lower-rated bonds they feel are on the path to future upgrades. They'll choose a company's bonds instead of its stock because they're paid a substantial yield while they are waiting for the company to perform. In the finance industry this is called "being paid to wait."

Sectors

There are different corporate bond market sectors.

Industrials Manufacturing, energy, mining, retail, and service industries are affected by consumer demand and economic cycles. These industries are also referred to as *cyclical*.

Airlines/transportation Airlines, trucking, and railroads are affected by oil prices, economic conditions, and safety records.

Public utilities Telecommunication, water, electric, and gas pipeline systems are affected by weather conditions, consumer demand, changes in government regulations, and technology.

Banking/finance Banks, savings and loans, brokerages, insurance, mortgage, and finance companies are affected by interest rate changes and economic conditions.

Maturities

Corporate bond maturities fall into three categories:

- *Short term*—up to four years
- *Intermediate term*—five to twelve years
- *Long term*—thirteen to forty years

Creditworthiness

There are two broad credit classifications for corporate bonds: investment-grade and high-yield (also referred to as junk) bonds. *Investment-grade bonds* are those ranked in the top four ratings categories (AAA through BBB) by national credit-rating services like Standard & Poor's (S&P) and Moody's. At one time, banks were allowed to invest only in bonds in the top four ratings categories, which is why such securities acquired the moniker investment-grade bonds.

High-yield bonds were made famous in the 1980s by the marketing prowess of the infamous Michael Milken. Although illegal trading practices landed Milken in jail and left his firm, the now-defunct Drexel Burnham Lambert, insolvent, Milken's efforts created alternative avenues for young companies to raise much-needed cash when more traditional methods of borrowing were closed to them. This sector of the fixed-income market offers investors the greatest opportunity for growth if the start-up takes off. It also offers the best chance for a big loss if the start-up fails.

You will find corporate bonds listed on the New York Stock Exchange (NYSE). However, the vast majority of corporate bonds aren't traded on the floor but are traded between dealers over-the-counter (OTC).

Some traders make the distinction between top-tier high-yield and low-grade high-yield bonds. In the heyday of high-yields, folks in the business joked that top-tier bonds were junk spelled "junque."

When a company gets into serious financial trouble and stops paying interest on its bonds, the bonds are said to be trading without interest—and they trade at a fraction of their face value. The hope is that they will begin to pay interest again and will be able to repay the principle at maturity. If they restore their interest payments, their value will move higher again.

Indenture Information

Corporate bonds are assumed to have a $1,000 face value unless otherwise stipulated. A 9 percent bond with a $1,000 face value would pay interest of $90 a year. The bond's indenture specifies the all-important facets of the bond issue, including coupon, maturity date, and seniority, meaning where this debt (bond) ranks in the debt hierarchy on the company's balance sheet. Seniority is important: You want to know where you stand if the company goes bankrupt. Senior debtholders are second in line, with all banks standing in front of them in the creditor queue. Subordinated debtholders are further back in the line. If a bond is subordinated, it will say so in the bond's description.

WHAT ABOUT RISK?

Lower ratings, lower coupons, and longer maturities increase bonds' risk. You also assume additional risk when you invest in nondollar-denominated bonds. If you are risk-averse, limit your exposure in these categories and focus on bonds with higher ratings, larger coupons, and shorter maturities. These tend to be less risky.

Don't let the possible risks of bond ownership paralyze you. Identify the degree of risk you are comfortable with, assess the risks different bond alternatives offer, use common sense, and then diversify your portfolio by adding some bonds.

HOW ARE BONDS BACKED?

A bond's indenture tells you what, if anything, is backing the bond. Bonds that are not backed by any collateral, that rely solely on the issuer's name or goodwill to attract investors, are called *debenture bonds*. These bonds are unsecured and rely on the issuer's ability to make money to pay investors. If the issuer fails to pay its bond investors, there is nothing to secure the bonds.

Many companies cannot issue debenture bonds due to their poor credit histories, so they have to post collateral to attract investors. *Equipment trust bonds* are secured by equipment. For example, a construction company may need to borrow money to buy a huge crane. If the company were to go bankrupt, the crane would be sold and the proceeds would be distributed to the equipment trust bondholders. Equipment trust bonds are often serial bonds, where the issuer's debt burden declines as the equipment is depreciated over time. As the value of the equipment depreciates, the company owes less money because it has fewer bonds outstanding (for example, older bonds mature) and so owes less interest than it originally did.

If a company has no hard assets to put up as collateral and the institution that issues the bonds demands that the bonds be secured, stocks, notes, and other paper assets can be used to back the issue. These bonds are known as *collateral trust bonds*. A company

> The market is incredibly efficient. If a bond's yield is too low, demand for the bond will dry up until the price falls far enough that the yield rises to a more tempting level. If the yield becomes too high, investors will swoop down, gobbling up the issue until demand forces the price higher and the yield falls to a point that makes sense in light of what other bonds are yielding.

can also put aside money on a regular basis in an escrow account that is earmarked to retire portions of the bonds on specific dates. These are *sinking junk bonds.*

HOW ARE BONDS PRICED?

How does the market assign value to fixed-income securities and determine what their yield should be? Market participants look at the bond's fixed characteristics: coupon and maturity. They then evaluate how these characteristics could be affected by the market's outlook for interest rates, as well as the issuer's financial prospects. All of these factors work together to determine a bond's relative value.

If you want to know a stock's price, you get a quote. However, with bonds you don't ask for a quote. Instead, you ask for the bond's bid/ask spread, which is displayed like this: 101/102. The bid (101) is on the left and the ask (102) is on the right of the slash. The bid is the highest price that someone is willing to pay for that bond. The ask is the lowest price that any current bondholder is willing to sell that bond for. The bid is always lower than the ask.

The bid/ask spread can be as wide as three points or more (i.e., 100/103). A wide spread indicates the bond is illiquid and is inactively traded. Conversely, highly liquid bonds, such as U.S. Treasuries (bonds backed by the full faith and credit of the U.S. government), can have small spreads of just a few pennies. When you buy a bond, you can either pay the ask or you can put in a bid at the price you would like to pay. Conversely, if you're going to sell your bond, you can either sell at the bid or you can submit an asking price. Don't waste people's time by putting in a ludicrous bid or ask price. Your bid or ask should be somewhere near the market price.

Here's an example of how this works: The bond you are interested in is 101/103. You are willing to pay 102, so you put in a bid at that price. The spread is now 101/102. Your bid is now the current offer.

If the bond is listed on an exchange, then all entered bids and asks are kept there. If the bond is traded over-the-counter, traders keep their own bid/ask ledger. When you are given a bid/ask spread, the prices are for normal-sized trades, meaning trades of $20,000 face values or more. If you are interested in prices for smaller lots, you'll find they're different than the bid/ask spread. You'll have to pay a higher price than shown in the bid/ask spread and you'll receive a lower price when you sell. If there's a chance that you might have to sell your bonds before they mature, avoid buying lots because they tend to be illiquid. Investment firms do not want to get stuck with little pieces, and since they don't want to own them, traders offer them for lower prices. However, if an investment firm ends up with a *bond-o-let*, as these are referred to in the industry, you can often get a good deal on it.

FINDING GOOD BOND BUYS

Sometimes investment firms will have bond positions in their inventory they want to unload. It could be they've owned the bonds for a long time or that they own too much of that type of bond.

Perhaps they need to move the bonds to make room for something else: A dealer's inventory is like a self-storage unit. There's a limited amount of space, and it's costly to keep stuff there.

Whatever the reason, traders who are highly motivated to sell their position may let it go cheap. Just make sure the reason that the bonds are cheap isn't because the issuer is in financial trouble. Do your research before you buy. Bond specials sell quickly, giving you limited time for research. That's why if you're interested in investing in bonds, it's good to stay up on what's going on in the economy and the bond market so that you can quickly use your common sense and experience to make a judgment call. Even when you rely on an investment adviser for guidance, it's important to understand the investment so you know what questions to ask to make sure it's right for you. It also makes your adviser's job easier and will give you added peace of mind.

When you've agreed on a price, don't whip out your pen and start writing a check just yet. First, the accrued interest needs to be calculated. This is the interest the former owner earned but hasn't yet been paid. Since you, the new owner, will receive this interest in your next semiannual interest payment, you pay the bond's seller the interest accrued to the point at which the bond traded hands. The investment firm will do this calculation for you and will include the accrued interest in the bond's purchase price on your confirmation statement.

Your confirmation statement will arrive sometime between the trade date and the settlement date. Unlike stocks, when you trade bonds you don't pay a commission. Instead, in the bond market, the purchase price is marked up and the selling price is marked down. This markup or markdown is how brokers are paid. This payment is transparent to investors because it's included in the price.

WHEN CAN YOU BUY BONDS?

Unlike stocks, bonds aren't always available when you want them. With listed stocks, there are always shares available to buy. With bonds, the best approach is to look for a certain type of bond at an acceptable yield. If you're looking for a specific bond and won't accept an alternative, you may be disappointed. There are three places investment firms can look for bonds to fulfill your request: their own inventory, other firms' inventories, and their client accounts. Much of an issue's securities are squirreled away in broker accounts, and there's no way to find out where they are without asking your broker. So, if you're set on a particular bond issue that you may have read about, there may not be any available at any price.

An investment firm may present an interesting bond to you, and you will probably find it difficult to locate the same bond at other firms to compare prices. What you can do is ask the firm that has the offering if it has bonds with similar ratings and maturities and what their yield-to-maturity is.

HOW DO YOU SELL BONDS?

Bonds are generally sold through brokers. If you want to sell a bond, ask your broker to get bids. You can get very different bids from different dealers. The reason is that one dealer may already own a lot of bonds like yours and may not want any more unless the price is right (that is, low). Another dealer may really want your bond and be willing to pay a reasonable price for it.

There have been a number of articles written about how difficult it is to price bonds since there is no exchange where they trade. You can call a number of investment firms or look in the newspaper at benchmark Treasuries. A few bonds are listed in the *Wall Street Journal*. Discover Brokerage Direct, a division of Morgan Stanley Dean Witter and Company, presents the bid/ask spread so that you can see both sides of the market.

SHOULD YOU PAY PREMIUM OR DISCOUNT PRICES?

Many investors refuse to pay premium prices for bonds. A premium price is an ask price that is higher than the bond's issue price. They feel paying a premium means they are paying too much for the bond. Yet all a premium price tells you is that interest rates have fallen since that bond was issued, justifying the premium.

Some investors allow their ignorance to keep them from premium bonds, which often have higher yields than similar bonds. Keep your eyes peeled, and you may find a good deal. If a bond's yield seems unusually high, double-check the financial health of the issuer to make sure that shaky credit is not the reason for the additional yield. If it's not, and the only reason the yield is higher appears to be investor reluctance to pay the premium, then snap up the bond. Premium bonds are like older folks. They react slowly and a bit more wisely to events. Premium bonds offer investors another benefit: Their higher coupons can help protect their price from falling as much as those of other bonds when interest rates rise. Bonds with large premiums are known as *cushion bonds* because the extra coupon size buffers the price.

Should you buy discount bonds? The answer is yes. Discount bonds offer you a nice way to buy a larger face value for the amount of money you are investing. For example, you might be able to buy a $20,000 face value for $8,000. Remember, buying at a discount doesn't in itself mean you're getting a great deal. You have to look at the yield, not the price, to determine that. But, it does mean that you can buy a significant face value even if you don't have piles of cash lying around. Discount bonds enable you to get into the game with a smaller investment.

Deep-discount bonds are also more price-sensitive to interest rate moves. This is a desirable trait when interest rates are headed lower. Discount bonds will appreciate more in value as rates drop. Of course, these bonds lose value when rates are going up, so avoid deep-discount bonds in rising-interest-rate environments. Remember that although discount bonds look attractive and have a lot of appeal, they're a lot like kids. They have plenty of energy, but they tend to jump around and overreact to much of what the economy throws at them.

THE LEAST YOU NEED TO KNOW

There's more to investing than stocks. Bonds offer investors a tool for diversifying their investment portfolios and for moderating risk. Bonds also let you adjust your portfolio's behavior should your needs change or the investment environment alter course.

Savvy investors shouldn't fear paying a premium for the right bond. Nor should risk-tolerant investors shy away from deep-discount issues. Should you decide to concentrate on corporate bonds, you can diversify by varying the types of businesses your bond issuers are involved in. For example, you could buy bonds of airline, technology, utility, and retail companies; or you could buy those of oil, finance, and construction companies.

I Buy on Feelings, Not Facts

When the bear is chasing everybody and there's
blood in the street, buy everything you can.

ALAN GWANT

*I*N THE STOCK MARKET, AN INVESTOR WITH MONEY IN HAND IS LIKE A KID in a candy store. There are well over ten thousand stocks and about eight thousand mutual funds to choose from. To put it lightly, you can afford to be picky. If your broker is pushing you to buy a stock or mutual fund that you're not comfortable with, insist on looking at other options.

If you're offered a complex packaged investment program (for example, one combining stocks, options, and bonds), look it over, but don't commit until you understand exactly how it works and why the broker thinks it's right for you. If your broker can't explain it, don't buy it. Investors have lost millions of dollars on complex investment deals that were high on commissions but low on returns. Make sure you understand exactly what you're buying.

As I've pointed out throughout this book, there are a lot of great investment opportunities out there to consider. Your goal should be to stock your portfolio with investments you understand and feel comfortable owning. This chapter reviews some of the important buying strategies we've looked at in our journey through the basics of stock investing. It also offers some new thoughts to keep you on track.

DON'T AVOID THE SMALL STUFF

Portfolio theory teaches that adding some risky assets to a portfolio can actually reduce risk and substantially improve overall returns. Yet many investors find it difficult to invest in small emerging-growth stocks because of their risk and volatility. Their concerns are certainly justified, but by playing the law of averages, you should be able to select enough big winners from the small-stock universe to more than make up for the losers that land in your portfolio when you follow this approach.

Throughout the stock market's history, small stocks have significantly outperformed the overall market. A study by James O'Shaughnessy, author of *What Works on Wall Street*, revealed that since 1951, stocks with market capitalizations under $25 million have grown about 20 percent per year. That is significantly higher than the roughly 11 percent per year growth of larger stocks. A $10,000 investment in small stocks in 1951, if continually reinvested in small stocks, would have grown to about $30 million by 1998.

The problem is that while the averages may favor small stocks, great performance as a group doesn't necessarily translate into great performance on an individual basis. So, what's the solution? Play the averages by buying several small stocks. You can expect a few small-stock duds as part of the game, but the law of averages suggests that some of your other picks will achieve excellent returns.

Consider the fact that, in the worst-case scenario, a bad $10 stock can cost you at most $10. But a good $10 stock could very well grow to $50 or more in a relatively short period of time. If just one out of every five small stocks grows fivefold, which is not unusual based on historic averages, you're assured of coming out ahead in your small-stock portfolio even if your other four picks drop to just $1 a share.

Identify Tomorrow's Leaders Today

By the time the major magazines catch on to a company with a hot new product, you may have missed the biggest price gains in its stock. Do your own sleuthing. Each day, *Investor's Business Daily's* "The New America" features two or three companies with enterprising products or services and good fundamentals, often before they are widely known. These are companies that exhibit the characteristics found among the market's biggest leaders of the past. Many of today's leading industries were in their infancy when they were first featured in "The New America."

What would happen if you bought a portfolio of six $10 stocks and half dropped by 50 percent while the other half rose steadily from $10 to $30? You would end up with three losers and three winners in your portfolio, which doesn't sound so great. But if you add it up, you'll find that your $60 investment would be worth $105, a 75 percent gain in a portfolio that includes as many losers as winners. Although small companies can be risky, by playing the averages and spreading your assets over several small stocks, you should be able to beat the overall market averages with a small-stock portfolio.

BUY WHAT THE INSTITUTIONS ARE BUYING

Although we covered institutions in some detail in Mistake #22, let's revisit them again because institutional buying plays a major role in making stocks winners. Institutional investors—the mutual funds, pension funds, banks and other financial institutions—are estimated to account for about 80 percent of all trading activity on any given day. So when institutions target a stock for purchase, it's more likely to go up in price thanks to the increased demand they create. This professional stock buying is called *institutional sponsorship.*

Institutions make a living buying and selling stocks. They employ analysts, researchers, and other specialists to gather comprehensive information about companies. They meet with executives, evaluate industry conditions, and study the outlook for every company they plan to invest in. That's why their stock selections are widely watched. Now, wouldn't it be great if you knew exactly what stocks institutions are buying and when?

How to Identify Institutional Activity

Although mutual funds and other institutions don't disclose their buys and sells frequently, you can track their moves by watching for clues in trading activity. One of the most useful ways to spot current institutional trading is to study volume percent change figures, or how much trading increased or decreased in a day compared with what is normal. By normal, we mean the average daily trading volume over the past fifty trading days.

Because this data comes out daily, it's the quickest way to detect institutional trading in a stock. When trading volume spikes up 50 percent or more at the same time a stock's price rises, that's generally a clear sign that major investors are moving into the stock.

Trading volume increases usually precede a significant rise in a stock's price. If, instead, a stock's price drops on heavy volume, it's a sign large investors may be moving out of the stock. If a stock's trading volume advances but its price goes nowhere, it could mean the stock is reaching a peak. You can't afford to ignore the influence professional money managers exert on stock prices. Information about volume changes appears in *Investor's Business Daily's* (*IBD's*) stock tables. Stocks with the largest increases or decreases in trading volume are also listed each day on *IBD*'s Web site (investors.com) under the title "Where The Big Money's Flowing Now."

AVOID BUYING PITFALLS

Don't limit your stock-buying decisions to one factor alone. Where a stock is in relation to its fifty-two-week high and low price should be just one part of the stock-selection checklist. Other important ingredients are its earnings-per-share rating, its price–earnings (PE) ratio, and its return on equity (ROE).

INSIST ON HIGH ROES

Return on equity (ROE) measures how well a company utilizes its investors' dollars. Put another way, ROE indicates how well a company produces earnings with the capital entrusted to it by its shareholders. ROE is one of the most popular ways to evaluate the financial performance of a company. It indicates whether corporate management is able to produce a profit with shareholder money. It's also a reliable indicator of what a company can earn in the future. High ROEs, year after year, tend to reflect increasing profitability and superior management. Cyclical stocks, those that move roughly with the economy, usually show mediocre ROEs.

ROEs vary among industries, but avoid companies with less than a 17 percent ROE. And be sure to compare a company's ROE against those of others in its industry to get a realistic comparison. In most industries, the top-performing companies tend to have ROEs of 20 to 30 percent. Occasionally, companies will boast ROEs of 40 percent or even higher. The higher the percentage, the more efficient the company is at utilizing its capital. ROEs have been increasing over the past several decades, largely because technology has helped cut costs and boost productivity.

LOOK FOR NEW HIGHS ON HIGH VOLUME

Be cautious about stocks that make new highs on less and less trading volume. This could be a sign of a stock that's reaching its peak, especially if the stock has gone up at least 50 percent in a few weeks after an extended advance. When a stock goes up on low volume, it's a gain produced by relatively small purchases. It's much safer to go with a stock that makes a new price high on higher volume, which indicates broader support for the stock.

Quality stocks making new price highs just as they emerge from sound bases on higher volume are likely to continue climbing, while stocks making new lows are probably headed even lower. Therefore, focus on the new price highs for the best potential opportunities. Think of a stock's price as a measure of its quality and potential.

How to Spot Stocks Making New Highs

IBD publishes a list of stocks making new highs each day. It also lists, on its "Industry Groups" page, those industries with the greatest percentage of stocks making new highs. *IBD*'s "52-Week Highs & Lows" table also provides insight into which industry groups are asserting market leadership. By watching these leaders, you can position your investments in industries that are poised to advance. Leading stocks within the leading groups are shown each day. The list of new price lows is a good place to check for industries and stocks that are weakening. Avoid these. The number of new price highs compared with new price lows provides a measure of the overall market's health.

New Price Highs Mean New Opportunities

To own the stock of a fast-rising company, you'll have to pay a premium. Many investors have passed up great stocks because they had reached new price highs. But that's when many of the best stocks begin their major climbs. One reason new highs represent good opportunities is because of something market experts call *overhead supply*. Suppose a stock that once traded at $50 falls to $25. If it starts to make its way back up, investors who bought near $50 start hoping the stock will return to the old high so they can sell and break even. This presents selling pressure near the $50 mark. But once the stock clears that $50 hurdle, it's no longer burdened by disappointed investors looking to wipe out their losses.

Great Stocks Reflect Success Stories

Stocks don't double, triple, or move even higher in a vacuum. There's usually something new behind a stock's major price advance. Usually, new products, new services, or new management propels a stock to a leadership role and a new high. A study evaluating the greatest stocks dating back to 1953 found that 95 percent of those winners had breakthrough products, new management, or a new way of doing business that boosted them to staggering heights. That's why it's important to keep up with developments that could launch the next great stock.

Where would Microsoft be today without its Windows operating system? Look through a list of the greatest stocks and you'll find plenty of breakthrough products that fueled those stocks' advances. Here are some examples:

- Syntex rocketed 450 percent in six months during 1963, when it began selling the first oral contraceptive pill.
- McDonald's surged 1,100 percent from 1967 to 1971 as its low-cost fast-food franchising business model swept the nation.
- From 1978 to 1980, Wang Labs' shares grew 1,350 percent with the development of word-processing office equipment.
- International Game Technology surged 1,600 percent from 1991 to 1993 thanks to the development of microprocessor-based game technology.
- Accustaff rose 1,486 percent from January 1995 to May 1996 as outsourcing grabbed hold of corporate America, sending this temporary-staffing firm's profits soaring.
- America Online surged 593 percent from September 1994 to June 1996 as the company became the leading Internet service provider to a nation eager to log on to the Web.
- Qualcomm rose 376 percent from February 1999 to December 1999 on the rising popularity of the company's Code Division Multiple Access technology for wireless telephones.

These and other success-story companies didn't achieve greatness without proven products. Watch out for companies promising a cure for cancer or some other breakthrough technology. It's wiser to wait for the product to prove itself in the marketplace before investing. If a product really hits it big, there will be strong demand for the stock for a long time to come because great companies never stop innovating. As soon as one product is out the door, they're working on the next generation, evaluating the future of the marketplace, and looking for new ways to sustain their leadership.

Annual reports often overhype achievements and developments, creating unrealistic expectations. Those who write these reports may be adept at glossing over shortcomings. Carefully scrutinize promises in annual reports. Many Internet chat rooms and bulletin boards are notorious for stock hype as well. Take anything you read at these sites with a big grain of salt. You never know who's posting the information, what their motives are, or if the information is even true. Rumors are cheap and plentiful.

TAKE THE TIME TO SHOP AROUND

It pays to shop around in the stock market. If stocks with high PE ratios have you worried, you might consider low-PE stocks and other stocks that no one else wants. Some money managers specialize exclusively in low-PE stocks with good success. In fact, studies have shown that low PE stocks, as a group, tend to outperform the overall market. There is evidence that portfolios of stocks with

---

The Importance of Acceleration

Focus on those stocks making major earnings advances and those that have accelerated over the previous three or four quarters. Acceleration represents an increase in the earnings growth rate quarter over quarter. Improving bottom-line growth nearly always precedes a burst in stock price. Rising earnings alone aren't enough to make a good stock. The key is to focus on companies whose accelerating earnings are drawing the attention of professional investors. This is when the stock is likely to spring higher.

---

relatively low earnings multiples often produce above-average rates of return. It has also been found that stocks selling at low multiples of their book value have tended to produce higher subsequent returns than stocks with high multiples of their book value. This finding is consistent with the views first expounded on by William Graham and Phillip Dodd in 1934 and later championed by Warren Buffett.

TAKE ADVANTAGE OF WALL STREET'S WRATH

Even good companies can go through a tough year or a tough quarter. And when they do, Wall Street punishes them mercilessly. A disappointing earnings report can cause the price of a stock to tumble far beyond what it should. Bad news about a company can also cause the stock price to drop. In 1994, when Intel reported that its Pentium chip was causing some mistakes in large calculations, its stock price dropped from $65 to $56 a share. But once the company resolved the problem, the stock not only moved back up to its original high, but continued to climb—to $156 a share in just seven months.

In 1996, America Online instituted a new unlimited-use policy for customers willing to pay $19.95 per month. The response was so overwhelming the company couldn't meet demand. That

---

Where can you find low-PE stocks? PE ratios are listed in the stock tables of the *Wall Street Journal*, *Investor's Business Daily*, and the business section of most major newspapers. An easier way to find cheap stocks is through the *Value Line Investment Survey* (which should be available at your public library). *Value Line* publishes a list of the lowest-PE stocks in each of its weekly updates.

seems like exactly the kind of problem most businesses would love to have, but Wall Street hammered the stock, knocking it from a high of $71 to a low of $25 in just two months. A year later, the stock had bounced back into the $70s, and investors smart enough to have bought the stock in its time of trouble earned a return of more than 180 percent in just one year.

John Rogers of the Ariel Funds likes to buy stocks when no one else wants them. He notes:

> We like to buy smaller and midsize companies when they're cheap and out of favor. We look at the private market value of the companies. We look at discount of future cash flows of companies and what comparable companies are being sold at if someone's taking them over. When talking about private market value, we really are trying to get a sense of what a rational, informed buyer of the entire enterprise would pay for the company. The heart of the process is the cash flow. Typically, less than eight times cash flow is something we feel comfortable buying. That's the high end for us. If it is at six or seven times cash flow, that is clearly a better bargain.

Smart investors watch for the same types of opportunities, when the market pushes down the price of a stock because of a temporary problem that may have no bearing on the company's long-term prospects. That's when they swoop in, buy the stock, and hold it until the company rebounds. What could be simpler? Yet as elementary and logical as it may sound, buying low and selling high is much easier said than done.

What makes the concept so difficult is that it clashes with every fiber of human impulse and emotion. When stocks are blazing through a strong bull rally, and every news show reports a new market high, it's hard to resist the impulse to jump in while the market is hot. Then, when stocks begin to go south and the economic outlook dims, emotion prods us to pull the plug and sell out before things get even worse. The result for the uninitiated is that they buy when stocks are pushing new highs and sell when they've sunk to their lowest levels.

The truth of the matter is, it takes nerves of steel to buy low, to put your money on the line when the market is floundering, and to sell out when everyone else is buying in. But that's what separates the winners from those whose performance is only so-so.

Only when you understand the psychology of the market and know its history does it become easier to get in and out of the market at the right time. There will be fluctuations in stock prices, with high points and low points every year. Try to use these fluctuations to maximize your returns, bolstering your holdings when stocks are down and lightening up your positions when euphoria has driven up prices beyond reason.

SEARCH FOR UNDERVALUED STOCKS

Look for undervalued stocks that the market has punished or forgotten. Try to use the emotion of the market as an opportunity to buy good companies at low prices. There have been times when a single negative earnings report has cut the price of a stock by 50 percent. Those are the stocks that should grab your interest. Obviously, you don't want to invest in every stock that takes a hit, but take a close look to see if there's a chance it can rebound. If there is, buy it.

Look for a company that has done something to correct whatever the immediate problem seems to be. Don't invest in the stock unless you believe the management team has figured out how the company is going to bounce back. Maybe it's new management, maybe it's a new subsidiary, maybe it's a new product or some cost-cutting measures.

Always remember that Wall Street ultimately values every stock accurately relative to every other stock. Watch for windows of opportunity when prices are out of whack with the rest of the market. Over the short term, emotions can cause the stock of a good company to drop further than it should. Disappointing earnings, a failed product launch, or other bad news can cause the market to overreact. That's when you want to make your move. It's a lot like photographing a bird. You have to be patient and sit back quietly. Let the bird settle nearby before you use your camera. You just need to click the shutter when the price is right.

THE LEAST YOU NEED TO KNOW

Great stocks to buy come in many different sizes and styles. They aren't necessarily the trendiest high-tech stocks. Some of the dullest companies make great stocks. For example, RPM Corporation manufactures paints and coatings. Although it's not glamorous stuff, the company has posted forty-nine consecutive years of record earnings, while its stock price has moved up 15 percent on average per year. Dull can be very profitable.

Narrow your industry focus. Rather than buying a little bit of everything to make sure you have all the industries covered, focus on the industries that have the most predictable earnings streams. Watch out for high-technology companies because they're volatile and unpredictable. Commodity-oriented companies, such as gold and silver or oil and gas, are also unpredictable. Companies such as autos, machine tools, and heavy manufacturing can be cyclical.

Look for companies in household goods, such as the ones you see in your grocery store (Procter & Gamble, for example). Consider concentrating on small to mid-sized companies such as Clorox, First Brand, McCormack Spice Company, Herman Miller, General Binding, and American Media.

These companies generate positive cash flow, have high returns on assets and equity, and have a strong brand name in their specific industry niche. When it comes to bleach, we think of Clorox. When it comes to tabloid journalism, we think of the *National Enquirer*. Warren Buffett talks the same way about Gillette and Coca-Cola and other companies with strong brand names.

MISTAKE 25

I Never Know When to Sell a Stock

I don't like money. However, I do like what money will buy.

BEN FRANCE

ONE OF THE BIGGEST ADVANTAGES OF STOCK OWNERSHIP IS THAT YOU pay no taxes on your gains until you sell a stock. So, if you hold a stock for many years, the stock can grow fivefold, tenfold, or more without any tax consequences while you own it. There are a number of great blue-chip stocks, such as Coca-Cola, Kellogg, and Merck, that have continued to perform well for many years. If a company maintains a strong financial performance, increasing its earnings and revenue year in and year out, why sell it? It's exactly the kind of stock you want to own.

On the other hand, circumstances change—and corporate performance may change with them. There are times when selling stocks that have served you well is the best course. How do you recognize those times? It's also important to get rid of losers before they drag down your whole portfolio. A review of selling strategies seems an appropriate way to close this book—because knowing when to sell can be one of the most difficult hurdles for many investors. This chapter will help you make the hard decisions.

IF THERE'S SMOKE, DON'T PANIC

As uncertain as stock investing may seem, there are still many certainties in the market. One such certainty is that no matter how robust the economy or the market may seem, the next correction is always just around the corner. There's a fine line between a correction—a substantial drop in stock prices when the market gets too high—and a crash. Most analysts consider a market decline of 5 to 20 percent to be a correction, and more than 20 percent to be a crash.

In the past century, there have been hundreds of market corrections. They generally occur several times a year. Whenever the market corrects, the press and the TV financial talk shows tend to treat the occasion like the second coming of the 1929 market crash. They talk in dire terms of the possible consequences of this unexpected bombshell, striking fear into the hearts of novice investors.

Veteran investors know that corrections are no reason for panic. They're just a natural part of the stock market process. But the media frenzy that accompanies the more severe corrections tends to spook inexperienced investors into selling their holdings to complete the classic "buy high, sell low" scenario. Experienced investors know better. They wait patiently for these corrections and instead coolly use them to add to their holdings.

In the stock market, there's often smoke, but seldom fire. When the market drops, follow the experts and focus on the long term. Shop around for bargains on quality stocks. Sell your losers so that you have the money to buy winners at great prices.

TAKE PROFITS EVERY CHANCE YOU CAN

An old Wall Street adage is you can't lose money taking a profit. Even with your best stocks, it sometimes pays to sell, take the profit to the bank, and move the money into other investments.

Top money manager Lee Kopp says he sometimes sells out a portion of his holdings in his best stocks for no other reason than to bring his portfolio into balance. When one of his stocks rises quickly, it can suddenly account for a disproportionately high percentage of his portfolio's assets.

If you sense a correction looming, it can be prudent to pare back your winners. But do it carefully because it's hard to find the big winners. If a large share of your investment dollars is in one stock and the prospects for that stock suddenly change, sell and spread your risks over a broader universe.

WATCH OUT FOR COCKROACHES

The cockroach is the most feared creature on Wall Street. According to the cockroach theory, when you see one, there are probably others hiding in the cupboards. When a company reports disappointing earnings, do what many experts do and consider it a sign to get out quickly. The cockroach theory is particularly relevant to smaller growth stocks, which can be very volatile.

William Berger, founder of the Berger Funds, prefers to get out of a stock when a company has disappointing earnings. Berger says, "We think one surprise may beget another surprise, so we get rid of the stock." Parkstone Small Capitalization Fund manager Roger Stamper takes the same tack when one of his stocks takes a turn for the worse. Stamper says, "Even if we have to take a 30 percent loss, we'll get out. It's the cockroach theory. I've seen too many times when you wait around a quarter or two to see if the company improves, and it just gets worse."

George Vanderheiden, manager of the Fidelity Advisor Growth Opportunities Fund, confesses to a fear of cockroaches. "As soon as I see the first crack, I get out. I want to sell my mistakes quickly. If I buy a stock thinking the company's new concept will do well, and it doesn't work out, I'll sell. Usually the first piece of bad news is not the last piece of bad news." When many of Wall Street's finest managers all reach the same conclusion, it's worthwhile for individual investors to consider the strategy as well.

WATCH THE INSTITUTIONS

Just as you would when you are buying (see Mistakes #22 and #24), pay attention to institutional selling trends. Learn how to recognize what institutional sponsors are doing. Lagging stocks without institutional sponsorship are likely to remain underperformers. If you have any in your portfolio, sell them.

ACT ON DETERIORATING FUNDAMENTALS

Don't hold on to a stock whose return on equity (ROE) is dropping rather than increasing. Replace it with a better opportunity. You want to own today's and tomorrow's winners. If any of the companies in your portfolio don't fit this description, get rid of them.

BEWARE THE SOARING PE

The higher a stock's price–earnings (PE) ratio, the more you stand to lose if its earnings suddenly go south. A high-PE stock that is starting to lose growth momentum can spell trouble. Some of the highest-flying stocks of the 1990s, when the technology sector was skyrocketing, became some of the biggest losers of 2001, when many of those stocks returned to earth. In a number of cases, the stocks fared poorly not so much because of any real weakness in their earnings,

Corporate managers want to portray their companies as strong. When results slip, they try to minimize the damage, sometimes reporting only part of the problem in hopes that things will turn around in the ensuing quarters. Most of the time, the problems persist and earnings continue to dip, pushing the stock price down even further. So when bad news breaks for one of your stocks, bail out. Otherwise, you too may face an army of cockroaches.

but because of their exorbitant PE ratios. In many cases, the stock price dropped even though earnings continued to rise.

If you own stocks in an overpriced sector, save yourself from potentially heavy losses by unloading those stocks before they begin to plummet. There have been several times in recent history when the PEs of certain stocks became dangerously high. The rationale for the high prices from Wall Street experts is almost always the same: "It's different this time. These stocks can support exorbitantly high PEs because . . . [you fill in the blank]." Don't believe a word of it. Their decline is imminent.

What History Tells Us About PEs

Here's a brief history lesson on PE ratios. In the early 1980s, high-tech start-up stocks and biotechnology stocks were the rage with investors who believed that there could be no end to their spectacular growth. Little matter that many of those companies had no earnings, or very small earnings, and no track record. Investors

Having a stock buying and selling checklist that highlights the most important traits you want in a stock will help you know when to sell. If you find that a stock you own no longer meets the expectations in your checklist, sell it. And never buy anything that doesn't meet all your criteria.

kept bidding up the prices. PE ratios climbed into the 100-plus range. And the rationalizations from Wall Street's experts began. "These stocks are different from the blue chips. They can support higher PEs because of their potential for rapid growth." When the rapid growth never materialized, investors lost interest in the sector, and prices fell through the floor.

In the late 1980s, Japanese stocks soared to record levels. Many stocks carried PEs of 200 or more, levels unheard of in the history of the Japanese stock market. But unfazed investors continued to buy, while Japanese brokers continued to tout the stocks. "This time it's different," they repeated. "This is the great Japanese financial empire, an empire that is taking over the world's financial markets, the world's manufacturing markets, and the world's high-technology markets. These stocks can support the higher PE ratios because they are part of this great Japanese economic machine."

The machine suddenly ground to a halt, the bottom fell out of the Japanese economy, and hundreds of stocks dropped to a fraction of their former highs. A decade later, Japan's Nikkei Stock Exchange is still trading at about half of its peak levels in the late 1980s.

In 1991, medical stocks caught fire. Merck climbed 80 percent. Pfizer went from $40 to $84 a share. Stryker went from $16 to $50. Across the board, medical stocks were climbing far faster than the market averages. PEs were moving into the 40 to 70 range. And again, the rationalizations from Wall Street analysts began to fly. "This time it's different. The world's population is aging, and the need for medical products will continue to expand. That's why these stocks can support high PEs." But in 1992, when presidential candidate Bill Clinton started talking about health care cost containment, Wall Street began to take another look at medical stocks. And suddenly, those stocks began to plummet.

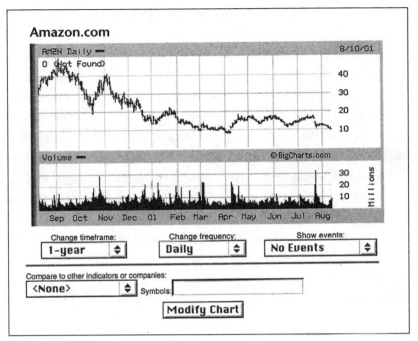

FIGURE 25.1 Amazon.com

Stocks like Amazon.com, which was trading at over a hundred dollars a share in the fourth quarter of 1999, plummeted to below $10 a share in the first quarter of 2001 (figure 25.1). Amazon's meltdown was typical of what was happening to the rest of the dot-com industry. Most of the dot-coms were trading at exorbitant prices, and very few were making a profit, including Amazon.com. That combination is a guaranteed formula for an investment disaster.

If you own stocks in a sector whose PEs seem way out of line, lighten your position. When you hear Wall Street pundits begin to say, "But this time it's different," that's your signal to take your profits and move on. Invoke the "greater fools" theory and let the next guy take the fall.

THE LEAST YOU NEED TO KNOW

Recognizing when to sell a stock is as important as knowing when to buy it. Not every market dip is a sign to run for the exits. But a bad earnings report or other negative news from a company whose stock has been a good performer should set off the "cockroach" alarm. Take your profits before any more insects creep out of the corporate woodwork.

Generally, houseclean your portfolio of any stock whose ROE is declining. And keep your eye on institutional activity in the stocks you own. If the big holders are running for the exits, so should you.

Reducing your holdings in a high-flyer may make sense to keep your portfolio in balance. Use the profits to take a chance on tomorrow's next great stock. Also, if a stock's PE is skyrocketing, consider unloading it while it can still make you a nice profit.

Epilogue

PUTTING IT ALL TOGETHER

Most of us would like to be rich someday. Some of us will try any get-rich-quick scheme that comes along, including the lottery. Others will invest in some bogus "ground floor opportunity" to make it happen. Still others will seek out the advice of an investment broker and buy the recommended stock or a mutual fund without much thought. Even though our investment approaches differ, most of us share two common failings. Our investment plans are not consistent, and if we manage to set investment goals, we don't follow through with them to achieve the financial security we desire.

As a result, most of us won't become rich from our investments in the stock market. Yet there are now more new entrepreneurial companies in America than there are in any other country in the world. Many are in the technology, communications, and Internet sectors. Others are in biotechnology, retail, leisure, and a variety of other industries. To become an astute investor, you need to develop the skills to recognize and invest in the fast-growing, innovative companies that are shaping America's growth economy. How do you do that without spending countless hours of painful research?

At the beginning of this book, I warned you that if you aren't willing to develop a systematic investment plan and take an active role in managing that plan, you're wasting your time investing in the stock market. The irony is that it really doesn't take that much effort to make a plan and carry it out. I have provided you with step-by-step strategies to follow and have shown you how to spot the most promising stocks and mutual funds for your portfolio. I have also shared with you some of the tips the top Wall Street money managers use to manage their portfolios.

Investing your money the smart way takes discipline, time, and patience. If you start with a well-thought-out set of financial goals, a solid investment plan, and a commonsense approach, you're well on your way to making money in the stock market. I wish you the best of luck on the journey!

Appendix

ANNUAL REPORTS AND COMPANY PROFILES

To get a company's investment package, call them. You can get their phone number from *Value Line*, a magazine article, the Internet, or directory assistance. On the Web, try typing www.NAME OF COMPANY.com to find the company's site. For instance, you'll find IBM at www.ibm.com and Ford at www.ford.com.

Best Calls (www.bestcalls.com) provides access to companies' quarterly earnings press conferences.

Companies Online (www.companiesonline.com) provides links to more than one hundred thousand corporations with online presence. You enter the company's name and their search engine will find its Web site.

Investor's Relations Information Network (www.irin.com) offers over twenty-five hundred company annual reports online.

Public Register's Annual Report Service (www.prars.com) offers both online and hard copy annual reports.

Thompson Investor Net (www.Thompsoninvest.com) covers over seven thousand in-depth company reports that are updated twice a month.

Wall Street Research Net (www.wsrn.com) provides annual reports for more than sixteen thousand publicly traded companies.

ANALYSTS' EVALUATIONS

Finding out what stock analysts are saying about a stock you're considering can help you determine if it's the right time to buy. Here are several sites that will get you the information you need.

S&P Advisor Insight (www.advisorinsight.com) allows you to review Standard & Poor's reports for the major stocks.

Zacks Investment Research (www.zacks.com) reports on what analysts are saying about most of the stocks on the U.S. exchanges.

ASSOCIATIONS

Unfortunately, there are not many good national investment associations that cater to online investors. Here are two good ones to check out.

American Association of Individual Investors (www.aaii.org) offers a variety of valuable services to their members including local chapter meetings in the major metropolitan areas.

The National Association of Investors Corporation (NAIC) (www.investing.org) is a national association with local chapters throughout the country. Their goal is to help investors develop a disciplined approach to successful investing.

BONDS

Although we only talked briefly about bonds in the book, they can be an attractive investment alternative to stocks. Here are several sites that can get you started in the bond market.

Bonds Online (www.bondsonline.com) provides charts and historical data that compare the various bond market sectors.

The Bond Market (www.bondcan.com) specializes in investing in Canadian bonds.

The Bond Market Association (www.bondmarkets.com) is loaded with information about thousands of bonds and their respective trading history.

BROKERS (ONLINE)

Accutrade (www.accutrade.com) 1-800-494-8939

American Express (www.americanexpress.com) 1-800-658-4677

Ameritrade (www.ameritrade.com) 1-800-454-9272

Brown & Co. (www.brownco.com) 1-800-822-2021

CSFBdirect (www.CSFBdirect.com) 1-877-355-5557

Datek (www.datek.com) 1-888-463-2835

Discover Brokerage (www.discoverbrokerage.com) 1-800-688-3462

E*Trade (www.etrade.com) 1-800-387-2331

Fidelity (www.fidelity.com) 1-800-544-8666

Muriel Siebert (www.msiebert.com) 1-800-872-0444

National Discount Brokers (www.ndb.com) 1-800-888-3999

Net Investor (www.netinvestor.com) 1-800-638-4250

Quick & Reilly (www.quickwaynet.com) 1-800-837-7220

Schwab (www.schwab.com) 1-800-435-4000

Suretrade (www.suretrade.com) 1-800-394-1452

Wall Street Access (www.wsaccess.com) 1-800-925-5782

Waterhouse (www.tdwaterhouse.com) 1-800-934-4448

CHARTS AND COMPANY PROFILES

Always remember that a stock's chart is your friend and that a picture is worth ten thousand words. At a quick glance, a stock's chart can quickly tell you not only where it has been historically, but in all probability, where it's going.

Hoover's Online (www.stockscreener.com) provides information on over eight thousand companies.

Money magazine's Web site (www.money.com) offers an excellent fund and stock charting service.

Research magazine (www.researchmag.com) offers you both a charting and company profile service.

SmartMoney magazine (www.smartmoney.com) offers free charts and quotes on all U.S. stocks and most funds as well. The Web site features company profile articles and timely comments on market trends.

DIRECT PUBLIC OFFERINGS

Direct public offerings (DPOs) are programs where a company agrees to offer its stock directly to the public when it initially issues stock (IPO or initial public offering). The advantage to the shareholders is that they pay no broker fees. Check out these Web sites to learn more about DPOs.

Direct Stock Market (www.dsm.com) provides information about companies that offer direct public offerings.

Netstock Direct (www.netstockdirect.com) is an online source for purchasing stocks directly from a company.

DIVERSIFIED PLANNING

Diversifying your portfolio is the best way to insure you're covered when the different segments of the market fluctuate in different directions. The following sites will help you put together a diversification plan that's right for you.

Fidelity's Asset Diversification Planner (www.fidelity.com) offers diversification advice, a risk questionnaire, and five model portfolios.

Frank Russell Company (www.russell.com) features a Comfort Quiz to help you allocate your investments.

The Intelligent Asset Allocator (www.efficientfrontier.com) offers comprehensive information on how to build a diversified portfolio.

Legg Mason's Web site (www.leggmason.com) provides an online questionnaire to help you develop a diversification plan.

DIVIDEND REINVESTMENT PROGRAMS

Dividend reinvestment programs (DRIPs) allow you to purchase shares of stock directly from participating companies without having to pay broker fees.

DRIP Advisor (www.dripadvisor.com) lists most of the companies that offer DRIP programs.

Netstock Direct (www.netstock.com) not only lists companies that offer DRIPs, but its search engine will allow you access to companies within industries that interest you.

Stock One (www.stock1.com) offers advice and suggestions on how to get started in DRIPs.

EARNINGS ESTIMATES

How do you find out what the experts estimate the earnings will be for a company that you want to invest in? The following Web site will help you find the answer.

Zacks Investment Research (www.zacks.com) provides estimated earnings based on broker opinions.

ECONOMIC INFORMATION AND TRENDS

To find out how the economy is doing today and is projected to do in the future, check out these Web sites.

The Bureau of Economic Analysis (www.bea.doc.gov) calculates economic indicators such as the gross domestic product and other regional, national, and international data, all of which are displayed on their Web site.

Census Bureau (www.census.gov) provides information about industry statistics and general business conditions.

STAT-USA (www.stat-usa.gov) is sponsored by the U.S. Department of Commerce and provides financial information about economic indicators, statistics, and economic news.

EDUCATION

Over the past few years, significant improvements have been made in the online education investment field. It's not great, but it's getting better. Check out these sites.

The American Association of Individual Investors offers advice on funds and portfolio management on their Web site at ww.aaii .com.

Bloomberg Personal Finance (www.bloomberg.com) offers online training when you click on the Bloomberg University module.

Investing Basics (www.aaii.com/invbas) offers feature articles about how to start successful investment programs, pick winning stocks, and evaluate your options.

Investor Guide (www.investorguide.com) features over one thousand answers to frequently asked questions.

Invest Wisely (www.sec.gov/consumer/inws.htm) is a feature educational article for new investors from the Securities and Exchange Commission.

Money and Investing (www.eldernet.com/money.htm) offers tutorials and advice on investing in stocks, mutual funds, and bonds.

Money 101 (www.money.com) offers an interactive online investment crash course.

Morningstar's University (www.morningstar.com) offers a comprehensive investment education program.

The Motley Fools offer an investment seminar on their Web site at www.fool.com.

The Mutual Fund Education Alliance (www.mfea.com) is the trade association for no-load funds and offers advice on how to select funds .

Vanguard (www.vanguard.com) offers online courses that cover the fundamentals of investing in mutual funds.

EXCHANGES

Both the NASDAQ and New York Stock Exchange offer a wide variety of investment features that will appeal to you.

American Stock Exchange (www.amex.com)

The National Association of Securities Dealers (www.nasdaq.com)

The New York Stock Exchange (www.nyse.com)

EXPERTS' ADVICE

In-depth research and savvy advice from the Wall Street experts are available to you at no charge if you know where to look. Here are several great sites that will get you started.

Merrill Lynch (www.ml.com) allows you to download research reports by such well-known experts as Merrill's chief economist Bruce Steinberg. Click on the research tab on the right side of their main menu to get to the reports.

Morgan Stanley (www.morganstanley.com) provides free advice from the firm's top names like Barton Biggs, Byron Wien, and Stephen Roach. Just go to their Web site and click on the Global Strategy Bulletin.

Paine Webber (www.painewebber.com) provides specific analytical reports by company even if you're not a customer. The firm's top-ranked strategists produce the reports.

Raymond James (www.raymondjames.com) was recently named by the *Wall Street Journal* as one of the top stock pickers in the country. A weekly commentary about the market and the economic outlet plus other great features are available at his Web site.

FINANCIAL TOOLS AND CALCULATORS

The Web sites listed in this section offer a multitude of solution-oriented features.

Altamira Resource Center's Net Worth Calculator (www.altamira.com) helps you determine your current net worth and track changes over time.

Charles Schwab (www.schwab.com) helps you develop a financial plan with his online calculators, tools, and advice.

The Financial Center (www.financialcenter.com) has a Savings icon. Click on it and then click the calculator titled, "What will it take to become a millionaire?" Enter the required data and click Calculate. The results show how much you need to invest today to be a millionaire in the future.

FUNDAMENTAL ANALYSIS

Visit the following Web sites to find the fundamental data you need to have before you buy a stock.

Financial Engines (www.financialengines.com) is a Web site developed by Nobel prize–winning economist William Sharpe.

411 Stocks (www.411stocks.com) offers a simple one-stop shopping site with lots of fundamental information about a stock, including pricing data, news, charting, financial statements, and more.

J&E Research (www.jeresearch.com) is a site that specializes in financial modeling, research, and analysis. Their stock analysis program uses an Excel spreadsheet that you can use to complete the fundamental analysis of any stock.

GAMES

If you're interested in testing your skills as an online trader with Monopoly money, check out these adult investment game sites.

Hedge Hog Competition (www.marketplayer.com) allows participants to build on a $1 million stock portfolio as they compete
against other contestants.

Virtual Stock Exchange (www.virtualstockexchange.com) is a
stock simulation game that allows you to trade shares just as you
would in a real brokerage account.

INDEXED FUNDS

There are literally hundreds of mutual funds that index every segment of the market. Here are two of the better funds to consider.

Fidelity Spartan Market Index Fund mirrors the Standard &
Poor's 500 (S&P 500) index (800-544-8888).

T. Rowe Price Equity Index Fund mirrors the S&P 500
(800-638-5660).

INDUSTRY INFORMATION

The Web sites listed here allow you to compare the performance of
investment candidates to their industry.

ABC News (www.abcnews.com) features articles on current
industry news and market expert commentary.

American Society of Association Executives (www.asaenet.org)
provides high-quality industry overviews including briefing of
industry trends.

Hoovers Online (www.stockscreener.com) offer excellent information on industries at their Web site.

Research magazine (www.researchmag.com) features Industry Spotlight module on their Web site with in-depth industry analysis.

INTERNATIONAL INVESTING

The Internet is a rich source for information on foreign companies. Three Web sites with useful information are www.bankofny.com, www.jpmorgan.com, and www.globalinvestor.com. Here are several additional sites to visit.

FT Market Watch (www.ftmarketwatch.com) provides up-to-the-minute news on offshore companies and foreign markets.

Worldly Investor (www.worldlyinvestor.com) is the international investor's forum. A daily column is featured on their Web site along with international trends in stocks, mutual funds, and bonds.

INVESTMENT STRATEGIES

Developing an investment strategy that's right for you is a critical component in your overall planning. Here are two sites that will help you get started.

Bank of America (www.bankamerica.com) offers a survey of twelve questions on their Web site. Enter your answers and the online calculator suggests an investment strategy that suits your current needs and situation.

Investor Home (www.investorhome.com) provides information about the investment process and how to bulletproof your portfolio.

MAGAZINES

There are several excellent investment magazines on the market that cover everything from expert advice to hot stock and mutual fund tips. Most of the better magazines also support Web sites that you can review before you subscribe.

Business Week (www.businessweek.com) is available online to all of its subscribers.

Forbes (www.forbes.com) is available online featuring articles on personal finance and investing.

Fortune (www.fortune.com) includes special market reports as well as stock and fund quotes.

Kiplinger's (www.kiplinger.com) has a broader scope than either *SmartMoney* or *Worth*. Instead of talking just about investing, *Kiplinger's* moves into other issues of personal business, such as credit card spending, loans, college tuition, and vacation planning. For subscription information, call 800-544-0155.

Money (www.money.com) does an excellent job of keeping its readers informed about what's happening in the mutual fund market. For subscription information, visit their Web site.

Newsweek Online (www.newsweek.com) not only covers the general news but also covers the latest news about the stock market.

SmartMoney (www.smartmoney.com) is the "*Wall Street Journal* Magazine of Personal Business" and it's excellent. For subscription information, call 800-444-4204 or visit their Web site.

Worth magazine columnists are second to none, including Peter Lynch's column, and its regular features are dynamite. For subscription information, call 800-777-1851.

MARKET INDEXES

Market indexes are relied upon by financial analysts and investors alike to gauge the direction of a particular market segment. The most popular indexes are covered in this section.

American Stock Exchange Market Value Index tracks roughly eight hundred companies that trade on the American Stock Exchange.

Dow Jones Industrial Average (DJIA or the Dow) is one of the most closely followed indexes that's made up of thirty primer companies on the New York Stock Exchange. The sum of their respective stock prices is reported throughout the market day to reflect on the state of the overall market.

New York Stock Exchange Composite Index tracks all stocks traded on the New York Stock Exchange.

S&P 400 and **S&P 600** are two indexes that were designed to track smaller companies than those in the S&P 500.

Standard & Poor's 500 Index contains five hundred of the largest companies' stocks from the New York, NASDAQ, and American stock exchanges. The index is derived from the market capitalization of its component stocks rather than price, which is the case with the DJIA.

MUTUAL FUNDS: GENERAL INFORMATION

There are almost as many mutual funds to choose from as there are stocks. The following Web sites will help you find the best ones that are out there.

CBS Market Watch (www.marketwatch.com) provides articles, news, and market data on funds. Click the Super Fund icon to see the fund information.

Invest-O-Rama (www.investorama.com) is an extensive, well-organized site that lists fund-related web links.

MaxFunds (www.maxfunds.com) specializes in offering news and statistics on small and little-known funds.

Morningstar (www.morningstar.com) is a premier site providing all kinds of information about mutual funds.

Mutual Funds: Screening

There are an infinite number of ways to screen through the mass of mutual funds that are on the market to find the one fund that's right for you. Check out the Web sites covered in this section to learn how to fine-tune your screening criteria.

Find a Fund (www.findafund.com) publishes a list of the weekly top-performing funds and lots of other fund-selection information.

Morningstar (www.morningstar.com) evaluates and ranks over seven thousand funds.

Mutual Fund magazine (www.mfmag.com) offers feature articles and tools for selecting funds that are right for you.

Mutual Funds Interactive (www.fundsinteractive.com/profiles. html) provides recommendations, analysis tools, and profiles of many of the top funds.

Quicken (www.quicken.com) offers a mutual fund screener. Click on the Mutual Fund Finder to get there.

Quote.com Mutual Fund Screen (www.quote.com/screening) offers a fund screener where you can also find out how different funds did in bull or bear markets.

Research magazine (www.researchmag.com) allows you to search for funds based on forty search variables.

SmartMoney magazine (www.smartmoney.com) provides an easy search tool for finding the top twenty-five funds in specialty areas.

Mutual Funds: Ordering Online

Most of the major funds allow you to order their funds online or over the phone. Obviously, you will need to set up an account before you can do that. Here are several Web sites to review:

Fidelity (www.fidelity.com) offers direct purchase plans for its funds.

Janus (www.janus.com) has a family of no-load funds that you can purchase or apply for online.

***Mutual Funds* Online** (www.mfmag.com) provides access to fund family guides, performance rankings, and a weekly E-mail newsletter.

Strong Automatic Investment Plan (www.strongfunds.com/strong/learningcenter/aipbroch.htm) has an automatic investment program for many of their funds.

T. Rowe Price (www.troweprice.com) offers direct purchase plans for its funds.

Vanguard (www.vanguard.com) has over eighty funds that you can purchase directly from the company.

NEWS ONLINE

One of the biggest advantages of getting your news online is that you can go to the specific news sector (i.e., Market Watch) without having to thumb through a bunch of paper to get there. Here are several excellent sites to try.

ABC News (www.abcnews.com) features business and industry news and market commentary.

Bloomberg Personal Finance (www.bloomberg.com) is loaded with timely business news, data, and an analysis of the market.

CBS Market Watch (www.marketwatch.com) offers feature articles on the market and breaking news targeting investors.

Company Sleuth (www.companysleuth.com) will send you news updates each day on companies you're following via E-mail.

NEWSLETTERS

If you're short on time and are willing to pay someone else to search for great stock bargains, then subscribing to a newsletter may be for you. Most of them will send you a free copy to check out before you subscribe.

Dick Davis Digest is chock-full of information. Companies covered in each issue are listed alphabetically on the first page, making it easy for you to monitor the latest on stocks you own or are watching. For subscription information, call 800-654-1514.

First Capital Corporation (www.firstcap.com) offers two free newsletters. *Market Timing* presents a short-term technical approach for the stock and bond markets. *Global Viewpoint* provides a weekly technical analysis of world markets.

John Dessauer's *Investor's World* is a good general-purpose newsletter that discusses global investment issues and stock recommendations. For further information, call 301-424-3700.

Louis Navellier's *MPT Review* publishes performance numbers on hot stocks. It is one of the top-performing newsletters around, listing hundreds of volatile growth stocks from which to choose. For subscription information, call 800-454-1395.

Louis Rukeyser's Wall Street is one of the best investment newsletters around. It's a good balance between Dessauer's conversational letters and the hard data contained in other newsletters. For subscription information, call 800-892-9702.

Newsletter Access (www.newsletteraccess.com/subject/invest.html) offers a searchable directory for specific types of newsletters.

The Neat Sheet lists hot stocks to watch and caters to people who do not have a lot of time to research and monitor stocks. Subscribers also receive a straight-shooting annual report. For subscription information, call 800-339-5671 or visit their Web site at www.neatmoney.com.

Outstanding Investor Digest is a collection of the best ideas from the most successful investors. For subscription information, call 212-777-3330.

The Red Chip Review is a comprehensive small-cap investment publication. For more information, call 800-733-2447 or visit their Web site at www.redchip.com.

Outlook weekly is published by Standard & Poor's. It is one of the most widely read investment newsletters. For further information, call 800-852-1641.

Standard & Poor's Stock Guide is a professional publication that lists vital information about stocks. For more information, call 800-221-5277.

The Value Line Investment Survey, the premier stock-research tool, is published by Value Line. It covers over seventeen hundred companies. Almost everything you could want to know about each company is condensed to a single page. For information, call 800-634-3583.

NEWSPAPERS

Financial newspapers are still a way of life in the stock market's paper-oriented world, although some of them are beginning to make the migration to the online world. Here's a rundown of the best papers out there.

The Financial Times (www.ft.com) provides special reports on the market and the different industry sectors.

Investor's Business Daily (www.investors.com) is a great financial newspaper that publishes important information in determining the value of a stock. For subscription information, call 800-831-2525 or visit their Web site.

News Page (www.newspage.com) allows you to customize daily news abstracts it sends to your E-mail address.

The New York Times (www.nytimes.com) provides a business section that includes quotes and charts, a portfolio management tool, and breaking business news.

USA Today (www.usatoday.com) features a money section that includes investment articles and news, economic information, and information on industry groups.

The Wall Street Journal (www.wsj.com) is the Big Kahuna among investment newspapers, although its authority isn't as unquestioned as it used to be. For subscription information, call 800-778-0840 or visit their Web site.

PORTFOLIO MANAGEMENT TOOLS

There are several portfolio management tools you can use to manage your portfolio. Check out the following Web sites:

Financial Portfolio (www.finportfolio.com) tells you how to construct your portfolio to meet your financial goals and evaluates your investments to determine how much you should buy to keep your portfolio in balance.

Morningstar (www.morningstar.com) provides a portfolio setup menu that is easy to use.

Quicken (www.quicken.com) offers a variety of financial tools, including an excellent portfolio management program.

Reuters Money Net (www.moneynet.com/home/moneynet/homepage/homepage.asp) offers a wealth of financial data and one of the best portfolio management programs on the Web.

Stock Point (www.stockpoint.com) offers a free personal portfolio tracking program.

QUOTES (STOCKS AND MUTUAL FUNDS)

The Internet provides several quote servers that provide real-time and delayed quotes on stocks, mutual funds, and bonds.

American Stock Exchange (www.amex.com) offers quoting services on their Web site for stocks that are traded on its exchange.

Data Broadcasting Online (www.dbc.com) can retrieve up to seven ticker symbols at one time.

Individual Investor Online (www.iionline.com) offers delayed quotes, stock prospecting tools and screens, portfolio management tools, and financial news.

Microsoft Investor (www.investor.msn.com) offers a free stock ticker that you can personalize along with portfolio tracking tools.

The National Association of Securities Dealers (www.nasdaq.com) offers quoting services on their Web site for stocks that are traded on its exchange.

The New York Stock Exchange (www.nyse.com) offers quoting services on their Web site for stocks that are traded on its exchange.

PC Quote (www.pcquote.com) offers current stock prices, a portfolio tracker, company profiles, and broker recommendations.

Personal Wealth (www.personalwealth.com) features quotes and research along with expert advice.

RETIREMENT PLANNING

To bone up on the basics of retirement planning, check out these Web sites.

Hoover's Online (www.stockscreener.com) provides a special module for retirement planning.

Money Central (www.moneycentral.com) walks you through the process of setting up a retirement plan, including calculating your living expenses and determining your income requirements.

Schwab Investor Profile (www.schwab.com) offers an investor's profile questionnaire that matches you to one of six retirement-oriented portfolios.

SEARCH AND SCREENING TOOLS

There are over eighteen thousand stocks and mutual funds to choose from, a number that is overwhelming to most investors.

Fortunately, there are several excellent tools on the Internet that will help you substantially cut down that number to get at the few stocks and funds that are of interest to you.

American Association of Individual Investors (www.aaii.org) has a downloadable library of stock screening software for members.

Daily Stocks (www.dailystocks.net) offers an advance stock screen that allows you to enter important criteria to select stocks that meet your needs.

Hoover's Online Stock Screener (www.stockscreener.com) allows you to enter up to twenty variables for selecting stocks. The results are then sorted and displayed alphabetically.

IQ Net Basic Stock Scan (www.siliconinvestor.com/help/iqc/) allows you to use twelve variables to screen for stocks.

Market Guide (www.marketguide.com) allows you to screen for stocks by using any of twenty variables.

Money Central (www.investor.com) allows you to download information on stocks that you're interested in buying. You can create your own screens that weed out stocks you have no interest in owning.

MSN Investors (www.investor.msn.com) shows you how to use twelve prebuilt stock screens and how to set up your own screens.

Quicken (www.quicken.excite.com/investments/stocks/search/) has prebuilt screens for stock searches.

SmartMoney (www.smartmoney.com) magazine offers an excellent "search and find" tool for quickly finding the "TOP 25 FUNDS" on their Web site.

Vector Quest's (www.eduvest.com) features a database to help you find stocks that meet your selection criteria.

TAX ASSISTANCE

If you're struggling with taxes and the preparation of your return, these sites can help you out.

Internal Revenue Service (www.fourmilab.ch/ustax/ustax.html) enables you through this site to access the complete text of the U.S. Internal Revenue Code.

Secure Tax (www.irs.ustreas.gov) is a well-organized tax guide that allows you to print out tax forms.

TECHNICAL ANALYSIS

Technical analysis is the part of the analytical process where you determine when to buy and when to sell based on a stock's indicators. Here are several Web sites that will help you get through the process.

Equis International (www.equis.com) offers an excellent technical analysis program that you purchase. Check out their latest prices on their Web site and see a demonstration of their system.

Flex Trader (www.flextrader.com) is one of the best sites to get a quick look at a stock's technical outlook. It provides you with a rundown on a variety of indicators.

Quicken (www.quicken.com/investments) has an extensive investment section that covers stocks, mutual funds, and bonds.

Stock Trader (www.stocktrader.com) is an online brokerage firm with excellent technical analysis tools.

Glossary

American Stock Exchange (AMEX) Second in size to the New
   York Stock Exchange (NYSE). Trades mostly in small to
   medium sized companies.

Annual percentage yield (APY) The effective, or true, annual
   rate of return. Accounts for the effect of compounding.

Ask price If an investor owns a security and is interested in
   selling, he or she "asks" for a certain amount of money to
   part with the security. The ask price is therefore the lowest
   price an investor is willing to accept to sell a security. Also
   called the *offer price*.

Beta A coefficient that measures a security's relative volatility in
   relation to the rest of the stock market. For example, the
   Standard & Poor's (S&P) 500 Stock Index has a coefficient
   of 1. Stocks with betas greater than 1 are more likely to rise
   and fall with greater volatility than the general market;
   stocks with betas of less than 1 are more likely to rise and
   fall with less volatility than the general market.

Bid price Investors interested in purchasing a security "bid" to
   buy the security. Therefore, the bid price is the highest price
   an investor is willing to pay for a given security.

Bond A debt instrument issued for a period of time with the
   purpose of raising capital by borrowing from purchasers.
   When you purchase a bond, you are essentially lending the
   issuing party your money. The bond you purchase represents a promise by the issuing party to repay the borrowed

amount (principal) by a certain date (maturity). Some bonds are interest bearing and pay the interest periodically.

Buy The purchase of a stock, option, mutual fund, or other investment.

Call option contract A call is an option contract that gives the holder the right to buy a certain quantity of shares of a specified security at a specified price within a specific time period. You can either buy a call option, giving you the right to "call" away the stock from the seller, or you can sell a call option, giving someone the right to "call" away the stock from you. If you write, or sell, a call without owning the equivalent amount of the underlying stock, it is called an *uncovered call*. If you write the call and do own the equivalent amount, then it is called a *covered call*.

Certificate of deposit (CD) A short- or medium-term, interest-bearing, FDIC-insured debt instrument offered by banks and other financial institutions. A CD pays a contractual rate of interest over a specified period of time.

Exchange A central location where securities are traded. The most popular exchanges in the United States include the New York Stock Exchange (NYSE), the National Association of Securities Dealers Automatic Quotation System (NASDAQ), and the American Stock Exchange (AMEX).

Federal Deposit Insurance Corporation (FDIC) A federal agency that insures deposits in member banks. CDs are insured by the FDIC up to $100,000 (including principal and interest) for all deposits held in the same capacity per issuer.

Good 'til canceled Commonly referred to as "GTC," this trading choice means the order you place will remain open for a set period of time, unless the order is executed or cancelled.

Index Indicators of trends in markets, sections of the economy, or other economic indicators, such as precious metals or Treasuries. Some of the most common indexes include the Dow Jones Industrial Average, the NASDAQ Composite Index , and the Standard & Poor's 500 Stock Index.

Interest rate The rate that the issuer of a debt security is obligated to pay you until maturity, expressed as an annual percentage of the instrument's face or par value.

Limit order A trading choice that lets you set a price, or "limit," at which you are willing to buy or sell a security, regardless of the current market price. When buying, the limit is placed at a specified price below the market price. When selling, the limit is placed at a specified price above the market price.

Listed stocks Stocks that are traded on the New York Stock Exchange (NYSE), the American Stock Exchange (AMEX), and other regional exchanges. To be "listed," the companies must qualify and obey the rules that govern that particular exchange.

Load A fee imposed by a mutual fund family to buy or sell shares. There are two types of loads: front-end loads, where you pay a fee to purchase a fund, but nothing to sell it, and back-end loads, where you pay nothing to purchase the fund, but may have to pay a fee to sell it.

Long You are "long" in the market when you have purchased a security position but have not yet closed out that position through an offsetting sale.

Management fee This is the fee paid to a mutual fund's adviser for portfolio supervision and general management of the fund. The fee compensates the adviser for the expenses it incurs in providing its services, plus a profit that amounts to half of the fee or more. Some fees incorporate an incentive or penalty provision that ties compensation to performance to a correlating index or benchmark.

Margin Buying on margin means borrowing money to buy a security. The amount you borrow is also referred to as a "debit balance." A margin call will occur if the market value of the securities in your account falls below the required maintenance level.

Margin call A demand that a margin investor provide additional collateral. Occurs when the market value of the securities in your account drops below a certain maintenance level, relative to the equity in your account. Two types of margin calls are Fed calls and House calls.

Market order An order to buy or sell a stock at the current market price.

Maturity The date on which a lender can collect the principal and interest due.

Mutual fund A pool of investor money used by an investment company to purchase a group of assets for management. The investors own shares of the fund. The benefits to investors include diversification, professional money management, and capital gains and dividend reinvestment.

NASDAQ The National Association of Securities Dealers Automatic Quotation System (NASDAQ) is a computer system established to facilitate trading without a physical exchange. To accomplish this, the NASDAQ posts real-time broker/dealer quotes on OTC stocks. Approximately four thousand common stock issues are included in the NASDAQ system.

Net asset value (NAV) The per-share market value of a mutual fund, which in general is the price at which an investor purchases one share of the mutual fund. In most cases, the

NAV is calculated each trading day by totaling the closing prices of all securities held in the fund plus all other assets owned by the fund (including cash), subtracting all liabilities of the fund, and then dividing the sum by all the outstanding shares of the fund on that day. If the fund is a no-load fund, then the per-share offering price of the fund and the NAV per share will be the same.

New York Stock Exchange (NYSE) The largest and oldest (founded in 1792) exchange in the United States. It is located on Wall Street in New York City and trades more than two thousand common and preferred stocks.

No-load A class of mutual funds that have no fees associated with the purchase or sale of the shares. It is important to note, however, that there may be other fees associated with the fund, such as transaction fees and management fees.

No transaction fee (NTF) This is a class of mutual funds, either load or no-load, that have no extra fees associated with the purchase or sale of these shares.

Options Contracts giving the owner the right to buy (call) or sell (put) the underlying stock at a specified price (strike price). Options have a limited time value (expiration month) and can be extremely speculative investments. Special approval is required to trade options.

Over-the-counter stocks Stocks traded on the NASDAQ and other over-the-counter (OTC) markets. An OTC market is one where the dealers are not physically together, but rather connected via telephones and computers.

Price–earnings ratio (PE ratio) The ratio of the current market price of a stock to its trailing annual earnings.

Put option contract An option contract that gives the holder the right to sell a certain quantity of shares of a specified security at a specified price within a specific time period.

You can either buy the put option, giving you the right to "put" the stock to the buyer, or you can sell the put option, giving someone the right to "put" the stock to you. If you write, or sell, a put without being short the equivalent amount of the underlying stock, that is called an *uncovered put*. If you write the put while you are short the equivalent amount of the underlying stock, then it is called a *covered put*.

Sell short To sell a security that you do not own but are committed to repurchasing. In essence, after borrowing the stock and selling it in the open market, you are able to buy back the stock to cover, or close, the position. The strategy is to purchase the security at a price lower than that at which you sold it short. Investors employ this strategy if they believe the price of a security will decline.

Settlement date The date on which payment (in the case of a purchase) or securities (in the case of a sale) are due to settle a trade. The current settlement period is three business days after the trade date for stocks and mutual funds and one business day after the trade date for options.

Short A contract that one buys to establish a market position in a stock that can be exercised or "closed out" over a period of time.

Standard & Poor's 500 Stock Index (S&P 500) A market-value-weighted index of five hundred blue-chip stocks. Considered to be a benchmark of the market as a whole.

Stop order An order to buy at the market price when the price increases to the specified level or an order to sell at the market price when the price falls to a specified level.

Term The length of time a CD has until maturity.

Ticker symbol Letters assigned to a particular stock, option, or mutual fund to identify that security for trading or quoting purposes.

Total expense ratio The annual fee charged to mutual fund shareholders (usually as a percentage of the total investment) for the administration, operations, and management expenses associated with a particular mutual fund. May include management fees, 12(b)1, and other fees.

Treasury bills (T-bills) Debt obligations of the United States government with an initial maturity of one year or less. T-bills are generally issued with maturities of three, six, and twelve months. The minimum purchase size for T-bills is $1,000.

Treasury bonds (T-bonds) Debt obligations of the United States government with maturities of more than ten years. They are issued in a minimum purchase size of $1,000. T-bonds have a stated rate of interest, also known as the coupon rate, and pay interest to the holder semiannually.

Treasury notes (T-notes) Debt obligations of the United States government with maturities between two and ten years. T-notes are issued in a minimum purchase size of $1,000. T-notes have a stated rate of interest, also known as the coupon rate, and pay interest to the holder semiannually.

Zero-coupon treasury securities U.S. Treasury bonds that have been "stripped," or divided into principal and interest components, which are then sold separately. Often called *Treasury STRIPS*, zero-coupon securities make no periodic interest payments, but rather are sold at a discount from their face value. Accordingly, the difference between the discounted price and the face value represents the investor's return.